The BIG BOOK of LITERACY TASKS
Grades K–8

75 Balanced Literacy Activities Students Do *(Not You!)*

Nancy Akhavan

CORWIN LITERACY

FOR INFORMATION:

Corwin

A SAGE Company

2455 Teller Road

Thousand Oaks, California 91320

(800) 233-9936

www.corwin.com

SAGE Publications Ltd.

1 Oliver's Yard

55 City Road

London EC1Y 1SP

United Kingdom

SAGE Publications India Pvt. Ltd.

B 1/I 1 Mohan Cooperative Industrial Area

Mathura Road, New Delhi 110 044

India

SAGE Publications Asia-Pacific Pte. Ltd.

3 Church Street

#10-04 Samsung Hub

Singapore 049483

Publisher and Senior Program Director: Lisa Luedeke

Senior Acquisitions Editor: Wendy Murray

Associate Editor: Cynthia Gomez

Editorial Assistant: Jesssica Vidal

Production Editor: Amy Schroller

Copy Editor: Karin Rathert

Typesetter: C&M Digitals (P) Ltd.

Proofreader: Dennis W. Webb

Indexer: Wendy Allex

Cover and Interior Designer: Janet Kiesel

Marketing Manager: Brian Grimm

Printed in the United States of America

ISBN 978-1-5063-8963-9

This book is printed on acid-free paper.

Certified Chain of Custody
Promoting Sustainable Forestry
www.sfiprogram.org
SFI-01268

SFI label applies to text stock

18 19 20 21 22 10 9 8 7 6 5 4 3 2 1

What Your Colleagues Are Saying

This is a colorful gem of a book that should be on every literacy teacher's desk! Nancy Akhavan has always been a voice of reason, and so leave it to her to rescue the term *task* from its ho-hum baggage and reclaim it to mean all the authentic "doing" our students do as they learn new skills and strategies as readers and writers. I love that Nancy has organized these 75 engagements into Everyday Tasks that you can choose from depending on your students' needs, or what you're teaching that day, to Weekly Tasks, and then to the more multi-day Sometime Tasks, that you can sprinkle into your school year. But most of all I admire how she hand carved each one so to ensure you release students to do the task on their own within several minutes. So set your stopwatch, and get ready to see the results you want—students who love to read and write!

—Leslie Blauman, **Author of *Teaching Evidence-Based Writing***

Here's a resource we can all use! These strategies help us move readers and writers toward independent success. Beautifully organized, practically structured, this is a supremely user-friendly resource for busy teachers—and who isn't busy? I love the chart showing how each strategy is research-based, which helps us rely on strategies proven to work. Akhavan's voice shines through, telling us we've got this, and our students will, too.

—Berit Gordon, **Author of *No More Fake Reading***

The 75 practicable tasks in this book are like the Who's Who of literacy strategies. Any learner, in any classroom, needs them to read and write well. Dr. Akhavan masterfully demonstrates for teachers what to expect to see as learners practice each strategy. The strategies can be used as an instructional coach that doesn't encroach on students' independence. She provides the "what, how, and why" through brief lessons and authentic student examples that are applicable to all ELA and SED classrooms.

—Dr. Robin Shive, **Superintendent, Kernville Union School District**

How does a teacher make better use of class time? By rethinking strategies and habits. And for any teacher interested in improving general practice, Nancy Akhavan pinpoints the general problem of overteaching, and then shows us how to brilliantly underteach! If you are a teacher who recognizes in yourself a tendency toward "too-gradual-release"—Nancy helps you break that helicoptering habit. She shares a variety of strategies designed to let students launch into their own literacy moves more quickly, and with more visible results for all readers and writers.

—Gretchen Bernabei, **Author of *Text Structures From Nursery Rhymes***

This one is for Wendy Murray. Thank you for being my thought partner and friend. You inspire me to be all I can be for teachers and students. This book would not be a reality if it were not for your belief in my work.

Contents

Section Two: Weekly Tasks for Reading, Writing, and Thinking

Section Three: Sometime Tasks for Reading, Writing, and Thinking

This Book At-a-Glance

In each section of this book, I focus on engaging tasks that will help you move students to independence in the targeted activity. As much as possible, students need to do the engagements in the context of their own choice reading and writing, and they need to make their own decisions about going about it. I've laid out each task with the following features to make it easy for you to use this book as you are actually teaching.

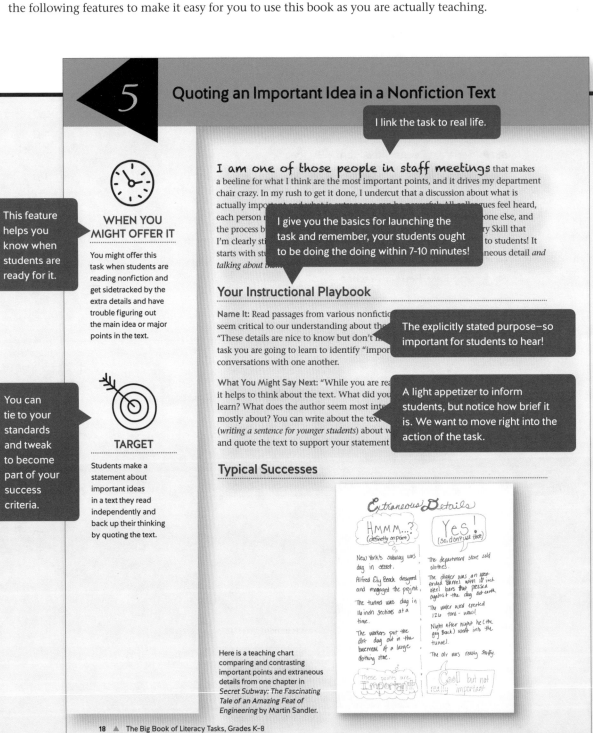

5 Quoting an Important Idea in a Nonfiction Text

I link the task to real life.

I am one of those people in staff meetings that makes a beeline for what I think are the most important points, and it drives my department chair crazy. In my rush to get it done, I undercut that a discussion about what is actually import~~ant and what is extraneous can be powerful.~~ All colleagues feel heard, each person r~~...~~one else, and the process b~~...~~ry Skill that I'm clearly st~~...~~to students! It starts with st~~...~~neous detail *and talking about th~~...~~*

I give you the basics for launching the task and remember, your students ought to be doing the doing within 7-10 minutes!

Your Instructional Playbook

Name It: Read passages from various nonfic~~...~~ seem critical to our understanding about the~~...~~ "These details are nice to know but don't h~~...~~ task you are going to learn to identify "impor~~...~~ conversations with one another.

The explicitly stated purpose—so important for students to hear!

What You Might Say Next: "While you are rea~~...~~ it helps to think about the text. What did you~~...~~ learn? What does the author seem most inte~~...~~ mostly about? You can write about the text~~...~~ *(writing a sentence for younger students)* about w~~...~~ and quote the text to support your statement~~...~~

A light appetizer to inform students, but notice how brief it is. We want to move right into the action of the task.

Typical Successes

This feature helps you know when students are ready for it.

⏰

WHEN YOU MIGHT OFFER IT

You might offer this task when students are reading nonfiction and get sidetracked by the extra details and have trouble figuring out the main idea or major points in the text.

You can tie to your standards and tweak to become part of your success criteria.

🎯

TARGET

Students make a statement about important ideas in a text they read independently and back up their thinking by quoting the text.

Here is a teaching chart comparing and contrasting important points and extraneous details from one chapter in *Secret Subway: The Fascinating Tale of an Amazing Feat of Engineering* by Martin Sandler.

> This section gives you ideas for how to demonstrate and also involve students but I purposefully didn't spell out your every move.

Model/Do Together: Launch with some vivid, contrasting examples of concise text and a treatment of the same topic that is bloated with extraneous details. It could be two YouTube videos showing how to bake or make something or an evening news segment that is taught. Now that your students get the gist, give students practice in knowing the difference between an important point and extraneous detail. Create a teaching chart with the students, discussing and recording the definitions and maybe samples of each from texts. You want what is recorded on the teaching chart to be a class-created definition, not just your definition written out for ease. You can also model how to quote from the text to back up your thinking. *It is the conversation you have with your students that helps them learn this for their own.*

Tweak: Language frames to jump-start conversation might include:

"When you think of (text topic), what do you already know about (text topic) and what did you learn that is new? (Quote from the text so we know what part of the learning is new for you)."

"What did you learn about (subject of the text)? Can you share your thinking? What part of the text made you think that? (Quote it.)"

"In the book _____, on page _____, new information for me is_____."

"On page _____, the author talks about _____. This reminds me about _____, but it is different and new. What is new is _____."

Release: Have students defi[...] [...]versation with one another. They ca[...] [...]g text or in texts you have in the cl[...] [...]with the whole class by quoting fro[...] [...]tant point or extraneous detail.

> Ideas for students doing the doing! The independent practice part that is the heart of this book.

Watch Fors and Work Arounds

Students are not quoting te[...] correctly. You might have to teach that skill directly, as appropriate for your grad[...]

> Ideas for reteaching and differentiating when students need your coaching in the midst of the task.

Students sometime[...] [...] don't make any sense or that ar[...] [...]hat it is in the text that is ne[...] [...]out the subject. You might h[...] [...]y say to be a good connection between known and unknown facts: What is important is if the student can explain their new learning and defend it by pointing to evidence in the text as support.

The Research Support for the Tasks

We are in this era when lessons, curriculum, and articles flood the Internet and are free for the taking, and yet paradoxically, teachers and schools are asking for—and deserve—to know the research behind the resources they use. Efficacy and evidence are terms that pop up in professional discussions often now, and I think it's a good thing. We can't afford to perpetuate routines and practices with students that research has shown are ineffective, and on the flipside, each hour of the school day should be filled with practices that have a strong research base. So with that in mind, I share this list to show you where each task comes from.

	Title	Reference
1	A New Spin on Who, What, Why, When, and Where	Clarke, P. J., Truelove, E., Hulme, C., & Snowling, M. J. (2013); Graham, S., Hebert, M., & Harris, K. R. (2015); Raphael, T. E., & Pearson, P. D. (1985); Wade, S. E., & Moje, E. B. (2000)
2	Making Predictions to Help Comprehension	Clark, S., Jones, C., & Reutzel, D. (2013); Graham, S., Hebert, M., & Harris, K. R. (2015); Raphael, T. E., & Pearson, P. D. (1985)
3	Journal Writing After Reading	Akhavan, N. (2008a); Marshall, J. (2000); Wixon, K. K. (1983)
4	Make a Connection to the World When Reading a Text Independently	Brock, C. H., Trost-Shahata, E., Weber, C. M., Goatley, V. J., & Raphael, T. (2014); Harvey, S., & Goudvis, A., (2007); Stevens, R. J., Lu, X., Baker, D. P., Eckert, S. A., & Gamson, D. A. (2015)
5	Quoting an Important Idea in a Nonfiction Text	Berger, R., Woodfin, L., Plaut, S. N., & Dobbertin, C. B. (2014); Clark, S., Jones, C., & Reutzel, D. (2013); Wade, S. E., & Moje, E. B. (2000)
6	Name Character Motives and Actions	Harvey, S., & Goudvis, A., (2007); Shashiredkha, S. M. (2014)
7	Name Rising Plot	Bohaty, J. J. (2015); Parsons, S. A., & Ward, A. E. (2011)
8	Name Plot Resolution	Bohaty, J. J. (2015); Parsons, S. A., & Ward, A. E. (2011); Shashiredkha, S. M. (2014)
9	Tell the Text	Clarke, P. J., Truelove, E., Hulme, C., & Snowling, M. J. (2013); Wade, S. E., & Moje, E. B. (2000)
10	Dig Deeper Into the Text	Akhavan, N. (2014); Davis, M. H., & Guthrie, J. T. (2015); Parsons, S. A., & Ward, A. E. (2011)
11	Guided Comprehension Talks	Davis, M. H., & Guthrie, J. T. (2015); Parsons, S. A., & Ward, A. E. (2011); Wade, S. E., & Moje, E. B. (2000)
12	Elaborate and Clarify Meaning	Akhavan (2016); Berger, R., Woodfin, L., Plaut, S. N., & Dobbertin, C. B. (2014); Taylor, B. M., Pearson, P. D., Peterson, D. S., & Rodriguez, M. C. (2003); Wade, S. E., & Moje, E. B. (2000)
13	Setting Routines for Independent Reading	Akhavan, N. (2008a); Mokhtari, K., Hutchison, A. C., & Edwards, P. A. (2010); Pressley, M., Mohan, L., Raphael, L. M., & Fingeret, L. (2007); Rasinski, T. V. (2017)
14	Fixing Up When Attention Wanders	Bohaty, J. J. (2015); Clarke, P. J., Truelove, E., Hulme, C., & Snowling, M. J. (2013); Mokhtari, K., Hutchison, A. C., & Edwards, P. A. (2010); Snow, C. (2002)
15	Communicating Your Heads-Up Ball Approach	Akhavan, N. (2014); Pressley, M., Mohan, L., Raphael, L. M., & Fingeret, L. (2007); Schirmer, A. (2010)
16	Answering a Text-Dependent Question	Akhavan, N. (2014); Berger, R., Woodfin, L., Plaut, S. N., & Dobbertin, C. B. (2014); Taylor, B. M., Pearson, P. D., Peterson, D. S., & Rodriguez, M. C. (2003)
17	Tell Why (You Think, Believe, Remember, Know) With Why Messages	Brock, C. H., Trost-Shahata, E., Weber, C. M., Goatley, V. J., & Raphael, T. (2014); Fisher, D., & Frey, N. (2015b)
18	Make a Bold Statement About a Text	Fisher, D., & Frey, N. (2015b); Parsons, S. A., & Ward, A. E. (2011); Taylor, B. M., Pearson, P. D., Peterson, D. S., & Rodriguez, M. C. (2003); Wade, S. E., & Moje, E. B. (2000)
19	Extend Thinking When Discussing a Text	Beers, K. & Probst, R. E. (2017); Block, C. (2004); Davis, M. H., & Guthrie, J. T. (2015); Harvey, S., & Goudvis, A., (2007); Parsons, S. A., & Ward, A. E. (2011)
20	One-Liners for Nonfiction Texts	Fisher, D., & Frey, N. (2015b); Harvey, S., & Goudvis, A., (2007); Wade, S. E., & Moje, E. B. (2000)
21	Crystal Ball Predictions	Shashiredkha, S. M. (2014)
22	Yesterday's News	Brock, C. H., Trost-Shahata, E., Weber, C. M., Goatley, V. J., & Raphael, T. (2014); Fisher, D., & Frey, N. (2015b)
23	Annotate Text	Fisher, D., & Frey, N. (2015a); Gentry, L. (2006); Houck, L. C. (2017)

	Title	Reference
24	Sentence Strip Statements	Akhavan, N. (2014); Tompkins, G. E., & Blanchfield, C. (2005)
25	Write Questions About Reading	Berger, R., Woodfin, L., Plaut, S. N., & Dobbertin, C. B. (2014); Raphael, T. E., & Pearson, P. D. (1985)
26	Super Cool Three Steps to Describe an Experience	Williams, C., & Pilonieta, P. (2012); Wood Ray, K. (1999); Yoo, M. S. (2010)
27	Getting Kids to Write: Wonderful Concentration	Graham, S., Hebert, M., & Harris, K. R. (2015); Donovan, C. A., & Smolkin, L. B. (2011)
28	Sketch to Write	Akhavan, N. (2009); Williams, C., & Pilonieta, P. (2012)
29	Getting Help From Another Writer: Write Dialogue in Narratives and Quotes in Reports	Clark, S., Jones, C., & Reutzel, D. (2013); Logue, C. (2015)
30	Getting Help From Another Writer: Write a Hook	Logue, C. (2015); Pytash, K. E., & Morgan, D. N. (2013); Wood Ray, K. (1999)
31	The Right Amount of Details, the Right Amount of Clarity	Donovan, C. A., & Smolkin, L. B. (2011); Graham, S., Hebert, M., & Harris, K. R. (2015)
32	Thinking Small to Write Well	Akhavan, N. (2004); Akhavan, N. (2009); Graham, S., Hebert, M., & Harris, K. R. (2015); Pytash, K. E., & Morgan, D. N. (2013); Zaragoza, N., & Vaughn, S. (1995)
33	Writing a Jot About What Was Read	Akhavan, N. (2008a); Clark, S., Jones, C., & Reutzel, D. (2013); Topping, K. J. (2001)
34	Works Too long and Never Gets Any Writing Done	Goldberg, G. (2016); Mokhtari, K., Hutchison, A. C., & Edwards, P. A. (2010); Zaragoza, N., & Vaughn, S. (1995)
35	Dialogue Journals	Akhavan, N. (2008a); Williams, C., & Pilonieta, P. (2012)
36	Analyze for Author's Purpose With a Text That Is a Little Too Hard for Students to Read on Their Own	Berger, R., Woodfin, L., Plaut, S. N., & Dobbertin, C. B. (2014); Lutz, S. L., Guthrie, J. T., & Davis. M. H. (2006); Taylor, B. M., Pearson, P. D., Peterson, D. S., & Rodriguez, M. C. (2003); Valencia, S. W., Wixon, K. K., & Pearson, P. D. (2014)
37	Create a Structured Outline of a Text	Bohaty, J. J. (2015); Yoo, M. S. (2010)
38	Collecting Research and Organizing Notes for Writing	Donovan, C. A., & Smolkin, L. B. (2011); Fisher, D., & Frey, N. (2015b); Lutz, S. L., Guthrie, J. T., & Davis. M. H. (2006)
39	Plot Summary Snapshots	Berger, R., Woodfin, L., Plaut, S. N., & Dobbertin, C. B. (2014); Fisher, D., & Frey, N. (2015a)
40	Writing Information in a New Format	Bohaty (2015); Berger, R., Woodfin, L., Plaut, S. N., & Dobbertin, C. B. (2014); Taylor, B. M., Pearson, P. D., Peterson, D. S., & Rodriguez, M. C. (2003)
41	Stay on Point in Writing	Harris, K. R., Graham, S., Friedlander, B., & Laud, L. (2013); Zaragoza, N., & Vaughn, S. (1995)
42	Productive Use of the Author's Chair	Goldberg, G. (2016); Jaeger, E. L. (2012); Parsons, S. A., & Ward, A. E. (2011); Pytash, K. E., & Morgan, D. N. (2013)
43	Write a Short Research Report	Akhavan, N. (2009); Brock, C. H., Trost-Shahata, E., Weber, C. M., Goatley, V. J., & Raphael, T. (2014); Donovan, C. A., & Smolkin, L. B. (2011)
44	Write an All About Text	Akhavan, N. (2009); Donovan, C. A., & Smolkin, L. B. (2011); Harris, K. R., Graham, S., Friedlander, B., & Laud, L. (2013); Wood Ray, K. (1999)
45	Your Students Have a Voice: Writing an Opinion Text	Akhavan, N. (2009); Harris, K. R., Graham, S., Friedlander, B., & Laud, L. (2013); Wood Ray, K. (1999); Zaragoza, N., & Vaughn, S. (1995)
46	Arguing the Solution to a Problematic Situation	Akhavan, N. (2014); Fisher, D., & Frey, N. (2015b)
47	Writing the Recipe for Success: How-to Texts	Brock, C. H. (2014); Brock, C. H., Trost-Shahata, E., Weber, C. M., Goatley, V. J., & Raphael, T. (2014); Donovan, C. A., & Smolkin, L. B. (2011); Fisher, D., & Frey, N. (2015b)
48	Writing Explanations, Be Like an Encyclopedia	Akhavan, N. (2009); Berger, R., Woodfin, L., Plaut, S. N., & Dobbertin, C. B. (2014); Taylor, B. M., Pearson, P. D., Peterson, D. S., & Rodriguez, M. C. (2003)
49	Inquiry for Smart Minds	Brock, C. H., Trost-Shahata, E., Weber, C. M., Goatley, V. J., & Raphael, T. (2014); Lutz, S. L., Guthrie, J. T., & Davis. M. H. (2006)
50	Responding to Literature With Some Kick to It	Akhavan, N. (2009); Duncan, L. G., McGeown, S. P., Griffiths, Y. M, Stothard, S. E., & Dobai, A. (2015); Harvey, S., & Goudvis, A., (2007); Zaragoza, N., & Vaughn, S. (1995)

	Title	Reference
51	Identify Theme in a Complex Text	Harvey, S., & Goudvis, A., (2007); Duncan, L. G., McGeown, S. P., Griffiths, Y. M, Stothard, S. E., & Dobai, A. (2015).
52	Posing Questions for Easier Inquiry	Akhavan, N. (2006); Nyberg, L. (2016). Taylor, B. M., Pearson, P. D., Peterson, D. S., & Rodriguez, M. C. (2003).
53	Writing a Fable or Myth	Akhavan, N. (2006); Harris, K. R., Graham, S., Friedlander, B., & Laud, L. (2013); Tompkins, G. E., & Blanchfield, C. (2005)
54	Writing a Fairy Tale	Akhavan, N. (2006); Harris, K. R., Graham, S., Friedlander, B., & Laud, L. (2013); Tompkins, G. E., & Blanchfield, C. (2005)
55	Justifying an Answer With a Claim and Evidence	Akhavan, N. (2014); Brock, C. H., Trost-Shahata, E., Weber, C. M., Goatley, V. J., & Raphael, T. (2014); Davis, M. H., & Guthrie, J. T. (2015); Duncan, L. G., McGeown, S. P., Griffiths, Y. M, Stothard, S. E., & Dobai, A. (2015Fisher, D., & Frey, N. (2015b)
56	Use Known info to Help Others Learn New info	Taylor, B. M., Pearson, P. D., Peterson, D. S., & Rodriguez, M. C. (2003); Moss, B. (2003); Yoo, M. S. (2010)
57	Connect Ideas Between Texts	Berger, R., Woodfin, L., Plaut, S. N., & Dobbertin, C. B. (2014)
58	Identifying Real Facts From Made-Up Facts: Fallacious Reasoning	Clark, S., Jones, C., & Reutzel, D. (2013); Moss, B. (2003); Topping, K. J. (2001)
59	Brainstorming Multiple Valid Answers/Responses	Brock, C. H., Trost-Shahata, E., Weber, C. M., Goatley, V. J., & Raphael, T. (2014); Topping, K. J. (2001)
60	Concept Mapping Between Big Ideas	Harvey, S., & Goudvis, A., (2007); Yoo, M. S. (2010)
61	Make Me Ponder: Questions That Get the Thinking Juices Flowing	Akhavan, N. (2009); Beers, K. & Probst, R. E. (2017); Raphael, T. E., & Pearson, P. D. (1985); Taylor, B. M., Pearson, P. D., Peterson, D. S., & Rodriguez, M. C. (2003)
62	Writing Compare and Contrast Response to Literature	Akhavan, N. (2009); Fisher, D., & Frey, N. (2015b); Harvey, S., & Goudvis, A., (2007); Marshall, J. (2000); Tompkins, G. E., & Blanchfield, C. (2005)
63	Peer-to-Peer Analysis and Response	Clarke, P. J., Truelove, E., Hulme, C., & Snowling, M. J. (2013); Henry, L. A., Castek, J., O'Byrne, W. I., & Zawilinkski, L. (2012)
64	Critique a Functional Document or Text	Berger, R., Woodfin, L., Plaut, S. N., & Dobbertin, C. B. (2014); Goldberg, G. (2016); Taylor, B. M., Pearson, P. D., Peterson, D. S., & Rodriguez, M. C. (2003); Valencia, S. W., Wixon, K. K., & Pearson, P. D. (2014)
65	Visible and Visual: Use Known Concepts and Vocabulary to Understand a Text	Bohaty, J. J. (2015); Harvey, S., & Goudvis, A., (2007); Lutz, S. L., Guthrie, J. T., & Davis. M. H. (2006)
66	Summarize a Text That Is a Little Too Hard for Students to Read on Their Own	Fisher, D., & Frey, N. (2015a); Valencia, S. W., Wixon, K. K., & Pearson, P. D. (2014); Yoo, M. S. (2010)
67	Student Think-Alouds	Fisher, D., & Frey, N. (2015b); Harvey, S., & Goudvis, A., (2007); Henry, L. A., Castek, J., O'Byrne, W. I., & Zawilinkski, L. (2012); Jaeger, E. L. (2012); Wade, S. E., & Moje, E. B. (2000)
68	Separate Central Idea From a Big Idea	Brock, C. H., Trost-Shahata, E., Weber, C. M., Goatley, V. J., & Raphael, T. (2014); Moss, B. (2003)
69	Writing in Different Genres or Multimedia to Engage and Persuade	Clark, S., Jones, C., & Reutzel, D. (2013); Donovan, C. A., & Smolkin, L. B. (2011); Ediger, M. (2000); Fisher, D., & Frey, N. (2015b)
70	Creative Debate	Fisher, D., & Frey, N. (2015b); Taylor, B. M., Pearson, P. D., Peterson, D. S., & Rodriguez, M. C. (2003)

About the Author

Nancy Akhavan is an assistant professor in the Department of Educational Leadership at California State University, Fresno. She has held various positions as teacher, principal, and district office leader. She has led literacy programs for schools, Grades K–12. She currently consults with teachers, as well as school and district leaders, to implement effective reading and writing instruction to close the achievement gap and increase reading achievement for all students. Nancy is the author of numerous professional books, including *The Nonfiction Now Lesson Bank, Grades 4–8* (Corwin, 2015).

Acknowledgments

When I finish a book, I feel as if I am floating. There is so much hope. Hope that I will be able to help you, teachers all over, guide and mentor your students to deep learning and success in reading and writing. Hope that the work will have relevance and hope that you, the reader, can see my heart on the pages, and that I truly care about the success of your students. This hope floats.

I am able to hope in these ways because an entire team of people believes in me. First, my husband, Mehran, who stands by me during all my teaching and writing endeavors. My editor, Wendy Murray, holds my hand and pushes me, as any good coach does, to run that last lap and make that last edit (after about a million edits—because I always need to revise!). My publisher, Lisa Luedeke, has believed in me for *years* now. I will always be indebted to her from coming to visit my school and wrapping herself into our magical literacy world at Pinedale Elementary School. I also am able to float because of Nicole Shade and Jess Vidal, who put up with me sending snips and bits of student writing; they help make everything beautiful. Also, to the rest of the team who makes the book beguiling and useful for the teacher, thank you. This includes Julie Nemer, Janet Kiesel for cover and interior design, Karin Rathert in copyediting, and Amy Schroller in production. Of course, this book wouldn't be in your lap right now if it weren't for Rebecca Eaton and Brian Grimm in marketing who help the book float into the world.

Last, but not least, thank you to you for trying out all the tasks with your students and to all the teachers who have shaped my thinking and teaching, including teachers at Storey Elementary School and their principal Gayle Fredinandi; teachers at Standard School District; and all the teachers at Pinedale Elementary School in Clovis Unified School District and Lee Richmond School in Hanford Elementary School District, who created a magical literacy learning place at Lee Richmond School and Pinedale School, where many of these ideas took root and grew.

Introduction

For a few years now, I have suggested in my workshops, classes, and, yes, even in my books that explicit instruction helps students reach the end goal, the *learning*. And clear learning intentions, demonstrations, and modeling do have a strong research base (Fisher, Fry, & Hattie, 2016). But I didn't emphasize enough that *the learning happens when the students are doing the work, not you.*

You see, in my heart and my head that idea was a given, that students were doing the work, but in classrooms, the teacher I'd coached so earnestly went into the explicit modeling so deeply that it crowded out the students' work time. Yikes! So I am saying it here: Your students need to do the work of the lesson, not you.

So this book is your guide for getting students to do the work. I am a teacher. My partner in life, my husband, is a coach. When he immigrated to the United States and had to learn English, he had coaches that helped him (he was an adult, and there were no teachers to help him then). He connected with people that coached him how to get another degree in the United States (in English, when he spoke Farsi); he connected with people that coached him to realize his dreams. He certainly had teachers along the way too, but the coaches, those people that gave him time to try on his own, to learn for himself by doing, were the people that helped him reach the American Dream. He coached competitive high school girls' soccer for years. We used to go out on the field at all hours of the day and his girls would play. I watched him coach these young women to win numerous championships over the fifteen years. I was fascinated by the coaching approach. He would teach but not tell. He would show but not bore. He would support but not enable. He stood by the team, pointing out what they did well when they executed a play and how a play went wrong. Sometimes he would point out that a play went wrong simply by how they held their bodies in relation to the ball. He coached, scaffolded, and nurtured, but he never *did* the playing for them, because he was the coach and not the player. He could not go in and play the game for them, and even if the girls copied him the first time they tried a new move, by the second or third try, they were starting to own the new move for themselves.

Coaches show us what to do then release, immediately, to let us try for ourselves. But they don't just let go; they stand beside us and watch us as we try, then they point out what we could do to keep getting better and also ask questions that help us reflect on what we learned from our own actions. Coaches rarely ask, "What did you learn from watching me?" because coaches know that idle hands don't lead to deep learning. They also know that hands (and feet) that copy don't learn without trying on their own first.

So with the gradual-release model—also known as the I Do, We Do, You Do sequence—we have to make sure it *doesn't* go like this: I do (for a long time or quickly, without a think-aloud, or loudly, if I am saying it for the umpteenth time as the students still didn't learn it). We do (for too long or too much, which seems almost like an I do again because, as the learner, I am just copying you without you letting me try it my own way, adding my own twist to help me own it). You do (for too short of a time, when just as I am starting to *get it,* it is time to move on to the next lesson because we spent too long in the I do and we do phases). I release you from this. Yes, me. I give myself the authority to do this, as I am going to suggest a new focus. Anne Lamott spoke at TED 2017 (Lamott, 2017a), and she spoke about things she knows for sure. One of those things is about helping our children. She says, "We can't run alongside our children with Chapstick and sunscreen on their hero's journey. You have to release them. It's disrespectful not to."

So if we think about this and our teaching, we have to stop running alongside with scaffolds that hurt and don't help. We have to release to independence. We have to release sooner in the lessons we teach. Anne Lamott goes on to say, " Our help is usually not very helpful. Our help is often toxic, and help is the sunny side of control." [Lamott, 2017a] Let's focus on not being toxic. Let's focus on not disguising our *control needs* in lessons and tasks and other classroom endeavors as *help*. We need a new focus.

The new focus is I do, you do (with me standing beside you coaching you), or I suggest, we do (quickly, just until you get it so we can move to you trying it yourself) and then you do.

Let's get started helping you ensure your students do the doing, not you. You work too hard as it is!

Tasks and Coherence: What Research Has to Say

The place I love to be most second to my classroom is *in someone else's* classroom learning. (Well, it is probably third best because my favorite place to be is home, and then in my classroom!) I love to learn as much as I take joy in helping others learn. In 2012, I had the opportunity to learn a lot about school coherence and tasks. At the university, I was part of a two-year professional learning opportunity called Building Coherence in Instructional Improvement (BCII), which was led by Richard Elmore, Michelle Foreman, and Leisy Stosich from Harvard. It was a powerful learning setting for me, as the Harvard team would fly to Fresno, California, to work with a coaching team and then with a school district. For me, it was a jump-up-and-down thrilling opportunity, as I had followed the work of Elmore for many years, and now I was working with Elmore and his team at my very own university.

In this project, I learned about how to help schools prepare for instructional improvement by considering the leadership practices of a school, examining the whole school improvement efforts and organizational processes, looking at the team processes and beliefs, and teaching for student learning. For me, the most powerful part of this the professional study was on helping teachers experiment with new ways of interacting with content and with students. Elmore, Foreman, and Stosich guided me and my colleagues to consider how to raise the level of academic tasks in order to do things: to make a difference with the connection of teachers with students and to make a stronger connection between students and the academic tasks. During this focus on coherence, we revisited the idea of tasks as defined by Elizabeth City: Academic tasks are what the students are actually doing during instruction, not what we hypothesize that they are doing. The more aligned our academic tasks are to high-quality implementation, the more students will learn (City, Elmore, Fiarman, & Teitel, 2009).

So it began. Tasks. In the work with Harvard, Elmore, Foreman, and Stosich, my team looked at the tasks students were completing in the classroom and helped teachers have conversations about the tasks they were assigning. All this consideration of tasks and how tasks lead to learning springboarded me to a great big idea: I would conduct my own research with students and find out what they thought about the reading and writing tasks they were doing in classrooms. So I launched into a large research project where I surveyed nearly seven hundred students about literacy tasks and interviewed thirty students about their thinking about reading and writing tasks in the classroom. The findings include the following: Tasks can be good and can be bad. Tasks can be mundane and tasks can be engaging. Tasks that are purposeful, appropriately scaffolded, and at the students' readiness level lead to student excitement, engagement, and most importantly, learning. I also learned that statistically significant numbers of students want to be involved in engaging tasks that give them ownership of their learning. I call these types of tasks *engagements*. I learned that statistically significant number of students in the study were read to or completed worksheets on reading but *did not* read in class and *did not* want or *like to* read outside of class. Also, a statistically significant number of students did not use the most commonly taught reading comprehension strategies in or outside of class, and they wanted their teachers to teach them how, in essence to help them be able to do things on their own. In interviews, students told me about what kind of instruction they wanted to be part of. The students said they wanted teachers that believed that they were worthy of the work, to help them do the work on their own and to see them as people and as capable and to believe in them. When we focus on academic tasks where students are doing the doing, we squarely put student ownership of learning first.

Academic Tasks: Reclaiming Them as Engaging Actions Students Do

Cluttered curriculums can bog us down and make it hard to teach in the ways that we want—focused, purposeful, and productive. Having too much to do each day with students puts you in a race with yourself and your own skills to get it all done. Did you cover the standards today? Did you assign all workbook pages aligned to the books your students read? Did you correct all of the work produced by students at workstations? Did you read all their journal entries? We can get buried by the jobs we are giving students and not realize that we are wasting the most valuable resource available to us: time.

This book is about coaching students to learn for themselves. We do this day by day, hour by hour, as we instruct and interact with our students. The seventy-five tasks in the book are, in essence, what gets done on the journey of each school year and the longer journey of being a third grader reading *Junie B. Jones* and arduously writing a few sentences to being a literate adult whose life is enriched by her literacy.

My editor and I joke that I am hijacking the word task and redefining it for a new generation of teachers, getting rid of its heavy connotations of drudgery or teacher-directed, teacher-pleasing mindsets. Because the thing is, I think it's okay for teachers to give a task; that doesn't have to mean the student doesn't get enough choice or voice. I am talking about purposeful engagements—academic moves that carry your students away with their work in a way that they forget that they are working. I am talking about tasks that are wings to independence because they exercise the big and small skills and strategies that add up to a learner being able to tackle the major endeavors of literacy in every discipline. Some of the tasks in the book have the glamour and depth of a major endeavor (say, comparing two novels; designing an experiment that compares the drinking water in two adjacent but economically different towns), but many are the more workaday literacy pursuits that we all need to do the grander stuff. Here is a sampling:

Identifying patterns in text

Collecting research and organizing research notes

Note taking in jots on complex text

Compare/contrast

Write an explanation

So you see, in defining tasks, I've got a kind of high/low thing going—I want us to consider the quality of them, and I want to use tasks with the greatest degree of student choice and ownership possible (that's the "high), but I also want to say with unabashed conviction that there are some times and some tasks that the whole class will do because they need practice with a particular skill. It augments the authentic unit of study but isn't necessarily fully embedded in it. It's OK because the task is engaging, differentiated for the students, and leads to learning rather than busywork.

Active Tasks–Not Passive Tasks

A good task inspires creativity and passion; at the very least, it will spark some interest and get the neurons in the brain firing, getting ready to learn. A good task once learned is then something a student can choose to do, when it seems natural to him. For example, on page 116 there is a task "Responding to Literature With Some Kick in It." Once I have introduced the task and students have practiced it and explored it, it's up to them how they do it and how often. It would become a bad task if it were something they were compelled to do every day. A bad task dulls the senses, diminishes thinking, and decreases student passion to learn.

Engaging tasks sit at the center of the classroom dynamics and day-to-day routines. Tasks also create the glue that connects teacher and students. This is because, when the teacher works with students on learning, he is usually working on getting students to do something (a task) in order to get them to open up to new information, then practice doing something with that information (another task), so they can own the information or skill for themselves (an engagement). Engagements and tasks are the glue holding together the classroom community.

There are three premises to designing great tasks. The first premise to designing great tasks for your students is that the students should be "doing the doing." The second premise is that students learn by doing. The third premise is that effort pays off. You won't be nurturing strong, independent learners in a classroom that fosters passivity. You *will* be nurturing strong, independent learners in a classroom that fosters independence! Some tasks we assign to students reinforce passive interactions: prepare, listen, watch, talk when called, and copy down what she writes on the board. There are differences between active and passive tasks; these differences focus on the type of activities students are doing. The *tasks* students are engaged in. Let's take a look at the following table.

A Comparison of Task Types	
Independence Fostering Tasks	**Passivity Fostering Tasks**
Students think about the previous night's homework.	Students prepare their notebooks to take notes.
Students talk about their reflections.	Students sit quietly while waiting for the teacher to start the lesson.
Students read with the teacher.	Students watch the teacher read.
Students read.	Students listen to the teacher read.
Students think about what is important in what they read reading.	Student think about what is important in what the teacher read.
Students write notes about what they think is important.	Teacher writes notes on the board about important ideas and details; students copy the notes.

In the end of this example, both groups of students have notes in their notebooks, but the process of getting the notes is qualitatively different. In the independence example, students actively engaged in the tasks and practiced on their own. In the passivity example, the students passively engaged (by watching and copying) and did not practice on their own. The active tasks evoke different thinking, reading, and writing skills than the passive tasks, and they are higher-level tasks where students apply close reading skills, sort and select information, synthesize information, and summarize. In the passive classroom example, these things are going on, but it is the teacher who is doing them (she is the expert) while the novice learners only watch.

Every Day, Weekly, and Sometimes

The tasks are arranged in sections. The first section is Everyday Tasks. The tasks in this section are activities you might do every single day in reading, writing, listening, and speaking. The tasks in the everyday task section do not necessarily take as much time, thinking, or effort (for students of course!) as tasks that are considered weekly or occasional tasks. These are tasks that help with the smooth running of your classroom and of your literacy time. These are tasks students could and should be engaged in everyday.

The next section of the book is Weekly Tasks. The tasks in this section are harder to complete than the tasks in the daily task section. The tasks might occur over several days or might have precursor activities that take place before the students can work on the task being discussed. In essence, these are tasks that take different types of thinking than the tasks in the daily task section. They require deeper thinking, repeated attempts, and extended time to practice. Essentially, they build for students the ability to persevere.

The third section of the book is the Sometime Tasks. The tasks in this section are more difficult and take more time. Students may not be able to complete them in one day, or you might assign the tasks over time. These are tasks that students must persevere at; they take time. They take effort.

The Good, The Bad, and The Ugly

Each section of the book ends with a chart called The Good, The Bad, and The Ugly. It's a blog-like review of implementing the tasks! I include it to show you how it looked when it went great, how it looked when it didn't go too well, and how it looked when it was downright horrible. I want you to see that guiding students toward independence is always a work in progress.

Now, let's get started. Enjoy.

EVERYDAY TASKS

for Reading, Writing, and Thinking

Getting students to do the doing each and every day is part of us practicing what Anne Lamott (see Introduction, page 1) encouraged us to do: release. When we release to students independent work sooner, with us there to coach, they learn more in the end. Remember that Anne Lamott said that with, our "over active helping," we can fall into a pattern of doing just the happy side of control (Lamott, 2017a). We don't need to control our students. We need to control the setup for the work, the development of the skill, and the scaffolds we provide.

The tasks in this section are designed for daily use. You obviously don't need to use all of them every day! You pick and choose based on your student needs, your current unit of study, or the topic in your reading program. In the tasks that follow, you will see a variety of tasks that build different skills. You can choose which task to engage in with your students based on the skill the task builds. The task inventory, pages 8–9, gives the title of the task on the left and describes the skill on the right. So you can choose which task to engage in with your students based on the skill you are working on currently with them or by looking at the task and thinking about what type of practice they need right now. You can also choose by the genre of text you are working with.

The Everyday Tasks help develop stamina in thinking, speaking, listening, reading, and writing. The task inventory will show you which tasks develop which skills and how the tasks transfer to independence, so you can easily choose tasks that align to your objectives.

The Everyday Tasks are tasks that require less time commitment than the tasks in the Weekly Tasks section or the Sometimes Tasks section. The Everyday Tasks can easily fit into your daily plans, if you are using a published reading curriculum, or can enhance your units of study, if you are working in reading and writing workshops. If you are implementing Balanced Literacy, the tasks can provide structure for the shared reading, independent reading, shared and guided writing, and independent writing.

Section I ● Everyday Tasks for Reading, Writing, and Thinking

	Task	Genre	Skill	Transfer to Independence! Learners can:
1	A New Spin on Who, What, Why, When, and Where	Fiction (chapter books), literary nonfiction	Identify important information in text	Reflect on how arrived at answers and why answers are supportable.
2	Making Predictions to Help Comprehension	Fiction	Make predictions	Confirm prediction through reflection.
3	Journal Writing After Reading	Fiction, literary nonfiction, nonfiction, informational text	Write about reading	Self-select topic after independent reading.
4	Make a Connection to the World When Reading a Text Independently	Nonfiction	Make text-to-world connections	Make perceptive and well-developed connections with challenging topics.
5	Quoting an Important Idea in a Nonfiction Text.	Nonfiction	Identifying main idea or major points	Make statement on main idea/major point and back up thinking by quoting the text.
6	Name Character Motives and Actions	Fiction	Name character motives	State character's actions that portray the motives.
7	Name Rising Plot	Fiction	Identify plot	State plot and how the actions move the plot forward.
8	Name Plot Resolution	Fiction	Identify plot	Discuss resolution of the problem.
9	Tell the Text	Fiction	Retell	Sketch chronological order and use the graphics for oral retell.
10	Dig Deeper Into the Text	Fiction, literary nonfiction, nonfiction	Make inferences	Ask and answer questions about text that requires more than recalling of facts or information.
11	Guided Comprehension Talks	Fiction	Ask questions of text	Ask and answer deep questions about text that focus on wonderings.
12	Elaborate and Clarify Meaning	Fiction, literary nonfiction	Conversing at length on a topic	Make statements about a text, providing details or elaboration to clarify meaning.
13	Setting Routines for Independent Reading	Fiction, nonfiction, literary nonfiction, informational text	Sustain reading and writing for long periods of time.	Develop self-selected work routines.
14	Fixing Up When Attention Wanders	Fiction, nonfiction, literary nonfiction, informational text	Use fix-up strategies	Use self-monitoring strategies when reading challenging texts requiring students to stretch beyond their current range for accuracy and fluency.
15	Communicating Your Heads-Up Ball Approach	Fiction, nonfiction, literary nonfiction, informational texts, nonfiction	Manage sustained reading	Manage reading time and read across range of complexity and genres.
16	Answering a Text-Dependent Question	Fiction, nonfiction, literary fiction, informational text	Answer text-dependent question	Refer to or quote text to support response.
17	Tell Why (You Think, Believe, Remember, Know) With Why Messages	Fiction, nonfiction, literary fiction, informational text	Answer text-dependent question	Extend ability to discuss text with accountability by referring to or quoting text.
18	Make a Bold Statement About a Text	Fiction, nonfiction, literary fiction, informational text	Make statement about a text	Restate own ideas with clarity using information that is accurate and relevant.

	Task	Genre	Skill	Transfer to Independence! Learners can:
19	Extend Thinking When Discussing a Text	Fiction, nonfiction, literary fiction, informational text	Make a statement about text-extending ideas from discussion. Ask questions of others ideas about text	Discuss text using comparisons and analogies, referring to knowledge built during discussion. Ask others questions requiring them to support their claims.
20	One-Liners for Nonfiction Texts	Nonfiction	Use relevant information from text to summarize	Write one short thought-provoking sentence summarizing a point in the text.
21	Crystal Ball Predictions	Fiction, literary nonfiction, nonfiction	Make predictions	Use context clues and known facts from text to make predictions.
22	Yesterday's News	Longer fiction and nonfiction	Summarize important points	Capture meaning from text and restate it succinctly and in an engaging manner.
23	Annotate Text	Literary nonfiction, informational texts	Annotate text	Write margin notes to aide comprehension or text.
24	Sentence Strip Statements	Informational text, nonfiction	Identify main idea	Identify possible main ideas and discuss with other students, providing evidence to back up statements.
25	Write Questions About Reading	Fiction, nonfiction	Ask questions	Question in order to understand using concepts from the text in nonfiction or plot, setting, or character motivation in fiction.
26	Super Cool Three Steps to Describe an Experience	Personal narrative	Writes narrative on self-chosen topic	Generate own topics and spend time to refine writing.
27	Getting Kids to Write: Wonderfully Concentrating Minds Generating Ideas	Personal narrative	Writes for extended amount of time on one chosen topic	Routinely choose topics, rework, revise and edit writing.
28	Sketch to Write	Personal narrative	Plan writing with beginning, middle, end	Share an event with a sequence of events that is in a logical order.
29	Getting Help From Another Writer: Write Dialogue in Narratives and Quotes in Reports	Personal narrative, report writing	Use dialogue or quotes text	Effectively use dialogue in narratives and quotes in reports when reporting on interviews.
30	Getting Help From Another Writer: Write a Hook	Personal narrative, report writing, response to literature	Write beginning that engages the reader	Include a hook at the beginning of a piece that moves into the thesis and is more than a question.
31	The Right Amount of Details, The Right Amount of Clarity	Personal narrative, report writing, response to literature, functional writing	Write with details and clarity	Create believable world in fiction or includes relevant information for nonfiction. Avoids use of extraneous detail.
32	Thinking Small to Write Well	Personal narrative	Write with detail, engages the reader and has a beginning, middle and end	Write on one topic with control and focus.
33	Writing a Jot About What Was Read	Nonfiction, informational text, literary nonfiction	Write one fact/point at a time	Write a short, succinct text about information read.
34	Works Too Long and Never Gets Any Writing Done	Personal narrative, fantasy, report writing	Writes without repeating the same concept over and over	Routinely generate writing and routinely rework, revise, edit, and proofread work.
35	Dialogue Journals	Communication	Write thoughts and message to the teacher, and respond to teacher's comments.	Communicate ideas and thoughts to an appropriate audience conveying meaning and reflection.

WHEN YOU MIGHT OFFER IT

You might offer this task when younger readers are ready to dig into nonfiction text or students are beginning to read fiction texts with longer chapters or sections. You might offer it when older readers are reading more complex pieces of text or longer chapter books or nonfiction books with multiple sections.

TARGET

Students will identify important information, including who, what, why, when, *or* where, after reading a text independently and reflect on how they arrive at their answers and why they are supportable.

The other day, I was in a classroom and students were working, independently, to answer questions at the end of the text in their anthology. I leaned over a student's shoulder to take a peek, and they were the typical who, what, why, when, and where questions. *How boring!* I thought, and indeed, I began hearing a rhythm band of tapping pencils, sighing, shifting chairs. Don't get me wrong—these recall questions have a place, but the flaw was that students were merely working to prove they had read. Here is a task that puts a livelier, more metacognitive spin on identifying *who, what, why, when, and where* of any text.

Your Instructional Playbook

Name It: In this task, you will read with a partner and then use the different colored highlighters or markers to mark up your text and identify the five points you have been discussing (the five W's). Most importantly, you will state why you made your decision to label a section with one of the Ws.

What You Might Say Next: "When reading, it is important to think about who is doing what, when is it happening, and where it might be taking place. When we think about the five Ws (who, when, what, why, and where), we are checking that we understand what the text is about. Today we are going to practice finding these five parts of a text together and then justifying our thinking by pointing out what part of the books helps us know we are correct!"

Typical Successes

A page from *Radiant Child: The Story of Young Artist Jean-Michel Basquiat* (Steptoe, 2016)

Model/Do Together: Give students two or three different colored highlighters and a copy of the text. Or when working with younger readers, have a few different colored sticky notes handy. Facilitate reading the text and deciding on which parts of the text to highlight with a marker or by placing a sticky note. As you read the text together out loud, highlight the parts of the text that tell who, what, when, why, or where. It is best if you read the text the first time uninterrupted and look for the sections of text to highlight on the second or third read. Elicit a lot of discussion from students. Encourage them to decide one or more of the five Ws for themselves, and discuss their thinking about their choice by using the text to justify the answer. Older students can add a sticky note or write the justification in the margins. Younger students can add it to their sticky note or write it in a reading journal. Don't just show them the answers (because then you would be doing the "doing," and we want the students to do the thinking).

Release: Using a *new* piece of text (it could be the next section from the book you took the first excerpt from) remind students to recheck their text as they decided what is what in the text they are reading. Have a couple of groups of students share out what they were thinking. If they are younger readers, have them come up to the shared read-aloud text and highlight the part of the text they think shows a point they worked on (highlight by putting a sticky note under the sentence). Then, encourage them to write out what they discussed with their partners in journals or on additional sticky notes.

Watch Fors and Work Arounds

Students don't highlight anything or don't offer their ideas about the five Ws. Make sure they know it is OK to not get the answer "right" and that it can be helpful to share their thinking with a partner or in a small group, to get the others' take. Have kids talk and negotiate what they think the five Ws are in a given text. Or have them tackle just one of the five Ws, for example "What is this text about?"

Students highlight everything with marker lines or sticky notes all over the text. Help students make decisions for themselves by displaying the following prompts on a chart or on sentence strips: What is in the text that tells us what might be important? Let's find the sentence. How do we know this is *who* this text (or what) is about? Can you find the sentence and circle it?

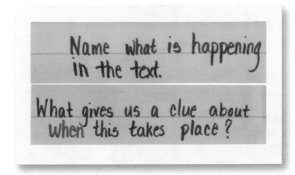

Name what is happening in the text.

What gives us a clue about when this takes place?

WHEN YOU MIGHT OFFER IT

You might offer it when students need practice with making predictions. With younger readers, model the task with a shared book before having students practice predicting on their own, doing more modeling as needed. For older readers, use when the text level increases or any time you want to check on the accuracy of their predictions.

TARGET

Students will comprehend and add new information to memory by making predictions about what a text will be about and then confirming through reflection.

I have seen many lessons where the teacher sets up the students to predict, the kids do, and then they power on through the story. I dubbed these lessons "predict and run." Don't do it! Slow down and savor the hypothesis and keep reflecting on it as you read on. Ask, Was I right or wrong? And why? How do I know? The comprehension boosting isn't in the guess but in stopping after reading to check the prediction. It is really important that you set this task up with your students as an inquiry. Make them excited to predict, then read and check.

Your Instructional Playbook

Name It: When we make a prediction about a text before reading it, we are waking up our brains and getting them ready to figure out what is happening in the book. The graphics, heading, and words in a text give clues to what the text will be about. In this task, we are going to make a prediction by waking up our brains and predicting what we will read and then stopping after we read to see whether our prediction was correct or incorrect.

What You Might Say Next: "You know when you are reading a good story or watching a suspenseful movie, maybe a mystery, and a character does something or acts odd all of a sudden, you say to yourself, 'Ooh, I bet something is about to happen! I bet that other guy is about to cause trouble!' When you do that, you are making a prediction. You are guessing what is going to happen next, based on clues. Good readers make predictions all the time, whether they are reading a story or a science book. Readers scan a cover and opening pages to predict what kind of book it is and if they will like it. And then as they read, they pause whenever the author seems to be inviting them to slow down and think and make an inference. An inference is a prediction, a guess based on what you know. We are going to start by flagging some stopping points for ourselves."

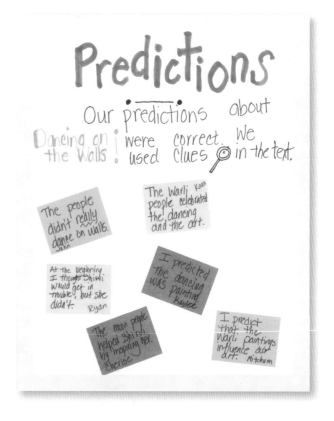

Owns It! Notice how the students are correctly making predictions about the text that they had read.

Model/Do Together: Take a bunch of sticky notes and talk with the students about where would be good places to stop and make predictions. Place them on the text and let the students know that the little sticky notes are going to be little stop signs for you as you read. The sticky notes will remind you and the class to stop and make a prediction. For younger readers, use a big book or enlarged text; for older readers, use text under a document camera. As they are choosing good stopping places in the book, invite students to come up and place the sticky notes on the text for stopping points. Then, read the text together and stop where there is a sticky note. Ask something like, *"Based on what we read (or see in the pictures or the headings), what is a prediction we could make right now? What do you think will happen next? Or what else is going to happen now that _____ happened? How can we be sure our prediction is plausible or could really happen? Should we reread what happened already in the text to make sure our prediction makes sense?"*

Release: Once students have practiced this a few times with you, have them try it for themselves. Stop at a stopping point and make a prediction about what will happen next, how the text will end, what the character is going to do, and how the information you are learning is going to change or develop.

Have students share their predictions. Ask, did their predictions come to pass? How do they know? These reflective questions will take students back to the text to think about what they read and how it gives them clues about what might be next.

Watch Fors and Work Arounds

Students' connections don't have anything to do with the text. Guide students to go back to the text to point to the text sections that back up their prediction. If and when they cannot find a text section that supports their thinking, invite them to reread the section, think about it, and make a new connection.

Students cheer when their prediction is confirmed and get down when their prediction is not. Remind the class that predicting isn't about winning or losing and that authors sometimes throw curve balls, so it's not useful to think of a prediction as wrong. The important thing is to keep helping one another learn to recognize strong supporting details that back up their hunches.

Students cannot make a prediction; they are stuck. Have students work in groups. To get them started, they can scan and make a prediction before they even read any of the text. Do a brief think-aloud if needed and then, for nonfiction, guide them to use the illustrations and headings to help them consider what the text might be about. For fiction, think aloud your process for rereading the final paragraph of a previous chapter, section, or sentence, for hints about the important parts and what it might mean for upcoming events and interactions. Use a prediction bookmark to prompt thinking.

I like to get kids thinking with Prediction Bookmarks they can put right in their books.

WHEN YOU MIGHT OFFER IT

You might offer it when you notice students need a refresher for purposeful writing in their journals.

TARGET

Students write in journals, on a topic of students' choice, 90% of the time after independent reading.

I have a vision for my classroom. I hope you do too. I see my students immersed in books selected from class book boxes or the library or on loan from a buddy. (Get the picture? They are reading!) I see some students writing about their reading in book journals and using t-charts and other note-taking and reflection strategies that work for them. However, more often than not, my classroom doesn't hum along the way it does in that dream scenario! And so this task helps me do little check-in and tweaking so that students are reminded of how to keep making the best choices for their reading and writing.

Your Instructional Playbook

Name It: We have been reading a lot during independent reading, but after a few minutes, we get distracted and forget to write about our reading. In this task, you are going to think for yourselves about what you might write about based on what you have been reading.

What You Might Say Next: "Once you finish reading your book each day, you should be writing in your journal. You can write about what we talked about during the minilesson today, or you can think first and then write about something else that interests you, like making a connection, for example. I want you to choose what you want to share in your journal. We have lots of teaching charts in our room that can help you choose what to write about in your journal."

Typical Successes

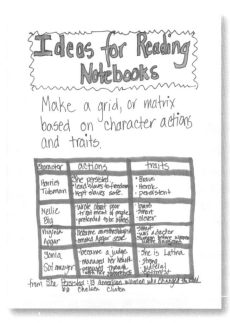

Examples of different teaching charts from minilessons that students can use to help them start writing.

Model/Do Together: Model how to write in the journal after reading. Have a journal and a book near your teaching area (on the floor for preK–3 and near your chair, stool, Promethean board or doc camera for 4–6). Talk about what you are doing as you model it. Model how you would finish reading a book, book section, or chapter. Then, while talking aloud so students can understand your thinking processes, make a choice about what you are going to write about in your journal. It might be directly from the minilesson you taught that day or a lesson from another day. Maybe you will write about a character or what is happening in the book thus far.

Tweak: Talk aloud about your choice so students know why you chose as you did. You can say: "I don't want you to do this for the teacher—for me, I want you to write for you, the reader. Writing helps us recall, reflect, and organize our responses to a text." Point to a teaching chart to support your thinking if applicable. Then model writing in your journal about what you had planned in your mind.

Release: Get students reading and writing. For preK–3, it could be what is in their book boxes, for fourth to sixth grade, it could be a book they have chosen on their own. You can also have them check their journal and turn to a page where they could start writing. Remind them that they can make a lot of different choices about what to write about after they read but that it is important to write and not sit idle or bug their neighbor and get distracted.

Watch Fors and Work Arounds

When you first introduce writing about reading or journal writing during independent reading time, students might be unsure how to jump in and do this on their own. They need modeling and examples of journal entries that are creative and serve different purposes. If students have been getting distracted during independent reading time or complaining that they don't have anything to do after they read their book(s), create a journal sample space in your room and mock up some journal pages and post them for students to refer to for help. You show them how to respond with inventive emoji charts, bar graphs, Venn diagrams, and other graphics.

GETTING STARTED WITH WRITING ABOUT READING

Find out the reasons why your students currently write about reading

- Introduce authentic reading notebook lessons to students.

- Explain and show students what a reading notebook is and why we create them.

- Show students different ways to record their thinking in notebook entries.

- Reflect with students and help them set personalized goals and intentions.

- Inspire creative notebook entries by showing them examples.

From *What Do I Teach Readers Tomorrow?* by Gravity Goldberg and Renee Houser (2017). Used by permission of the authors.

WHEN YOU MIGHT OFFER IT

You might offer it when introducing a complex text or when offering students to read nonfiction texts on topics that might be new for them.

TARGET

Students make perceptive and well-developed connections between what was already known about information and ideas in the world and the text read.

Lately, as I am out in classrooms working with teachers very focused on implementing new standards, I hear people talking about *rigor,* and also teachers tell me that they don't teach text connections anymore. That worries me a bit. In reaching for rigor, we forget the value of text-to-world connections. We need to connect to what we are reading in order to understand what we are reading, as this reinforces and grows what we know.

Your Instructional Playbook

Name It: Start by talking about how when you read you make connections to things you know about the world or about life in general. In this task, you are going to learn to make connections to things you know about the world.

What You Might Say Next: "When we are reading, sometimes we can connect what we are reading about to something we know or saw on TV or learned in school. Making a connection between what you know and what you are reading about will help make the text easier to understand. It also helps you grow smarter, as you will be adding to information you know."

Typical Successes

> This we know: All things are connected like the blood that unites us
> We did not weave the web of life.
> We are merely a strand in it.
> Whatever we do to the web, we do to ourselves.

I think everybody in the world has some of thare familys blod. I think the web of life cant brake because babys keep geting born and make and more and more. I think all things are conected I think there are so many people we dont die until a long time so we are conected and the blood is too. I think we are all living. I think when it say all things are conected I think the grass and the flowers are conected. I think when it said whatever we do to the web we do to ourselves I think if we do something to the web we are doing it to our selves because something bad will hap to us.

Owns It! Student writing in a reading notebook that shows he was relating what he already knew to what he was reading when working with the complex text, *Chief Seattle's Speech.*

Model/Do Together: Read passages from various nonfiction texts and talk a lot about what details seem critical to understanding the text. Share lots of examples of your thinking. Encourage students to share their experiences when they were reading along and the topic or something in the text reminded them of something they knew. Use prompts like those that follow to encourage students to connect the text to what they know. Create a teaching chart with the students, discussing and recording the definitions and maybe samples of each from texts. You want what is recorded on the teaching chart to be a class-created definition, not just your definition written out for ease. *It is the conversation you have with your students that helps them learn this for their own.*

Tweak: If their connection is far afield, don't shut it down but talk about it: Ask them why they think there is a connection.

- Have you ever heard or read about this information (or idea) before?
- Do you know anything about (*information in the text*)?
- What do you think about the big ideas in the text?
- How would you connect what you know to what you think the text is about?
- How does what you know or what you've heard or learned somewhere connect to what this text is about?

Release: Using sticky notes, have students record connections they make between what they are reading and what they know. It is better if they just put one connection on each sticky note so that they don't get confused about what they were thinking about. They can add a page number to refer them back to the text. Invite students to share their sticky notes and post the sticky notes on a teaching chart or recording wall.

Watch Fors and Work Arounds

Students get stuck and don't know if they have any connections they can make. This is all right, and sometimes it happens that a student doesn't have the background knowledge about the subject to make a connection in a direct sense. Encourage any other connection to the text the student might be able to make, even if it is about a process or something occurring. For example, a student might not know about the automaticity of an orange packing company, but they might have held or ate an orange and be able to imagine what texture the fruit is and how an engineer had to design a machine not to hurt the fruit when packing it.

Here is a favorite graphic of mine showing a few Banned Boring Connections.

5

Quoting an Important Idea in a Nonfiction Text

WHEN YOU MIGHT OFFER IT

You might offer this task when students are reading nonfiction and get sidetracked by the extra details and have trouble figuring out the main idea or major points in the text.

TARGET

Students make a statement about important ideas in a text they read independently and back up their thinking by quoting the text.

I am one of those people in staff meetings that makes a beeline for what I think are the most important points, and it drives my department chair crazy. In my rush to get it done, I undercut that a discussion about what is actually important and what is extraneous can be powerful: All colleagues feel heard, each person may discover that what is minor to them is major to someone else, and the process builds consensus. Now, this is a very grown up, 21st Century Skill that I'm clearly still learning, but ironically enough, I know how to teach it to students! It starts with students being able to determine important facts from extraneous detail *and talking about them.*

Your Instructional Playbook

Name It: Read passages from various nonfiction texts and talk a lot about what details seem critical to our understanding about the topic and what is extraneous detail—say, "These details are nice to know but don't make or break our understanding." In this task you are going to learn to identify "important point" and "extraneous detail" in conversations with one another.

What You Might Say Next: "While you are reading and when you are done reading, it helps to think about the text. What did you think about the text? What did you learn? What does the author seem most interested in about this topic? What was it mostly about? You can write about the text in your notebook by making a statement (*writing a sentence for younger students*) about what you read. It is important to go back and quote the text to support your statement (*or sentence*)."

Typical Successes

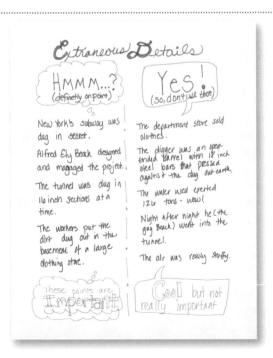

Here is a teaching chart comparing and contrasting important points and extraneous details from one chapter in *Secret Subway: The Fascinating Tale of an Amazing Feat of Engineering* by Martin Sandler.

Model/Do Together: Launch with some vivid, contrasting examples of concise text and a treatment of the same topic that is bloated with extraneous details. It could be two YouTube videos showing how to bake or make something or an evening news segment that is taught. Now that your students get the gist, give students practice in knowing the difference between an important point and extraneous detail. Create a teaching chart with the students, discussing and recording the definitions and maybe samples of each from texts. You want what is recorded on the teaching chart to be a class-created definition, not just your definition written out for ease. You can also model how to quote from the text to back up your thinking. *It is the conversation you have with your students that helps them learn this for their own.*

Tweak: Language frames to jump-start conversation might include:

"When you think of (text topic), what do you already know about (text topic) and what did you learn that is new? (Quote from the text so we know what part of the learning is new for you)."

"What did you learn about (subject of the text)? Can you share your thinking? What part of the text made you think that? (Quote it.)"

"In the book _____, on page _____, new information for me is_____."

"On page _____, the author talks about _____. This reminds me about _____, but it is different and new. What is new is _____."

Release: Have students define important point and extraneous detail in conversation with one another. They can come up with examples also in a shared reading text or in texts you have in the classroom library. Have students share their examples with the whole class by quoting from the text to back up their thinking about important point or extraneous detail.

Watch Fors and Work Arounds

Students are not quoting text correctly. You might have to teach that skill directly, as appropriate for your grade level.

Students sometime make connections between points of information that don't make any sense or that are incorrect. When this happens ask them to explain what it is in the text that is new and what they might already know or not know about the subject. You might be surprised. It isn't important that we deem what they say to be a good connection between known and unknown facts: What is important is if the student can explain their new learning and defend it by pointing to evidence in the text as support.

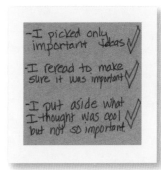

-I picked only important ideas ✓

-I reread to make sure it was important ✓

-I put aside what I thought was cool but not so important ✓

Name Character Motives and Actions

WHEN YOU MIGHT OFFER IT

You might offer it when students are beginning to read more complex text and or launching into chapter books.

TARGET

Students are able to name character motives and back up their claims by stating the character's actions that portray the motives.

When I read a novel, I relate to the characters as if they are real people. I want to counsel them about how to handle a situation, or I just want to kick them (only the villainous ones, of course!). Sometimes I feel sad when a book ends, as I feel like the contact with people that seemed so real has ended. This is the kind of involvement a novelist wishes for! It's hard to parse precisely what accounts for this empathy, this relating, between reader and character, but I think a big part of it is a by-product of a reader weighing the *motives* of a character against what their own motives might be in a similar situation.

Your Instructional Playbook

Name It: Story events are often propelled forward by the actions that the characters are taking. A character map is a graphic brainstorm where the student represents the character in pictures and words. In this task, you are going to learn to name character actions by starting with a character and creating a map about that character.

What You Might Say Next: "Understanding characters help us enjoy stories. When we know why the character is doing what he or she is doing, we can empathize with him more, better predict events, and know what he needs to realize or do differently to conquer his challenges. Knowing all these things helps us to get the author's themes."

Typical Successes

Owns It!

Model/Do Together: Consider the events occurring in a story and see if there are any connections between the character's motives and story events. In the character map, students can write what the character has done, how the character has felt, and even what the character has said. Then, you can do a gentle lead by having the students talk about their maps and try to decide together what the character's motives might be.

Help students launch into creating the character maps. Start by having the students draw or sketch the character in the middle of a blank page. Then have the students write the character's actions, thoughts, and things he or she said around the character, using words to illustrate the character's nature. Next, work with the class to name motives. For example, "When Charles helped up his fellow soccer player after he fell down shows that his motives are good. He could have run by the soccer player in order to score the goal by himself."

Tweak: Guide your students to be able to discuss motives as what the character wants or the reasons she is doing what she is doing. As they take turns doing this, they build the map together in a progressive brainstorm.

Release: As the whole class or in small groups, have students discuss actions and debate what the motives might be. Use the progressive brainstorm format (see below) to support students. After some discussion, have the students work with you to brainstorm a sentence that names the character's motives. A frame you use to support this might be the following: "_____ did _____ because_____." Or "_____might (do, say, make, think) _____because_____."

"The meeting of two personalities is like the contact of two chemical substances: If there is reaction, both are transformed."

—Carl Jung (1998)

Watch Fors and Work Arounds

Students are stuck and not adding ideas to the progressive brainstorm about the characters. Get students talking! Put them in groups of four to five, just for discussion, not for the progressive brainstorm. Using sticky notes and the book, have the students go back to the book and look for actions the characters are taking. Have them note the action, the page they found the action on, and add a jot about what they think the action means. Then, encourage students to talk about it. For example, "When Jenn ran outside to cry, after she found out about her grandmother, I think that it shows she is protecting her mom. She doesn't want her mom to feel worse. The sentence says . . . And it is because of this that I think she wants to spare her mom's feelings."

Progressive Brainstorm Directions

Pass out a large piece of paper to student groups, with four to five students in each group. Each group needs colored markers.

Have them add to the brainstorm paper: What we know about *character name.*

They brainstorm on their paper, then, when you signal them, they move around the room to add to the other groups' papers. After adding to other groups' papers, students return to original groups to add any new insights to their own papers.

WHEN YOU MIGHT OFFER IT

You might offer it when students are drawn into deep thinking about the text; they are ready to begin literary analysis.

TARGET

Students engage in discussion (versus talking a lot) about the plot in a fiction text, what is happening in the story to move the plot forward.

When I am reading a novel, I sometimes jump ahead and read what's going to happen to the main character because I cannot wait! I know, I know, I ruin it for myself, and my daughter scolds me about that all the time because I'm missing out on all that suspense-building, rising action. So I confess—I need this task, in which readers learn to relish and "track" the intriguing plot that is unfolding and deeply think about the character dynamics that go hand in hand with it.

Your Instructional Playbook

Name It: The plot is the problem of the story and the events that flow from the problem, leading to resolution. In this task, you are going to learn to focus on the events that create real tension, that contribute to the rising action.

What You Might Say Next: "We could check almost any story we have read and we would see *a lot* of events that lead up to the big problem or issue that the story is about. After several of these events, the story often suddenly gets full of tension and excitement—the term for this trajectory is called rising action. Today, we are going to learn to notice the important, interesting scenes and distinguish them from the "filler scenes." It is fun and interesting to map out these events, so we can see what is happening in order. We are going to name the events in _____ (State the title of the book you are reading). Let's put them in order on our story frame for rising action."

Typical Successes

Owns It! Here is an example of a story frame brainstormed by a group of students for *A Place Where Sunflowers Grow by* Amy Lee-Tai.

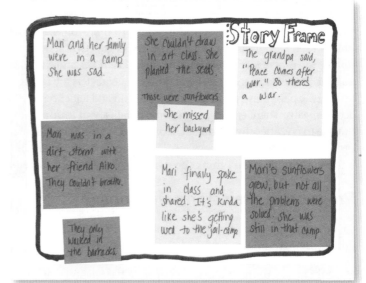

Model/Do Together: When you are partly into a fiction text that has a rich plot and sufficient tension, work on a story frame together. A story frame helps the students visualize what is happening in the plot by sketching out what has occurred and is occurring. See the preceding figure. Students will need guided practice and modeling from you in knowing how stories unfold in *a series* of events and that this unfolding involves conflict. You can, if appropriate for your students, get sophisticated in your discussion with them of the unfolding and talk with them about types of conflict (person vs. person; person vs. self; person vs. society; person vs. nature) or the fact that events sometimes don't unfold in chronological order. However, at first, focus on working with students in a story frame with a text in chronological order so they can get good at this task, before moving to more sophisticated forms.

Tweak: Students can build confidence by starting with the story frame in pictures only; doing so works well with younger readers. Older readers can jump right into the story frame in words or a combination of both as suggested above.

Release: Before students launch into working independently in a story frame, have them work in partners or trios to create a large story frame as a group using a different text. They can talk about their ideas together, referencing the text again and again as they go back and think through the plot. Encourage students to share with the class what they were thinking and what they added to their story frames.

> *"The most powerful words in English are, 'Tell me a story.'"*
>
> —Pat Conroy (2016, para. 3)

Watch Fors and Work Arounds

Students are confused about what is an action in the fiction text. Guide students in thinking about the text while having them think about a series of questions, so they can identify action that flows from the plot.

- What problem does the *character* have or is he or she facing?
- What do you think is most important in the story so far?
- How is the author showing what is happening?
- How has time changed in the story?
- Is the problem getting bigger (more difficult, complex)?

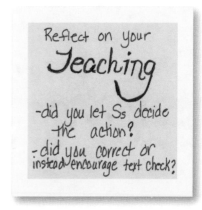

Reflect on your **Teaching**

-did you let Ss decide the action?
-did you correct or instead encourage text check?

WHEN YOU MIGHT OFFER IT

You might offer it when students have been engaged in deep thinking about the plot and they are moving to the end of the book to discuss how the text ends.

TARGET

Students engage in discussion about the resolution of the problem in a fiction text and finish a story frame.

Just like helping students map out the plot progression of a fiction text, reviewing the progression to the plot climax and the resolution of the problem can help students to understand what they are reading. On top of that, it can be deeply satisfying. I go over and over a book's ending in my head, thinking about well, this happened, then that . . . When I watch a movie, I am worse! I want students to get good at analyzing resolutions too, because it deepens their sense of theme.

Your Instructional Playbook

Name It: The events, as they happen in the sequence of a story, build up to the climax of the story. Sometimes people call this the *rising action.* Then, at the top of the rising action, is the climax, and then there is falling action, which leads to the resolution or the end. In this task, you are going to learn to identify the resolution in a story and create a story frame.

What You Might Say Next: "Stories don't just end. They end after a progression of events and after the climax of the story or when the 'big problem' happens. We call the ending a *resolution.* Usually but not always, the resolution makes sense based on what has happened in the story so far. (In the next sentence, give an example from a book you are familiar with.) For example, in *The Three Questions*, the resolution was Nicholai getting his questions answered. We can think of story plots as mountains. The events rise in the action or tension and then peak at the top of the mountain and go back down the mountain in falling action as the problem is solved."

Typical Successes

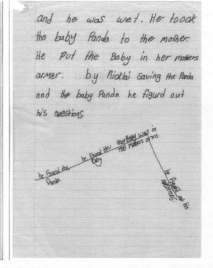

Not Quite There Yet! Student's writing showing part of the rising and falling action for the plot in *The Three Questions* by Jon J. Muth.

Model/Do Together: Draw the rising action, climax, and falling action in a line on a big piece of paper. Work with the students to name the events that fall along the time line and then label the events along the line. Have students fill in the blank spaces with the details from each event and then have them decide if the resolution was logical or expected from reading the book.

You can co-construct a plot map with the students, but make sure that you're a facilitator only. Students may depend on you for the answers, and it gets easy to answer your own questions about "What goes next" and forget to give wait time. In order for students to become independent at the task, they need practice with the task. Ask questions that facilitate student thinking like, "What happened first?" "What was the first big event?" "Where does that event go on the plot line?" "How did the problem get solved?"

Release: Have students work with a partner to discuss how they think the problem in the story was solved. Give them time to take jots about the ideas they share with their partners. Invite students to share out some of their ideas about how the problem in the story was addressed. Have them reference the text, and give the class time to discuss the thinking, adding whether they agree, disagree, or have more to add.

Watch Fors and Work Arounds

If you are reading a book as a whole class, the book is beyond the reading level of many students, and they aren't grasping all of the story events. In this case, read the book with the students or to the students and engage in lots of group discussions. Focus on being the facilitator, though, prompting students to think about what they know about the text, so they come up with the plot resolution themselves. Just because they cannot read it without support doesn't mean they cannot comprehend the text when supported.

Student Reflection
- What was first?
- What happened next?
- What happened after that?
- What was the problem?
- How was the problem solved?
- What wrapped it up at the end?

WHEN YOU MIGHT OFFER IT

You might offer it when students have been reading longer texts and need some help with remembering what they have read. Retelling can help them as they visualize what was in the text as they read.

TARGET

Using a circular story map, students will draw or sketch the main events in a story, in chronological order, and use the graphics to orally retell the story.

I hate to admit it, but sometimes I don't read all the way through an online article, blog, or even a long email. I stop halfway and I kick myself later because I usually miss something really important! Our students are just as vulnerable to this flightiness and like us, their reading demands have become more complicated. Think about the work involved in retelling a digital text, with its nonlinearity of hyperlinks, images, and text. What is considered key? What do they retell? Students need a way to check their own comprehension silently in their head by asking, "What did I just read?" Students need to be able to retell now more than ever.

Your Instructional Playbook

Name It: Retelling is an important skill. Retelling is a first step toward summarizing text. In this task, you are going to learn to draw or sketch the main events in a story, in order to orally retell the story.

What You Might Say Next: "Retelling what we've read helps us understand and remember it. But it is so easy to get lost in too many details when you retell a story. If you plan a retelling of a story you read and you have lots and lots of details, you are going to lose the interest of your listener or reader. Instead, when you retell, you want to make sure and put in the big events from the story and some of the details from those big events, to make sure you are saying enough about the story. But you don't want to get so bogged down in retelling all the parts that you drown in the details."

Typical Successes

Here is a circular story map created with a group of students.

Model/Do Together: Don't focus on retelling every single little detail, but start with the gist of the text and then add details to the retelling as students improve or as the text complexity increases. To guide students in gaining the ability to retell on their own, show them how to create a circular story map:

Starting at the top of a blank page, students draw or write out the beginning then going clockwise, they draw five to six main events from the story. As they round the circle, near where 11:00 would be on a clock face, they draw or write the ending.

Tweak: Remember that students need to come up with the main events themselves.

Release: Have students discuss in partners or trios what they would put on their circular story map as mental rehearsal before they dive into creating on their own. Or have them plan as a group about a text they have all read, and then have them go off and work on the circular story map together. Have a few students share out what they plan to do (or did) in creating their circular story map.

Watch Fors and Work Arounds

Your students either don't say enough or say too much while retelling. Reinforce their excitement to share, but remind them to keep on track and think about if they are sharing too much. Role-play with the class what happens when you say too little or share too much.

Students get stuck and don't know how to get started with their retelling, Give them prompts:

- At the beginning
- Share five to six main events
- Ending

Students get stuck and cannot think of the main details. Allow them to go back to the book or text to review the story.

This student's description of events could be added to a large circular group-designed map by cutting students' notes out of the notebook and gluing it on the map. The student's notes are from *Frindle* by Andrew Clements.

WHEN YOU MIGHT OFFER IT

You might offer it when students are ready to make inferences about what they are reading or when students are ready to explore the meaning of a book beyond just what they read in the words on the page.

TARGET

Students will dig deeper into the text to ask and answer questions about that text that require more than of recalling of facts or information.

I love interactive reading work with students. The more I can encourage students' voices in the room, the better. Now, that does *not* mean that I like a classroom in disarray or that I am a laissez-faire teacher when it comes to classroom management. No, I just feel most empowered as a teacher when I encourage my students to do the learning for themselves and from each other. A quiet classroom is not a classroom where students deeply comprehend what they are reading (or learning vocabulary or acquiring English, but those are topics for another day).

Your Instructional Playbook

Name It: Really expert readers go beyond what the text says, and they also figure out meaning about the text that isn't answered "right there" in the text. In this task, you are going to learn to dig deeper into what you are reading to ask and answer questions that require some thinking.

What You Might Say to Introduce It: "Alright, let's figure out what happened (for older readers bump up the vocabulary by saying, 'what came to light'or 'transpired') in the text. We are going to dig in here with some deep questions. I have a couple of questions to start us off, then you can ask questions also."

Typical Successes

> Motivashon
> The Emperors motivashon is to be a greedy man. Like when the part when the Emperor banished the nightinegale. And when He said "If I don't get the nightingale everyone will get punished."
>
> The nightingales motivashon is TO be free and not be a slave. When The Emperor got the toy of the nightingale, everybody got there attention to the toy. So She left.
>
> The primemenister's motivashon is He's worried because the Emperor told him to get the bird or he Or anybody else will get hurt.
>
> The Emperors and the nightingale Was amazed when Death went away and all the faces. The singing from the nightingale comfted the Emperor.
>
> [Teacher's question] → [What motivated each character?]

Owns It! This is a piece of student writing where the student was able to answer a deeper question asked by the teacher about the book *The Emperor and the Nightingale* by Fiona Waters.

Model/Do Together: Let's read a short text together (paragraph, poem, or a few pages from a picture book) and think about what we know about what is happening in the text. (Please note that K–3 students determine a lot of meaning from illustrations and pictures. This is fine; encourage this as it helps them to comprehend deeply.)

Do a shared reading (where students have copies of the text) of a short piece of text that is *not* from the text that you are currently reading in class. Facilitate a short group discussion about the text you just read. Make sure that the answers require students to draw conclusions about the text. If you don't know how to do this, ask a question and then ask "why?" Encourage students to ask questions that need them to dig into the text to answer. Give ample time for students to work through some of the questions. Intersperse the discussion with questions you ask as well, but only if needed.

Release: Pass out sentence strips or 12 x 18 paper cut longwise about 3 inches wide. Now, refer students to a text that you are currently reading in class or have read in class previously. (For K–3, this might be a big book or a picture book.) Have the students write questions that are not "right there" in the text on the strips and then have them show their question to another group of three to double check if their questions make sense.

Watch Fors and Work Arounds

When you ask a deep question, a question where the answer is not right there in the text, your students might just sit silently. Or maybe the few students who always answer will be eager to share, but others will be quiet.

Lean into that silence; don't be afraid. Your students just might need wait time. Watch that you don't rush into the silence and answer the question yourself. Pair students up and encourage them to share their thoughts first with a partner. Encourage partners to share their answers together. Turn the responsibility of asking the questions to your students. Have them work in groups of two or three to write the questions.

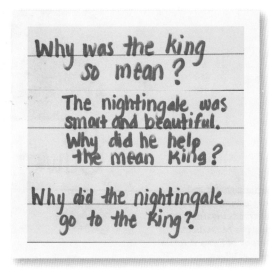

WHEN YOU MIGHT OFFER IT

You might offer it for use with younger readers, when you read complex texts to them, and for use with older readers, as they read their own texts.

TARGET

Taking turns with a partner or in a trio, students will ask wonder questions and respond to wonder questions while reading a text.

A few years ago, I was leading a session at a conference for parents about how to help their children comprehend what they are reading. I had an array of picture books scattered about, and I asked each group of parents to pick one picture book. They did, and I asked them to read the first five pages. Then I asked, *"What do you wonder about in this book right now?"* No one answered. So I rephrased my question. *"Now that you have started the book, what are you wondering? Do you wonder what will happen next?"* I received blank stares. My workshop on was falling flat quickly. A moment later (thankfully), a brave mom raised her hand and she said, "I never knew it was OK to 'wonder' about the book, I mean, don't you just read it?" That moment reminded me that I cannot take for granted that students wonder when they read, and that they know *how* to wonder.

Your Instructional Playbook

Name It: In this task, you are going to learn to wonder about and respond during and after reading a text or reading part of a text.

What You Might Say Next: "Find a partner. We are going to do some wondering together. When I wonder, I think about all of the lovely things that an author might want to be telling or showing me through their writing. You are going to get in the habit of stopping right where you are in a book and wondering about *why* or *how* something is happening. You are also going to get very good at answering your wonders. You can brainstorm all the maybes with your partner, and then by answering your own wonder question with *Maybe because . . . "*

Typical Successes

Teaching chart filled with students' wonder statements regarding the book *The Miraculous Journey of Edward Tulane* by Kate DiCamillo.

Model/Do Together: Choose a book or text that you want to read aloud to the students. Let the students know that they are going to be making *I wonder* statements about the text you are going to read aloud. Then, start by telling the students the title and author of the text. Give a short prereading introduction to the text.

Minimodel the guided wonderings and responses. A minimodel is when you model for short snippets rather than read really long passages. So start by reading a few pages, and then say *I wonder why . . .* and fill in with something from the book. For example, in reading *The Miraculous Journey of Edward Tulane* by Kate DiCamillo I might stop on page 29 and say, "I wonder why the grandma told such a dreary story?" Follow your first couple of wonders with a tentative response. Your responses can begin with *maybe* and *because.* I might say, "Maybe she is trying to teach Abilene something." It is important to give a tentative response using textual evidence. Use something in the text or illustrations to help you come up with your *because* answer. Continue reading, wondering, and allowing responses to bubble up from you and the students.

Release: After you have minimodeled a few *I wonder* statements and responses, let the students ask the *I wonder* questions. Allow their responses to unfold naturally; don't direct the conversation too much. Have the students work in pairs or triads.

After the small groups have been engaged in conversation for a while, have them share with the whole group what their *I wonder* questions and responses were. Have students jot different *I wonder* questions on sticky notes and add them to a teaching chart about how to have a book conversation based on wonderings.

Watch Fors and Work Arounds

Some students monopolize the wondering and responses.
Remind the class that all voices need to be heard and valued. Use a token like a poker chip to regulate conversation. Pass out two to three poker chips to the students. If a student wants to speak, he or she puts the poker chip in the middle of the table (or floor if students gather in different places around the room). Students cannot speak once they run out of poker chips, giving other students a chance to speak up.

Students don't wonder about anything. Often the partner or trio groups are reluctant to share their thinking. Join the group for awhile and offer some *I wonder* statements that are really obvious, with the answers right there in the text. Also, you can pretend to not be able to answer an *I wonder* question, modeling that every one gets stuck from time to time. These two actions will usually get the conversation going so students can see they don't have to ask hard questions or always know the answer.

Reflect on your
Teaching
- Did you give wait time before adding your own "I wonder"?
- Did you coach or tell?

WHEN YOU MIGHT OFFER IT

You might offer it when students are ready to go deeper into conversation about text and share their thinking. This task works well in first through sixth grade, when you are teaching with text complex enough at each grade level that students can participate in a shared reading and have something significant to discuss. Check out the text sample at the end of the task.

TARGET

Students can make statements about a text, providing details or elaboration to clarify their meaning if classmates don't understand the point being made.

Praise only goes so far. According to Carol Dweck, praise doesn't develop students into strong thinkers with a growth mindset. In fact, praise can make students feel like smart is something you are, not something you get. I used to be in the praise trap. I would tell my students "good job" or "nice work." These are hollow phrases and don't carry much meaning. Elaboration and clarifying go a long way in giving feedback. When I ask students to do something hard, like clarify the meaning of the text or elaborate on what they said about something they read, I actively remember to use coaching terms, not praising terms. So, I might say, "That makes sense, what else can you add?" or "I am not understanding, tell me more."

Your Instructional Playbook

Name It: Naming specific points that happen in a story helps readers comprehend. In this task, you will learn to have deep conversations about texts that you read in groups.

What You Might Say Next: "Sometimes we say things without being clear about what we mean. Yesterday, my husband asked me to go get that thing that he needed from the kitchen. I had to ask, what *thing*? I didn't know what he wanted. See, when we are clear, when we clarify our thinking, we can better understand what we are talking about. We do this too when we read books. I read in someone's journal that they liked what the character did to help his brother. But I didn't know what the character did to help his brother. You need to name it."

Typical Successes

This visually engaging teaching chart has students' sticky notes on it with examples of clarified meaning from the text *Effie's Image* by N. L. Sharp.

Model/Do Together: Model for students the difference between entries in a reading response journal where the writer used specific details from the text to make a point and elaborated. Then, show an example of a journal page where the writer was not specific and was not clear in exactly what was happening. You can use student samples for this (from former students, and with names deleted) or write an example yourself. Then, move students to a story or text discussion. Ask them to share what they think about the text, elaborating with details to provide clarity. Encourage students to do the talking about the text, not wait for you to jump in and lead the discussion.

Choose a text and read it as a shared reading with the class. After the reading, lead a class discussion about the text. Focus on asking questions, on coaching students to answer, not answering yourself. Focus on pulling the ideas from the students that encourages them to be clear in what they are saying. Ask questions like the following:

- What . . . ?
- How . . . ?
- Tell me one way.
- Tell me another way.
- Tell me another point.
- What else . . . ?
- Who else . . . ?

"If we want students to become highly expert readers, we must help them become independent and attentive noticers, questioners, and interpreters on their own."

—Wilhelm & Smith
(2016, p. 7)

As you focus on these questions, encourage students to elaborate with details from the text. Use specific prompts that help students get farther in their thinking. I might say, "What did you notice first in the text?" "Then what did you think?" "At the end, were you thinking the same thing as at the beginning? Why?" You need to offer students opportunities to work at complex thinking while you *coach* them as they work on this difficult task.

Tweak: As you are facilitating the discussion, focus on the role of the facilitator. If the discussion has a lull, pause before you rush in and elaborate on the story discussion. Remember you want students to be doing the discussion, not you. If the students are not elaborating and giving short answers, prod a bit. You can ask questions like "Can you tell us more?" "What specifically in the text makes you think that?"

Release: After practicing a few times together as a class in discussion, have the students work in small groups to have a discussion, focusing on sharing ideas with detail and elaborating as necessary to make their points.

Watch Fors and Work Arounds

Your students tend to talk in pronouns. For example, they say *him* or *her* instead of using the proper name of the character. Or they use pronouns to describe people, places, and things. Encourage the students to use the proper noun or noun. This will instantly clarify their meaning. For example, "I thought it was mean when the character Kara told Sally's secret to all of their friends," versus "I thought it was mean when she told all the secrets." This can be tricky to catch when you have read the same book or text as the students, as you will know what they are talking about. But insist on clarity. It deepens comprehension.

WHEN YOU MIGHT OFFER IT

You might offer it at the start of school year, to set up the literacy routines, or anytime that you need to revisit routines for productive literacy work.

TARGET

Students will able to sustain reading and writing on their own when given time for independent work.

When I go to a professional development workshop where there are lots of colleagues I haven't seen in a long time, I am *the worst* at talking too much and not paying attention enough. Sometimes, it feels so good to connect with those around us that our work falls aside. This happens with our students as well. Young readers and writers need help to satisfy their desire for peer relationships. Very young students have not yet developed good control over their emotions and impulses, so they might lean to talking more than reading, even if they think they are sharing about their reading.

Your Instructional Playbook

Name It: In order to shore up or expand work routines, you are going to discuss and decide what good reading and writing behaviors and actions look and sound like. In this task, you are going to check yourself to make sure you are focusing on good reader and writer actions.

What You Might Say Next: "It is so much fun to talk to each other while we are working, but I have noticed lately that we are talking to each other more than we are working. That makes it hard for us to get our reading and writing done. We want to get smart, so we need to read and write everyday! Today, think about how much you are talking to your friends and how much you are reading. I do want you to talk about your reading, but you have to read *first* so you have something to talk about."

Typical Successes

Use a catchy classroom management chart that can help students know (or choose) when they should talk and when they should just write or read.

Model/Do Together: Cheerlead about the great work ethic your class is showing (even if they aren't in the groove of good routines yet, it is better to start positive). Cocreate a chart that shows students' productive (and not!) reading and writing behaviors, and use emojis like happy, neutral, or sad faces to illustrate it. You can use this chart when you remind students of classroom routines.

Tweak: After a specified work time in class, reflect as a group on the work routines and behaviors that the class displayed. Ask students to be self-reflective, and consider the level that they were working at and if that level helped or hindered them as readers and writers. Ask the class if there are any new actions to add to the chart that will help them stay on task?

Release: Invite students to routinely reflect on their readerly behavior and decide where they should be at what time. Students have much more capacity than we anticipate they do for deciding what readerly behavior is appropriate when.

Watch Fors and Work Arounds

If students are still not reading and are spending too much time talking, revisit the discussion and talk about self-reflection and self-regulation. What do those terms mean? How might it help the class if all students acted "readerly" or "writerly" and learned to *share* with friends as appropriate?

"A schedule defends from chaos and whim. It is a net for catching days. It is a scaffold on which a worker can stand and labor with both hands at sections of time."

—Annie Dillard
(1989)

WHEN YOU MIGHT OFFER IT

You might offer it whenever you notice readers floundering or not reading as much. Remember that just because a student can fix up at one text level, he may not be able to do this at a harder text level.

TARGET

Students will be able to apply a fix-up strategy when they realize they don't understand what they are reading.

We've all heard the stories. Teachers feeling they have to read aloud the textbook because it's too hard for their class, or students read too-easy books all year because it's too daunting to try to get every reader to read challenging texts for themselves. I've been there, done that, way back, and it feels like when I'm driving in the rain and hit a curve that is sharper than I'd anticipated, and I grip the wheel, bracing for the fallout. We can't just squeeze our eyes shut and hope for the best for our readers. To bring about successful comprehension instruction, we have to give students strategies they can lean on when they read challenging texts.

Your Instructional Playbook

Name It: Launch with a positive statement: *When you get stuck reading, I know you know just what to do to help yourself.* In this task, you are going to think about fix-up strategies that work for you when you get stuck while reading.

What You Might Say Next: "Do you ever get partway into a chapter and you realize you have no idea what you read? It's like I'm whipping over the words but my mind is elsewhere! Today I'm going to show you some of the things I do to get myself out of that autopilot; you stop reading, you go back a few paragraphs or pages, and you double-check to make sure you know what the book is saying. To do this double-checking, you choose from what are called fix-up strategies. I think of them as a first-aid kit for readers."

Typical Successes

This is not your run-of-the-mill fix-up strategy chart. Use this teaching chart as a springboard for creating a vibrant chart that can be changed or added to over time.

Model/Do Together: Model using several different fix-up strategies with both fiction and nonfiction texts. Display a poster size Fix-Up Strategy Chart in your classroom that you begin with students and add to over time using your ideas *and* students' ideas. Have students jot on sticky notes their own fix-up tips and put them on the chart whenever the spirit moves them.

Tweak: Devote a few minutes to mental rehearsal before students try a strategy for the first time. Mental rehearsal is a strategy used in many fields, from sports to acting to surgery, when the learner envisions himself performing a new skill. Students are naturals at it, and it centers them as they think about which strategy they might try and visualize themselves going through the steps of the strategy.

Release: Periodically, encourage students to share what is working for them. Students can learn so much more from each other than they can often learn from us. Give them time to discuss what they tried, when, and how.

Watch Fors and Work Arounds

When your students talk superficially about what they read, for example, "Some guy, I think his name was Jeff, well he did some stuff in the story," or "A really bad thing happened, I think it was during a flood. Some people got hurt and some bad stuff happened," encourage the students to reread or make mental images while reading. They could also stop and think or stop and jot to help themselves track what they are reading as they go.

When you realize a text might be just beyond what students can read on their own, change out the text, it may be too hard. Use partner reading or read the text first together as a read-aloud.

Reflect on your **Teaching**

- did you encourage students to "fix-up" on their own?

- did you refrain from telling the word or text?

WHEN YOU MIGHT OFFER IT

You might offer it when your students are not digging into work for some reason; this task helps you redirect the behavior that you don't want to see, like students sitting, not trying, in a positive manner.

TARGET

Students focus on task completion and developing the ability to work independently and manage their time.

I went into yoga class this week, and I thought to myself, "I've got this," as I rolled out my mat. Then, as class started, I found that I felt listless and not really *into it*. I think we all have days like this, when we don't mentally focus on what we are about to do and how we are going to support ourselves to get it done. Our students experience the same thing. Some of this may be human nature, and we can't expect one hundred percent attention, but I think it's helpful to look at what we are saying—and how long we are saying it! Encourage awake and ready brains to take in new information by avoiding too much teacher talk where you tell them every last little detail they could ever need to know.

Your Instructional Playbook

Name It: I am going to give you highly specific directions, and I expect you to jump in quickly and try! In this task, you will learn to work to stay focused and get to work quickly.

What You Might Say Next: "It can be difficult to get started when I ask you to start working. I know that you might not be feeling 'into it' when I say, 'Ok, let's go.' But I really need you to give your work a try instead of sitting and waiting for me, after I go through our minilesson. You won't believe how much more sense my directions will make once you have dug into the work and given it a try. Then, let me know if you are stuck. Remember, I am here to help you do something you have not done before, not to do it for you. That's how we get smart, we do things we haven't done before! I don't want to solve problems you have the chance to solve yourself."

Typical Success

> I get distracted alot so I have to try this First, I will pinch myself because sometimes I daydream (my mom says so). Then, I will luok at the chart or my notes to see what I should do. I might not wirte stuff down if I was daydreaming, so I have to check the chart Mrs. G posts in front. I know if I mess it all up I can read and thats o.k.

Owns It! Check out this student's exit ticket reflection about what he will try when he gets distracted.

Model/Do Together: Have students repeat back to you (chorally) what you are asking them to do. Have them tell each other what they understand about what it is they are to do. Next, let supports like prompts and anchor charts do the teaching; help them take new information, ideas, and directions from processing memory (things that wash away quickly when we hear them if we don't have a reason to hang on to the information) to short-term memory so students can remember what to do when they start working.

Tweak: Ask a few prompts to get students thinking about their choices for action, but make it clear you expect them to do this kind of mental jumpstarting independently:

- Think to yourself, what are you going to do first when you get your work started?

- How will you approach your reading (writing) today?

- Make three jots about what your goals are during reading (writing) today.

- Reflect on what is hardest about what I am asking of you today, talk with your partner about what seems so hard. Can your partner help you figure out a good approach?

Release: Ask students to share with a partner what they could do to *be in charge* of their learning that day.

Watch Fors and Work Arounds

Students don't start working after the minilesson is over, but overwhelm you with hands up in the air and a chorus of "teacher" "teacher." Or the students are not building their stamina to try to work on their own. One-on-one conferences provide you a great opportunity for coaching. Usually, if a student seems to be depending too much on you to get started, she might be unsure about what to do. First, check your teaching. Reflect on the minilessons and make sure you have been clear and supportive. Then, sit with the student and have her talk through with you the various ways she can start working. You can ask, "What can you try?" Once the student answers, ask "What else can you try? I want to sit with you while you get started so I can see what you do to help yourself." Give encouraging comments as the student works through getting started on her own. Listen and support.

"Before each shot, I go to the movies inside my head."

—Jack Nicklaus (1972)

You might offer it when readers of all abilities are ready for this task once they are reading text on their own. Younger readers may use the pictures and the text to answer the questions. Older readers may use text features to guide and help them.

TARGET

Students justify their answer to a text-dependent question by referring back to the text.

Yes, yes, I know. *Text-dependent question* is one of those terms that has some baggage, but it doesn't have to mean that student-generated questions are therefore banished. And I have to admit, when I see students succeed in a task that helps them think on their own and be literate, it is like an elixir for my soul. Focus on text-dependent questions when you want students to reflect on something they've read and brush up on referring back to the text.

Your Instructional Playbook

Name It: A text-dependent question is a question that requires you to quote or refer to the text to support your response. In this task, by using text as evidence for an answer, you will say or write a justification statement in order to answer a question.

What You Might Say Next: "Sometimes you will be asked a question that you have to answer based on what you read in the text (or story). For example, if you are asked why you think a character did something, go back and find the page that has details that help you explain or prove your answer. What is in the picture or in the words on that page that helps you answer the question? You can put a sticky note on the page to help you remember what your answer is and why."

Typical Successes

Not Quite There Yet! This student answered a question in her reading journal, but the answer does not use the text to support it.

Teacher question:	What do we know about the character traits of the main character?
Student response from journal:	"I think it's because she is working hard for that guy. I think she has done a lot of hard work."

Owns It! An example of the student later on—this snippet shows how she thought about the question and added a quote.

Teacher question:	What do we know about the character traits of the main character?
Same student revised response from journal:	"Charlotte is hard working. At Ebenesser's ranch, Charlotte is the first one up working with the horses and the last one to bed at night."

Model/Do Together: During a read-aloud, start with asking a *juicy* question that cannot be answered just by remembering something simple from the text. For example, *Why was [the main character] so anxious? Why did the author keep repeating that word? What is the one thing [the character] wants but cannot seem to get?* Model how you skim to find the answer—and the supporting evidence. You could also model saying or jotting a "gist" answer on paper or a sticky note and then how you go back to the text to hunt for support. Tell students that a gist answer can be a partial or tentative answer, not yet with details from the text to confirm its accuracy. Then, demonstrate how proficient readers might underline or jot in margins or on a sticky note a fuller but still quickly worded response. Say aloud and point out which sentence or part bolsters your assertion. Finally, model how you turn your notes into a full sentence or two that answers the question and includes quotes from the text and/or page references.

Tweak:

- Use sticky notes as bookmarks to help students find pages that make them think of their answers.

- Practice with students to write jots on the sticky notes to remember their answers.

- Help students make their thinking visible by practicing a lot of classroom conversations where students go back to a page to answer a text-dependent question.

Release: Encourage students to log their thinking in a reading notebook or on a plain piece of paper. Set up the class to work in partners or triads to share their questions and their answers collaboratively. They will also need to have copies of the text with them to share accurately.

Watch Fors and Work Arounds

When students toss in ideas without deep thinking first or write their answer without backing up their thinking, you will need to guide them to go back to the text and highlight, underline, or put a sticky note on the place in the text that helped them make their decision and come up with their answer. If you are using a text that students cannot mark up, it might help to copy parts of the text when students are first learning this skill, so they can highlight and write on the copy.

"*You can't have come this far without knowing that my most urgent message to writers is that you are providing stimuli for the reader's experiences.*"

—Sol Stein
(1995, p. 196)

Tell Why (You Think, Believe, Remember, Know) With Why Messages

The other day I came across a box of letters between me and college friends and me and my family. OMG! Reading them, I was transported back to the mind and heart of an earlier me. Think about what a boon letters have been to historians of famous presidents, authors, scientists and such—what's going to happen now? Will we be combing through the hard drives of early Macs? Clearly, letter writing is becoming a lost art. So leave it to me to revive it for today's students—its yesteryear status actually makes the task more fun. The letters get our students reading; they get our students processing messages more deeply because unlike fleeting electronic text, the letters *stay*. A little permanence can go a long way.

Your Instructional Playbook

Name It: A *why* message is a class message from students to teacher or vice versa where we answer a *why* question posed by someone else. In this task, we will orally cocreate a class message to answer a why question.

What You Might Say Next: "When you are answering a question, you need to be able to say why you know or think something. In the world, we cannot say, 'just because,' or 'because I said so.' We need to explain what our take is based on, so that others can respond. What's great about learning to do this is that it's a way of communicating, connecting, and understanding ideas *and* one another better."

Typical Successes

Dear Mrs. Tollefson,

Today we are reading *Inside Out & Back Again* by Thanhha Lai. Although we have only read the beginning of the book, we think that the main character is going to feel great heartbreak. (Why is the character going to feel great heartbreak?) We think this because . . .

Dear Mr. Magdaleno,

Our class loves the Mars rover *Opportunity*. (Why do you love the Mars rover?) We love the rover called *Opportunity* for two reasons. First, we think the rover is amazing as it landed on Mars. Second, we think it is cool because it can take pictures and send them back to earth.

Model/Do Together: On big chart paper or a blank page on a projection screen, begin composing a why message while talking about your thinking. For example, Why did the patriots dump the tea in Boston harbor? Or why did Kate DiCamillo choose to have the tiger die at the end of *The Tiger Rising* (2015)? I start this task as a think-aloud because students are often shy or unsure in their answers at first. This activity opens the gate for students to confidently participate in class discussions. After you get the message started, pause and ask, "What might I (we) write next?" Students can share the pen with you and write part of the why message. The why message is a letter from the class to you, the teacher.

Tweak: To show that why questions are central to life in a fun way, play Woodie Guthrie's song "Why, Oh, Why" or a few minutes of Annie Lenox's song "Why." Youtube often has versions with the lyrics and great visuals! Your students might like creating their own video-based why messages. Also, cocreate a teaching chart with your students so they always have these jumpstarts. The possibilities are almost endless.

Release: Working in small groups—and mindful of mixing soft-spoken kids with peers who won't over talk—guide students to talk and then write why messages to you, one another, the principal, or whomever! In selecting the topic, students can draw from what they are learning, fiction, nonfiction, local events, school issues, or current or future events.

Watch Fors and Work Arounds

Watch out for overzealous students when co-constructing the message. Some students will offer up lots of ideas and answers about how to say why, but it is important to nurture all the voices in the room. Also, watch for your own voice. The message is co-constructed with the students, so there should be a balance between how much you are talking and the students are talking.

Check Out These Ways to Ask Questions

Question	Other ways to ask the question
"Why do you think . . . ?"	Why do you think that young girls like Caroline in *Long May She Wave* (Fulton, 2017) were chosen to sew instead of more experienced seamtresses?
"Why did the author . . . ?"	Why did the author write in poems in *Inside Out & Back Again?* (Lai, 2011)
"Why did the character . . . ?"	Why did Harry Potter go into the cave under the castle? (Rowling, 2000)
"Why do you think that is the most important part of the text?"	Why do you think that _____ was highlighted as an important part____?
"Do you know why . . . ?"	Do you know why pink *blobfish* float to catch their prey? (From *Pink Is for Blobfish*, Keating, 2016)
"Tell me why."	Why do we think wind power ought to be used in most states by the year 2025?
"Why do . . . ?"	Why do astronauts like Chris Hadfield go on multiple missions to space? (Langley, 2015)

Make a Bold Statement About a Text

WHEN YOU MIGHT OFFER IT

You might offer this task when students are ready to discuss complex text as a group. Text can be at the higher Lexile levels for the grade level.

TARGET

Students are able to talk in full sentences about what they read and with conviction because they have command of the facts.

One day I ran into principal Gayle Ferdinandi of Storey Elementary School in Fresno, California, and she said the teachers there were getting kids to talk about books in depth. A few days later, I sat in a first-grade classroom there and was bowled over as students popped up and talked. Such animation and smarts! Each child stated something about satellites. It was a super diverse class, with each child from different backgrounds with different languages as a first language, so their lack of shyness was all the more impressive. (So thanks to them for this task, and check out the examples shown below.)

Your Instructional Playbook

Name It: When we talk about books, we are making statements. In this task, you will be making a statement and adding to others' statements about what was read in a text by speaking in full sentences.

What You Might Say Next: "You are all really smart readers, and smart readers have deep conversations about texts they read. We are going to jump into having conversations about texts we read and think deeply about the text. We are all going to share our thinking together. And we are going to learn to be honest in what we really think and why, but we are also going to be comfortable in saying when we are still working to understand something or not getting it at all."

Typical Successes

S1	"This means satellite was moving around Earth in an orbit. And [now, reading from the text,] "Orbit is the path a spaceship that travels around other objects."
S2	"I read that people have sent hundreds of satellites around earth's orbit, and a satellite orbits the planet."
S3	"A satellite is something that connects with the power we have on earth. Like TV."
S2	[quoting the text] "I think a satellite is an object that tracks weather or sends signals."
S3	"I have a connection, and we learned about cell phones before and in this text they talk about satellites and cell phones."
S4	"I want to build onto this text. Maybe the satellite helps us because maybe that's how the weatherman tell us if it's gonna to be rainy or it's gonna be cloudy."
S5	"I wonder why they sent a satellite to space?"
S6	"So we can track weather and have signals to cell phones and computer."
S4	"Maybe that is how we get our electricity."
S1	"I want to add on to that, maybe it is because satellites have different jobs."
S8	"I want to add on, I think it's so there can be Wi-Fi and we can be connected."

Here is a snippet of a transcript of first-grade students having a conversation regarding a text about satellites.

Model/Do Together: Select a short paragraph or two of text and hand out photocopies to each student. It is best to select a chunk of text from a larger piece so the second day you can follow up with the remaining part of the text. Have students read the text on their own.

Next, ask students to pair share what they understood and emphasize that there is no correct answer! It could be simply something interesting, a wondering, a hunch about the main idea, a word that struck them as important, or something else. Then, have students reread the section together. What might they each say? Each student might write what they want to share in the margin, underlining or circling parts that are important for what they want to state. Now, choral read the text with the students so everyone has a last opportunity to absorb meaning. Finally, have students talk with their partner again to add any additional ideas they want to share.

Tweak: Prepare for the talk moves. Talk moves are the actions you take to facilitate students' conversation without overstepping with answers or by taking an authoritative role. Author Renee Houser suggests you hold a clipboard and jot notes to keep yourself from talking and suggests teachers use hand gestures and facial expressions to be the silent mime (Goldberg & Houser, 2017)! When you do talk, *put the question back out to the students*. For example, you might say, "Hmmm, that's an interesting question, what do the rest of you think? Where might we find the answer to Suzie's question?" Ask very open-ended questions to get the conversation started.

Release: On subsequent days with this task, facilitate less of the conversation and focus your role on helping shy students say more and students who tend to dominate give up the floor. Deepen the task by posting exemplary responses on teaching charts and debriefing on them. You can also up the ante by having student make connections between two or more entire texts.

Watch Fors and Work Arounds

Some quiet students do not share. Have those student sit closer to where you are so that you can check in with them frequently to make sure they understand the text and the discussion. If they are shy, then stop the free-flowing discussion to create an opening in the conversation for them to participate, and ask the class to support them as good listeners by showing good listening behaviors. You want the class to be encouraging of each other.

I want to build on to . . .

I have a connection . . .

I read that . . .

A _____ is _____

I wonder . . .

That text says _____

Provide students with discussion stems like these.

WHEN YOU MIGHT OFFER IT

You might offer this task when students know how to discuss complex text as a group and are ready to add on to the discussion by deepening the conversation. Text can be at the higher Lexile levels for the grade level.

TARGET

Participation in whole class discussion by adding on to other students' ideas.

She was sitting amidst classmates who kept bobbing up to talk. Her hand went up slowly, stopping first at her shoulder and then rising up fully. The students around her didn't see her; as I watched, my heart broke, but the girl's hand stayed raised, and she looked at the teacher.

The teacher's eyes met hers, "Alyssa, do you have something to share?"

Alyssa nodded slowly.

"Go ahead, then, what would you like to add?"

"Energy," Alyssa said.

"Tell us more, Alyssa—what do you mean about energy?"

"I am wondering about the energy. How does the satellite get energy up in space? I think it needs energy to do these things we are talking about."

"So you are wondering what powers the satellite to send the signals that Joanna and Ray discussed?" added the teacher.

Alyssa nodded.

Another girl sitting with a different group popped up. "I think that's a good wondering. Where do satellites get power? I wonder that too."

A boy at the same table said, "I don't see it in the reading. We need to read more."

"Let's get to it then," added the teacher.

This is a picture of first graders talking and adding on to the conversation that was started about a text they read together. It's real. Their teacher is in a word, brilliant. This task spells out how she set up this conversation so that first graders could thoughtfully add on to the conversation. Can you imagine what third graders or sixth graders or eighth graders could say!

Your Instructional Playbook

Name It: In this task, you are going to deepen a discussion about a text by adding on to other students' ideas and statements. You will do this by speaking in full sentences.

What You Might Say Next: "I get so excited when conversations get really deep, really smart about what we are reading. I also get really excited when I notice we are listening to learn from one another. We are going to start practicing listening to learn by really stopping to hear one another before we think about what we want to say."

Typical Successes

The transcript of a snippet of the beginning of the conversation can be seen on the previous page. To extend the students' thinking, this type of protocol works really well.

Extending Text Discussions

1. Cue students that they will be adding on to the discussion by looking at the subject from a different perspective or angle (for younger readers say "different way"). Remember to tell them build upon each other's comments.

2. Prompts to discuss new ideas include the following: "In what ways can we think differently about _____. We have been thinking about what it says in the text related to _____, but what do we know about _____ related to our world." (For example, the teacher went on to ask how the students thought the satellites were powered, as power came up in the first conversation.)

3. Another option to extend the discussion. Say, "Let's use our imaginations. Have we read anything that could help us think about how _____ might be in the future? What clues do we have that makes us think that, or what topic could we look up on a Google search to find out?"

4. Reminders for conversation include the following:

    "I would like to add on to what _____said. She said _____ and I am thinking _____."

    "I thought about what _____said, and I am sure/not so sure about that. We found out that _____ and that is same/different than _____."

    "I agree/disagree with _____ because _____."

Model/Do Together: Remind students they have been working really well together and getting into great discussions (see previous task). Share with the class how it is important to not just participate in a conversation by saying things but also by listening and taking into consideration what another person has said.

The focus is making the talk more productive and helping students to listen to one another. After completing the choral read and launching a discussion (see previous task), encourage students to listen to what each other is saying before coming up with what they want to say. You can encourage students to practice this first with their partner. Have students sit together and discuss the text, really listening to one another and adding one or more annotations to their text based on what their partner suggests. Then, they can share what they thought about by offering the ideas as the partners first. For example: "When Clarice and I were talking about alphabets and writing from *This is How We Do It* by Matt Lamothe (2017), first Clarice thought we wrote in an English alphabet, and I wrote "Latin," in the margin. That made me think of the different alphabets around the world and that I don't even know all of them.

Release: As students gain confidence with the conversations, introduce a written response layer by posing a closing question to the class for students to answer in writing (like an exit ticket). Your question could inspire their articulating a connection, an explanation, or an important idea or theme. You might give students a few moments to talk with their partners before they write their thoughts down, as this helps get the thinking juices flowing!

Watch Fors and Work Arounds

Students become repetitive in what they are saying, making the conversation shallow. Stop the conversation for a time-out and use this opportunity as a teaching moment. Share your thinking about what it is like to listen to them as they tussle over the same minor points. Encourage them; tell them you know how capable they are as thinkers and you know they can add deep thinking to the statements made. Model a couple of deeper statements.

> Sentence starters that may support students include the following:
>
> - Maybe . . .
> - Adding on to (student's name), . . .
> - I thought about what (student's name) said, and it made me think . . .
> - I agree with . . .
> - I disagree with . . . because . . .

Name:_____

Date:_____

Conversations About Texts
Checklist for Action

❑ **Did I make well-reasoned statements about what I read?**

A _____ is _____.

In this part, the text says_____ to support my thinking.

In the book _____, on page _____, new information for me is_____.

On page _____, the author talks about _____. This reminds me about _____, but it is different and new. What is new is _____.

❑ **Did I respectfully listen and connect to other's ideas?**

I want to build on to . . .

I have a connection . . .

I read that . . .

I agree, I noticed that . . .

I disagree, I think that . . .

I used to think that, but what you just said has me thinking that . . . .

❑ **Did I wonder, make a prediction, or make a connection?**

I wonder . . .

I predict that . . .

This reminds me of . . .

I know about this other thing that connects to this. It is . . . .

Earlier, I assumed this, but now this part makes me believe this . . .

❑ **Did I ask someone else a question to help them elaborate?**

What did you learn about (subject of the text)?

Can you share more of your thinking?

What part of the text made you think that?

WHEN YOU MIGHT OFFER IT

You might offer this task when students have begun working with nonfiction text independently, but they are not comprehending the text as well as they could or not able to recall big ideas from the text.

TARGET

Write down, in one vivid sentence, something learned from reading.

I have never been a jokester, but my husband is. He is great with off-the-cuff zingers and silly word play. I am glad that he is playful, even living with serious me. I tease him that it's like being married to Bob Hope. I am not very good at one-liners, so this task used to be harder for me—when I thought I had to be funny! But then I figured out I could deliver a one-liner that was just a cool fact. As you try this task, you will discover that some students are naturally funny and put a rib-tickling spin on what they say, and others will be gifted at just saying a lot in a few words. It's all good.

Your Instructional Playbook

Name It: A one-liner is a short joke or a witty comment. In this task, after reading a section of text, you will write one, short thought-provoking sentence that captures something that grabbed you. You are going to write a one-liner!

What You Might Say Next: "We are going to focus on having some fun and thinking hard about our reading today. We are going to focus on 'one-liners.' One-liners are a really witty (funny and smart) way to say something in just one sentence or one line. It doesn't have to be hilarious—aim for memorable! Say it in a way that you and classmates get the gist is of what you read. For instance, in reading *Our Earth* by Kenneth Walsh, I could come up with a one-liner to sum up a short paragraph. Here goes, "Earth, why so blue—are you blue from top to bottom because you are full of frozen and liquid water?"

Check out these one-liners a group of students brainstormed!

Model/Do Together: You might start with sharing some one-liners you find on the Internet. Next, riff some one-liners about topics close to home: For example, "The noise on the school bus is so loud, the driver wears soundproof clothing!" "Or "What are good dogs known as?—Doggone good!

Next, brainstorm thought-provoking sentences. Again, I recommend starting with something familiar. Here is one about the satellite cafeteria at my school, which is called Bulldog Bites. "If the cafeteria is the Bulldog Bites, what 'bites'? Us or the food?"

Finally, introduce students to one-liners that wrap up information into a memorable sentence. To do this, share a short text of two to three paragraphs. Read aloud the text and then, go back and read aloud just the first paragraph. Stop and brainstorm a one-liner that wraps up the information in a memorable way. It is all right to focus on only one big idea in the paragraph. Then repeat this with the second paragraph.

Watch Fors and Work Arounds

Students' one-liners are really paragraphs of two to three sentences. I strongly suggest that you create teaching charts with all the brainstorming you have done with students on one-liners during the Model/Do Together phases of the task. Then, you can refer students back to the processes the class went through together.

"The most important sentence in any article is the first one. If it doesn't induce the reader to proceed to the second sentence, your article is dead. And if the second sentence doesn't induce him to continue to the third sentence, it's equally dead."

—William Zinsser
(1976, p. 54)

Crystal Ball Predictions

WHEN YOU MIGHT OFFER IT

You might offer this task with fiction reading; use this task to sharpen students' ability to notice characters' patterns of behavior and predict. With nonfiction text that has a cause and effect structure, crystal ball predictions are a great way to have students see the pattern throughout the text.

TARGET

Predict in writing what will happen next in a text.

Not too long ago, my daughter went through a trying emotional "breakup" with a long-time friend. They had grown up together and also were close in college, and then all of a sudden, she said she couldn't be friends with my daughter any longer. For my daughter, this was one of those searing moments in life when you realize maybe you messed up, so when she called me, asking "Am I selfish? What did I do to drive her off?" I took a deep breath and didn't shy away. As a mom, I know logically that that our friendships in life ebb and flow, but my daughter was asking me to dig in with her and examine what she might have done, times when she might not have been a very good friend. This is not really such a bad exercise from time to time—to examine ourselves. It is like reading our own story. Based on how we grow and change over time as people, we can predict outcomes from our own stories. My daughter, as she worked through being a better friend, realized that in the future, she needed to work on listening, really hearing people. It is the evidence of her own story that helped her figure out what she could predict. The stories we read are not so different. We can use historic events in a narrative to predict the outcome of a current situation. It is almost like having a crystal ball.

Your Instructional Playbook

Name It: We can use the evidence the text provides us to predict what might happen next in the story. In this task, you will be able to predict what will happen next in the text. You will use context clues and known facts from the text to make the prediction.

What You Might Say Next: "You know how in some stories, there is a magical character who use a crystal ball to 'see' the future? We can see the future of stories and texts also! We can use the clues the author leaves to predict what might happen next. Now, we won't always be correct, but pondering, 'I wonder if . . . will happen next because the text just said . . . ' can keep us reading and eager to turn the page to find out!"

(If you are working with a group of students who don't know what a crystal ball is, then I would discuss it and perhaps show a picture on page 53 or bring one to class.)

Typical Successes

This is an example from a "crystal ball bowl" filled with prediction slips.

Model/Do Together: When reading aloud, stop at key points in a text and hand out "prediction slips." The prediction slips are blank, and students will write their predictions on the slip. Put the prediction slips in the crystal ball box and then, making a fanfare about how the crystal ball can answer a question, ask, "What will happen next in the text (story) _____?" Pull out one of the slips, and then pose to the class whether they think the crystal ball is right or wrong and why. Dig into the discussion and ask for textual evidence to back up the claims, yes or no. Pull a couple more slips from the box and repeat. See if the crystal ball is "consistent" with answers or not.

Once students are ready to make predictions on their own, model how you can make a prediction from a cause and effect text. *Volcanoes! Mountains of Fire* is a good example of a cause and effect text. It is important to have predetermined stopping points in the text as you can guide the predicting by stopping just before new or additional information is revealed. Model how to write out a prediction slip, using a sentence frame like, "I predict that . . . " as appropriate. Remind students that they want to make a prediction that the *text* invites them to make. So, they need to find textual evidence for their prediction and double-check their thinking before they write it down. You can model this by walking through it yourself. "I predict . . . and what is making me think this will happen next in the text is . . . on page . . . "

Release: Have students work in groups with a smaller version of the crystal ball box. As they work through the text (either fiction or nonfiction based on your current focus in class) have them stop at predetermined points in the text and (1) silently, without talking to a partner, write down a prediction on the prediction slip, then (2) have one student pull out one prediction from the box, and (3) have the group discuss. The group continues to pull out predictions until three predictions are pulled and discussed. The box is emptied, and students go on reading to repeat the process.

Watch Fors and Work Arounds

Students don't know what to predict or seem timid to make a prediction. In this case, first check the comprehension ability of the students with the text level. It might be a case where you need to take action as I described above. If not, then the student might need more guided modeling with you. Walk the student through making a prediction from a section of text read. Ask leading questions like, "Tell me about what you just read, what did you think about it?" "Why?" "Now, knowing what you know, what do you think might happen next?"

istock.com/OGphoto

Yesterday's News

WHEN YOU MIGHT OFFER IT

You might offer this task when students (or teacher reading aloud) are reading a text that takes more than one day to read.

TARGET

Summarizing one really important point from previously read material.

My husband and I chuckle when we watch the evening news and each night it begins with a graphic "breaking news" and the newscaster's expression making it seem like it was seconds ago that he learned of it. It's as if to say, this is fresh! Newer than the news on your smart phone! Of course, new news continues to break all night—right up to when we go to sleep—over our Facebook Feeds or whatever. But call me old fashioned, if I hear about a world event or a favorite actor who has died or even some feel-good story about a washed-up whale who was successfully sent back to sea, I relish reading the account in the newspaper the next morning too. It helps me recall it and reflect on it. This task helps learners use the news story in a similar manner.

Your Instructional Playbook

Name It: In this task, you will write a news story to another student explaining the most important points to know from the text read the day before.

What You Might Say Next: "Check out this news story I found in our local paper. (Read it to the class.) The news tells us all sorts of things that happened, usually the day before, because it takes about one day for the reporter to write the story up and the paper to be printed and delivered or posted online before we see it. The news keeps up-to-date on our town, our country, and our world. We are going to stay up-to-date with our reading in class by writing news stories about what we read so we can reflect and others can learn."

Typical Successes

Teaching chart of news stories that are class written on different texts.

Model/Do Together: Bring in short news stories—local newsfeeds provide a plethora of news you can download and share in class. For example, in the news today (Associated Press, 2017) is an article about seven Earth-side planets orbiting a star. It starts like this (see text, next page).

Alert! Lost Dog Boy finds lost dog after posting picture around town. It is a good day today for a boy who loves a German shepard. Peter's dog was returned to him after a neighbor saw the posters Peter had put up all over town looking for the lost dog. Peter is happy again, and the neighbor feels good for doing the right thing.

Not Quite There Yet! This student's news story is from a classroom-level reader about a dog. It is not quite on point yet is a good example of giving this task a try.

For the first time, astronomers have discovered seven Earth-size planets orbiting a single nearby star—and these new worlds could hold life.

This cluster of planets is less than 40 light-years away in the constellation Aquarius, according to NASA and the Belgian-led research team who announced the discovery Wednesday.

The planets circle tightly around a dim dwarf star called Trappist-1, barely the size of Jupiter. Three are in the so-called habitable zone, the area around a star where water and, possibly life, might exist. The others are right on the doorstep.

Next, model writing a short, one-paragraph news story or newsflash about this newsclip (which is actually much longer; I am using a short text here to illustrate). *Seven Earth-size planets found in a galaxy far away. They might have life on three planets.*

Practice creating short news stories with the students so they get the idea before you jump into creating news stories about books and texts students are reading in class.

Jump into creating news stories about the text read the day before to jog students' memories about what they read. It is fine to refer back to the text as needed for support, but the more you can write the news story from memory, the better. At first, work with students and do this together, then once students have worked with you a few times to write up news stories, have them write up their own news stories. The stories can be really short—the key is to have the students have fun with showing their understanding of the text.

Tweak: When students are reading their own texts and stories and are ready to write news stories on their own, they can compare with a partner to see how accurate they are in their memory or portrayal of the text and make revisions if necessary.

Release: If students had not referred to the text to write the news story, have them check what they wrote against the text for accuracy. Share thinking and possible revisions with the class. The key here is the *reflection*. You want your students to reflect on what they read, write it up, and then reflect on their writing to see how well they remember what they read.

Watch Fors and Work Arounds

The news story is not short; it is a retelling of almost all details in the text. Students can get confused about picking out important points to share and a retelling. Sometimes they think, the more detail the better. But in a news story, we don't want a retelling; the highlights are what is important. It won't help your students grow in their thinking if you take over, cross out what they don't need, and tell them to rewrite the news story. Instead, talk the students through the thinking. Ask them to identify one to three important points, circle those, and then recheck. Are these the most important ones you want to pick? Then, have the students redo the news story so they can feel the success of a short news story. Remember, students don't have to write what you think is important, they need to write what they think is important.

"Yet if we uncrumple that paper, the one with all the spelling errors and run-on sentences, what do we see? A boy writing about fishing trip with his dad, his language so vivid we can see the two of them on the lake, the trout flashing in the sunlight, the boy leaning forward earnestly his father talks."

—Adair Lara
(1999, p. 11)

WHEN YOU MIGHT OFFER IT

Offer this task when students are ready to make notes about what they are reading, in order to share thinking in a group, orally, or in writing.

TARGET

Place margin notes in a text to help with comprehension.

I am a supreme annotator. I circle, dash, and underline all over the texts as I am reading. This helps me understand, and it also helps me recall when I go back and skim it later. I also annotate e-books and e-texts using the annotation tools available in the reader or the device. I just need active comprehension while reading. Not everyone needs this, but it is a useful skill for students as they grow as readers. The secret to students finding annotating worthwhile is to model various types, but give students a lot of choice and freedom about when to do it.

Your Instructional Playbook

Name It: Annotating text is when we write notes in the margin of the text to help us understand. In this task, we are going to add marks and notes when reading independently.

What You Might Say Next: Project a couple of marked-up pages of a text that show notes and symbols you imagine your students will use—for example, underlines, ?, !, *W* for *I wonder,* and others and talk with students about them. Make the point that readers naturally mark texts, especially when they are studying it or working through a hard text (as opposed to pleasure reading).

Typical Successes

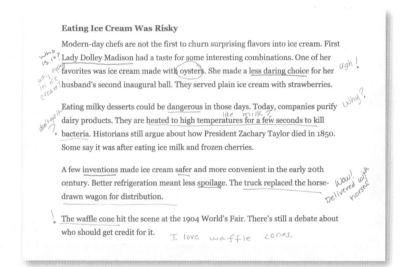

This is an example of an annotated text with notes and markings in margins.

Model/Do Together: Over a couple of lessons, introduce students to practical and appealing options for annotating and think aloud how they might especially apply to particular types of texts and purposes for reading. For example, if I am reading a cause and effect structure, I might simply annotate with a *C* and an *E* in the margins. If I am reading fiction, I might love using a few colored markers to highlight—say, blue for character, green for theme, yellow for literary elements/author craft.

That said, it is really important for your students to own and even invent the annotation marks themselves that they use rather than be compelled to use a particular one you recommend or a premade class chart. The key is for the students to do the thinking about annotation marks they could use, with you facilitating the conversation. So talk with your students about what marks would work and why, then create a class annotation chart so that you will have a common annotation.

Tweak: Have students try out the annotations for a few days and then revisit the chart or key and see if any annotation marks need to be added, removed, or revised. Again, it is important for students to own this process and be empowered to say what is working and what isn't working. You might be surprised by the suggestions for annotations the class comes up with.

Release: Post the class annotation chart in a prominent place in the room and have students try annotating a text with a partner. Double-check to see if the list they came up with is easy to use and has meaning for students as they mark their annotations.

Watch Fors and Work Arounds

Students annotate everything in the text and the margin is overrun with markings. Offer the students a chance for a "redo." Remind them first to breathe (deep breathing is good for students when they are frustrated). Sometimes everything might be highlighted, as they are unsure of what actually needs to be annotated. Start with one type of annotation—for example, "See if you have any areas where you have a question, and mark the questions." Or "Is there part of the text that was confusing? Mark that."

Suggestions for Annotating Text

A big idea	Capital B & I "BI"
A question	Capital "Q"
Something confusing	Question mark?
Something important	Capital I
Unknown word	Word
Key fact	Capital "FACT"
Important point	Capital "IP"
Key detail	Capital "KD"
Confusing part	Capital "IDK" for 'I don't know'

WHEN YOU MIGHT OFFER IT

Offer this task when students are reading nonfiction texts that have at least one main idea and two to three details. When working with older readers—it may be when they move to longer texts with multiple sections.

TARGET

Identify possible main ideas and discuss with partners what is the main idea of a text and why.

I feel like I'm doing a lot of confessing in these intros. Now I'll cop a plea to loving to read car bumper stickers, which is a good thing in California traffic. I sometimes will take a photo to share with my family if it's really good. Likewise, all those short inspirational quotes that go viral on social media? I'm more often inspired by them than irritated. So it won't surprise you when I say, sentence strips are not just for little kids. If you are a teacher of older readers you might be thinking, *What! That stuff is for teaching kindergartners!* Trust me, writing out text in chunks on sentence strips can be very helpful for readers and writers of all ages.

Your Instructional Playbook

Name It: In this task, using sentence strips, you are going to brainstorm possibilities for main ideas and write them out in full sentences, discussing with a partner to identify the actual main idea.

What You Might Say Next: "We need to be really good thinkers when we are reading. Good thinkers reflect on what they are reading, and one of the things they think about is the main idea of the text they are reading. The main idea is the point or information that is the center of the text. We are going to learn to figure this out by writing down our ideas."

Typical Successes

The first sentence was written by a kindergartner on a teacher-made sentence strip.

In Mongolia the holidays are children's day (June 1) and Tsagaan Star (White Month).

People in Mongolia speak Khalkha Mongol.

In Mongolia, life is different than in the United States.

This example is from a group of sixth grade students.

biens and allergaeters and

black widows. and sae

horses lay eggs.

Picture

Model/Do Together: The idea is for students to write out facts from the text they are reading and then work in a group to decide which fact is the main idea. They can write the facts out on sentence strips so they can move the sentence strips around as they decide what facts make up the main idea. Having students be able to manipulate the sentence strips is helpful for them to make their thinking concrete. Don't tell students what the main idea is; they need to work this out on their own.

If your students need demonstration first, model how to brainstorm what might be a main idea of a short text you all have just read. Write down a few ideas, one idea each on a sentence strip. Then, discuss with the class, putting one sentence strip up at a time on a whiteboard or in a pocket chart, and refer to the text to determine whether the fact/idea written on the sentence strip is the main idea. Once the main idea is determined, put that sentence strip on the board first, and place the remaining sentence strips below the first one. Help students understand that the main idea is the fact/idea/point that is the emphasis of the text they read. Do not focus on tips or tricks, like the main idea is the first or second sentence in a paragraph or section, as this isn't always true, and tips and tricks undermine a student's ability to think.

Release: Once students become more accustomed to talking through finding the main idea with a partner, they can move to just writing out their ideas on paper and skip the sentence strips.

Watch Fors and Work Arounds

Students fill out multiple sentence strips about a text read but do not figure out the main idea. Encourage the students to go back and look at the text and clues that can help them figure out the main idea (the title or the repetitive topic in each paragraph). Then, have them check and see if they have any sentence strips related to what they think the main idea is; they can add one if needed. Sometimes students who are younger readers may need you to point out the main idea, but only do that *after* they have tried to figure it out on their own.

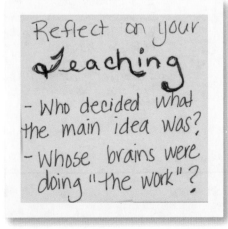

Reflect on your teaching.

WHEN YOU MIGHT OFFER IT

Offer this task when students are having trouble understanding text, both fiction and nonfiction.

TARGET

Question in order to understand the concepts in nonfiction text or plot, characters, and theme in fiction text.

I have a fiery personality. In our family, I am known for ranting after reading the newspaper if I read something that I disagree with—or agree with—or something that I just don't "get." Now that I have been married for twenty-five years, my husband will look up at me from his tablet (yep, we don't read paper newspapers anymore) and smile with me. There are some days that I want to ask the author of a news article or a piece in the *Smithsonian* or even *O Magazine* a question. Like, "What were you thinking when you wrote this?!" Even though the likes of me might not be as easy to live with as Queen Elizabeth or anyone more reserved, the truth is, we want to see this feistiness in our student readers.

Your Instructional Playbook

Name It: This task is about *author-and-you* questions. Author-and-you questions are questions that you ask in your mind or in your reading notebooks to the author while reading. In this task, you are going to write some author-and-you questions.

What You Might Say Next: "Readers tend to look over a text before they read it and ask questions in their minds about what they are about to read. They also ask questions while reading, to help themselves understand what they are reading. We ask questions about a text for all sorts of reasons: We might be confused, we might wonder what is going to happen next, we might wonder why an author shared a particular point in the text. We can ask lots of different types of questions while we are reading: questions can really help us to think about what we understand."

Typical Successes

This example shows questions a student asked while reading *Clues in the Woods* by Peggy Parish. Notice how the student revised the questions to make them author-and-you questions.

> Clues in the Woods
> Questions
>
> 1. I wonder why Jed and Bill are saying "I wonder if mom notices were gone" when they told her before they left? So did you use forshadowing? had ask
> 2. I wonder why Bill said "I've got to eat some? Because eating some is crazy, the berries are bad.

Model/Do Together: This task requires students to have read the text first to have some understanding of what the text is about, then the student can go back and reread, asking questions in parts of the text that are muddy or unclear. You could launch into an example of how fun it would be to have a conversation with an author about what he or she wrote. Model asking author-and-you questions. Students will need to refer to the text in order to ask these types of questions, so have the text handy when you model. In this example, I am using *Inside Out & Back Again* by Thanhha Lai (2011). I might ask how she chose to write in poems. The most beautiful poem is on page 82 about the water.

Release: Put out a bunch of texts that students can read on their own (younger readers might be reading by looking at the pictures or using leveled books). Also make sticky notes available for students. Having students work with a partner. Ask them to read a text once through, and then on the second read, stop and ask a couple of author-and-you questions. Have students write the question(s) on a sticky note and add to the page in the book that spurred on their thinking.

Watch Fors and Work Arounds

Students are writing questions on the sticky notes, but they are not author-and-you questions. Have students visualize themselves having a conversation with the author. What would they want to ask them? What did you love the most? What confused you the most? Have them write down the thoughts that bubble up as they visualize them.

WHEN YOU MIGHT OFFER IT

Offer this task when students need to write on their own, and you sense they are copying your modeled writing. Start using this three-step strategy to jumpstart narrative writing, and then students can apply it to other genres. The strategy works for all grade levels.

TARGET

A general planning strategy gets students writing their own narratives.

I have a daughter in her fourth year in college. A couple of weeks ago, she had to write a paper for philosophy class. This was no small feat, as she is an engineering student, and engineering students write lab reports, not essays. So I tried this task out on her. When she called me at 10:20 p.m. after staring at the computer screen for two hours, I told her to focus on three steps. "Write something, write anything, just three steps on scratch paper—write fast. Then, that becomes your outline." What usually gets us stuck is we overthink things, and then that little writing guy (or gal) who sits on your shoulder speaks up and tells you that you cannot write or organize your ideas. You have to write louder than the voice. My daughter tried it, and it worked.

Your Instructional Playbook

Name It: I have a super-cool, three-step writing strategy that will help you write. The three steps are: Step one, think; Step two, plan; Step three, write and write more. In this task, you will use this technique to draft a narrative on a topic of your choosing.

What You Might Say Next: "A lot of the authors of the books we love advise younger writers to write what they know—write based on your own experience. I think that is good advice! I am going to show you a mind map I made of all the memories I could write about (display your mind map). I know you can think about your lives right now and events would come up, some small, some funny, some really big, maybe even difficult. For example, I could write about the day my sister fell on a board with a bunch of nails in it and how she had to get stitches and how I was young enough that I worried she was hurt forever. The most moving (memorable) stories share meaning with the reader."

Typical Successes

- Have you described the setting, if they are showing what happened, with details?
- Have you shown how the main character's emotions, how he or she feels or thinks, with details and dialogue?
- Have you included action by showing what happened and when?
- Have you written a conclusion that is not *the end?*

Model/Do Together: After students have selected their own topics, the first step in this three-step strategy is to encourage them to consider the following: *Why am I writing the piece and who will read it?* This will help each student set some writing goals as he or she gets started. The next step is for the student to think about, *What will I say?* Students can brainstorm what they want to say on a blank piece of paper. The third step is for students to write and write more. Here, in step three, you can encourage them to think about a few things to encourage *more* writing. Nudge students to write more with a few prompts (see chart in Typical Successes).

Tweak: Hand out blank pieces of paper and a marker or a pencil. Ask students to close their eyes and visualize what they might write about and then either draw (younger writers) or create a mind map about their narrative. Encourage students to keep it to an experience they had themselves, making this a personal narrative.

Release: Give students time to fill in their pictures or mind maps with detail. What happened? How? Where? Why? How did you feel? What did you see, hear, or taste? What did you do? Have students share their mind maps or picture with a partner and tell their story aloud in order to prepare for writing their narrative.

"In rare friendships we know soul reaches out to soul, like deep calling to deep."

—Annie Dillard (1989)

Watch Fors and Work Arounds

Students don't know what to put on their brainstorm mind map. Pair students up or have them work in trios. Allow students with a lot of ideas to work with the student who is stuck. Ask him to think of just *one* thing to write on their mind map, then check in with the student and reinforce the student for thinking of one thing (wasn't too hard), and then encourage the student to think of *one more* thing. Sometimes, the enormity of lots and lots of ideas makes students freeze up.

The narrative the student wrote is either long and rambling or way too short. If the narrative is way too short, you can focus the student on the questions in the teach portion of the task above. Put those questions up in a visible place in the room or copy them on a paper and put them in a writing folder for the student. You can also have them visualize the scene in their head and then write out what they are seeing and hearing. For the student who rambles, sit with the student using a highlighter (the student uses the highlighter and makes the decisions, not you). Gently encourage the student to think about what really fits in the story and to underline or highlight the parts that will stay. Help him see that a lot of the detail he has written is extraneous and takes away from the power of his story.

Getting Kids to Write: Wonderful Concentration

WHEN YOU MIGHT OFFER IT

Younger writers can often think about a lot of topics to write about, but get snagged up when they have to pin their topic down to one idea or need to add detail and or information to their topic. Older writers sometimes get writer's block and just don't know what to write about. This task helps both types of writers brainstorm and concentrate about what to write.

TARGET

Generate topics for writing and concentrate on fully developing a topic.

In every endeavor in life, how one produces best often falls into two approaches. The first is what I lightly call the serendipity school—it's the creative, follow-your-muse when it strikes you, don't force it mindset. The second approach I've dubbed The Carnegie Hall camp, named after the old joke about a tourist stopping a man on a New York Street and asking, "How do you get to Carnegie Hall?" and being told, "Practice, practice, practice." In the writing classroom, too much serendipity can actually cause students to roam all over the place in their brainstorming without sufficient focus. And too much controlled practice of craft and planning can also cause writers to stall out. So, let's try to find just the right balance.

Your Instructional Playbook

Name It: Writers brainstorm ideas sometimes, and other times they gather ideas everyday, little by little, and write their ideas down in a notebook. In this task, you will think for as long as it takes in order to generate writing ideas so that you can write a good, solid text. You are going to keep your ideas organized and then write about them.

What You Might Say Next: "You might think that authors can sit down to write, and presto, out comes a story or an article. But it doesn't work that way. Writers have lots of ideas that they might want to write about, but they keep their list to come back to in the future, to see which ideas have staying power for them. We are going to act like real writers and do some brainstorming and then keep our ideas for future use."

Typical Successes

Check out this cool writing list an older writer brainstormed.

- Playing soccer
- Helping my mom with the cactus without getting poked
- The day I forgot my lunch money
- Going to my sister's high school graduation
- Wishing for the school dance
- Making spirit posters
- Marilee, my best friend

Model/Do Together: Set students up with a writing folder (or notebook, whichever works best for you) to record their writing ideas. First, introduce the folders and brainstorming paper (or notebook) and then model how to keep the folders organized, perhaps with brainstorming lists on the left and writing drafts on the right. As you go into the next phase of this task, you want to focus on *wonderful concentration*—the deep thinking students need to participate in to come up with topics that have meaning for and to them. Don't worry about grammar and language usage just yet!

Begin by modeling how to brainstorm writing topics. Using a doc camera or a large teaching chart, brainstorm a list of things you could write about and model writing out this list in front of students. Add details underneath or next to your brainstormed ideas so students can see you concentrating to add thoughts and ideas.

Release: Invite students to dive in and brainstorm writing ideas. Accept what they brainstorm, don't shut them down. If a student writes something outrageous that you think is not a topic they could ever write about, allow the student time to think about that topic and see what they can develop or research, instead of shutting down the idea. You want students to be able to concentrate on what they can write about, not what they cannot write. Invite students to share ideas from their brainstormed lists or maps.

Watch Fors and Work Arounds

Students' lists are short. Support the student thinking with encouraging activities. Do a think-aloud again of all the different things you might write about, facilitate a class conversation about writing topics, have students brainstorm together in pairs or trios. Post a class brainstorm list or "wall" where writing ideas are posted.

Students cannot yet write. If you are working with young writers, allow them to write using invented spelling. The message you want to send is that the student can independently create a list, not copy a list you have written. Allow students to write with invented spelling as they begin as writers. They can also create a brainstorm list by drawing pictures and writing with invented spelling and then having you write the word correctly beside the picture for future reference.

"All of us, in our daily speech to others, are not only trying to communicate information but to get something off our minds and into the consciousness of the listeners."

—Sol Stein (1995, p. 10)

28 Sketch to Write

In my garage, I have boxes and boxes of student writing from when I was a principal. I cannot part with the stories; they remind me of a very happy time when I worked with the teachers to hold writing workshops daily and writing celebrations often. When I go through these boxes, I marvel at how the youngest writers drew their stories first. Writers of all ages can draw out stories first; this strategy gives artistic students a way to use their gifts to structure a piece of writing. It gives all students, artistic or not, the chance to do what people in the advertising business know—that storyboards work to help flesh out ideas and thinking.

Your Instructional Playbook

Name It: A personal narrative is a story that is about something you have experienced. It is your story. In this task, you will draw your story before writing it out in words.

What You Might Say Next: "When you write your personal narratives, it is important to write small. But it can be very hard to get started writing when you have to think small. When we write small, we focus on one moment, one significant thing that happened to us, and we write about only that. Drawing your story can help you get started and stay focused. Draw what happened to you first; this would be how the story opens. Then, if it helps, you could jump to the end and draw what happened at the end of your story. So, you will have the story start and the story end sketched out. Next, you can fill in the details with a few sketches to remind you of the details you want to share in your writing."

Typical Successes

This example of a student's sketched-out story with text underneath shows how this second grader sketched first, then wrote.

Model/Do Together: Take a 12 × 18 piece of paper and fold it in half lengthwise, and then fold it into thirds. Open it back up and you will have a grid with three squares on top and three squares on the bottom. Keeping the paper lengthwise, label the first square *beginning* and the last square *end*. Using a short story that is well known to the class, sketch out what happens at first in the beginning box and then three to four events that occurred in the middle, and then sketch out the conclusion in the last box. (I am really bad at drawing, so if I can do this, you can to! Stick figures are fine!)

Tweak: Now it is time to dive into planning stories using the sketch to write idea. Set up your paper again, and this time, model for students how you could plan out a story that you have not yet written. After you model a few times (at least once, please!) you can share the pen with the class and co-plan a class story. Using one square each for beginning and end and four squares for details in the middle, facilitate a conversation with students about what the class could write about together. You might sketch the plan, or the students might sketch the plan, or you might share the pen and take turns sketching the story out. Once you have sketched the plan, write the story collaboratively on a chart, so it will be a co-constructed story. Go over the story and the sketched-out plan to see if you have left out any major points you had planned out. Here the point is to use the sketch to write in order to plan a new story that belongs to the class.

Release: Having students use one square each for beginning and end and four squares for details in the middle, encourage them to sketch out their stories. They can also share what they sketched in partners or in small groups. Once the stories are sketched and shared, have students use the sketch planning to help them as they write out their stories.

Watch Fors and Work Arounds

Students cannot clarify what they want to write or sharpen the details that they want to add to their narratives. We want them to have a starting place and an ending place. So if they visualize the start and the end (resolution), it makes it easier to focus on the important details that go in the middle.

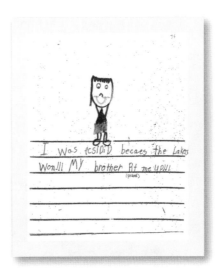

WHEN YOU MIGHT OFFER IT

Offer it when students have learned to add dialogue to their pieces and don't realize yet that dialogue has to move the plot forward in narrative or provide critical detail in nonfiction.

TARGET

Students are able to effectively use dialogue in narratives and quotes in reports when reporting on interviews.

I had a relative once that talked, just to talk. Needless to say, it made my brain tired to always be listening when the extended family gathered together. Sometimes I get trapped by a talker at a party, and I'm by turns furious and fascinated by how they can go off on these dog-after-a-squirrel tangents that provide useless asides. In the classroom, I'd say writers fall into this trap most often when it comes to dialogue. I'm always charmed (sort of) when I ask them why it's there, and they invariably reply, "just because." ☺

Your Instructional Playbook

Name It: Dialogue is what we call talking when we see it in print. Dialogue is what you see in stories you read when two (or more) characters are talking. We use quotation marks to show the dialogue. In this task, you are going to use dialogue in narrative. If you are writing an information report, we are going to add it in as quotes. A quote is what someone said about the topic of a nonfiction article. We also use quotation marks to show the quote in our writing.

What You Might Say Next

For Dialogue: "Writers have characters in stories talk so we can 'see' what they are thinking and feeling. The best way to learn about how to use dialogue well in our stories is to read stories (books) and texts that have dialogue in them. So let's dig in and start checking out how authors use dialogue to help make the story interesting."

For Direct Quotes: "Reporters add direct quotes to informational reports they are writing in order to give a better understanding of the topic they are reporting on. Direct quotes look like dialogue with the conventions we use, but they are not dialogue. The direct quotes are details to add dimension to the report."

Typical Successes

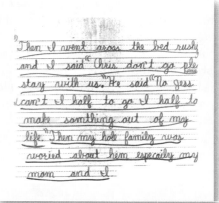

Owns It! We know older writers can get the hang of dialogue. In this example, a third grader uses dialogue well.

Model/Do Together: Share examples from the genre you are working on—read lots and lots of examples, pointing out quotation marks, commas, speaker tags, and other conventions. Students need to see and hear how dialogue looks in use and how direct quotes look and sound like in text. Students need to know inside and out that dialogue moves the plot forward like an engine. It often reveals the emotional state of the speaker and tension of some kind between characters. In nonfiction, direct quotes from people bring high quality information and expert opinion to a topic.

Tweak: Have students work in pairs and share ideas about adding dialogue to a narrative text. What could be added? Where? When? Why?

Release: If students are working on a report and don't have an interview or observation to add to their reports, then have them brainstorm who they might interview or where and what they might conduct an observation about. Give students time to make a plan.

Share around the room students' ideas for using dialogue or direct quotes in a report. Do a popcorn share to have students provide feedback to peers.

Watch Fors and Work Arounds

Dialogue is abundant and distracting, and students are quoting points that are irrelevant: Students tend to think that dialogue in a narrative sounds like when we talk, but it doesn't. Dialogue adds detail to move a story forward, usually showing what a character thinks or feels. One way to help students get dialogue correct is to play-act it out. Have the student think about what he could have the character say instead and then replace the dialogue. They also make mistakes with adding direct quotes from what a character said when the information added doesn't provide new or helpful information. Go over the direct quotes and have the student ask, "What detail is this adding to the piece?" "Is it necessary?"

Steps in the Process

1. Model the appropriate conventions for the use of dialogue or direct quotes.

2. Choose the appropriate modeling based on the genre you are working on; model when and where to insert dialogue or direct quotes.

3. Check the writing—writers don't write dialogue the same ways that people talk. Dialogue is more direct in providing information about what a character is thinking or feeling.

4. If using a direct quote, however, check that the quote is exactly as the sentence was uttered.

5. Show students that if they use direct quotes from an interview or observation they have conducted during an inquiry, then they only add in what provides information about ideas related to the topic.

WHEN YOU MIGHT OFFER IT

Offer this task when students are ready to focus deeply on the beginnings of their texts.

TARGET

Include a hook at the beginning of a piece that moves into the thesis and is more than a question.

A hook is like Superglue—in an instant, you are adhered! My favorite TV show is *Forensic Files*. I know, macabre, right? Anyway, I choose which episode to watch based on the hook line that Netflix shows under the title of the episode. I mean, do I want to watch how a man almost got away with murder or how a mysterious mold wrecked a family's home? Check out this hook from the book *Encouraging the Heart* by James Kouzes and Barry Posner. "Ask yourself this question: Do I need encouragement to perform at my best?" Ah yeah, I am thinking as I am carrying the book to the cashier at Barnes and Noble. Or when I peeked at Paula Hawkin's thriller *Gone Girl*, which all my friends had been raving about, "When I think of my wife, I always think of her head." *Eeeww, Creee-pyyy*. Yeah again, add that to my purchase.

Your Instructional Playbook

Name It: A hook is an invitation to the reader. Think of a hook, catching a fish, as a first step in reeling it in. In this task, you will write a hook that grabs the reader and lures him or her to read long enough to get your big idea. Sometimes, a hook is a question; sometimes, it is a cool image, or sometimes, an intriguing bit of dialogue. The hook gets us reading.

What You Might Say Next: "Writers strive to hook readers into their stories or articles so that they have lots of readers. Writing a hook takes some creativity, and we are going to work on writing hooks together. Invite students to share what they think a hook might be. If you are working with English learners, act out 'hooking' someone to capture their attention."

Typical Successes

One cold stormy night on August 17, 1999 Mr. McLarry was awakened by a sound in the pig pen. He went outside in his robe and slippers. He the sound again. It was 3:00 in the morning. Why could someone be here so earley?

when I was 4 yers old I went to new york beckuz it was Cismis. It was snowing. Me and my sister went ont sid to maek a snaw man.

Owns It! Here are two hooks from a first grader and a fourth grader. Both get the idea of catching the readers' attention early on.

Model/Do Together: Coach students to first reflect on what they want to write. They can ask themselves, "What is it that makes my story or report or essay totally different than everyone else's'?" "If I were to convince my friends to read my report/story, what is the one thing I would say about it to get them to read it?" and "What do I want my readers to remember after they finish reading my report/story?" These questions lead students to write a good hook. Read the first few lines of several articles (if you are working on nonfiction) or stories (if students are writing narratives) and explore the types of hooks that writers use to engage students to read the text. Read lots of hooks and collect the ideas on charts or sentence strips and hang these up on the walls in your room for reference.

Start by modeling for students your thinking aloud about a hook that you could write for a narrative or report. Ask yourself the three questions. Brainstorm a lot of different hooks, jotting them on a chart paper. Select your favorite, and then model writing a few sentences after the hook that reveal the big idea or the thesis of the paper if you are writing a nonfiction piece.

Release: After brainstorming, have them share with a partner what they think they might choose for the hook and why. Ask partners to provide feedback on the students' ideas for a hook, reminding them to double check that the hook isn't too long or too short (it's not just a question).

Watch Fors and Work Arounds

Students have learned to write a hook as a one-sentence question at the start of their papers. Time to ban questions as hooks! Perhaps make a sign and display it prominently in your classroom. Working with students, brainstorm other hooks; check out ways authors start their stories or their nonfiction texts and create a chart with prompts for other methods. These could include beginning a text with the following:

- A comparison
- A short story
- A rich text describing what the five senses sense with the topic
- A ratio
- A percentage
- A surprising or alarming fact

- "What is it that makes my story or report or essay totally different than everyone else's?"
- "If I were to convince my friends to read my report/story, what is the one thing I would say about it to get them to read it?"
- "What do I want my readers to remember after they finish reading?"

31 The Right Amount of Details, The Right Amount of Clarity

WHEN YOU MIGHT OFFER IT

Offer this task when students are writing abundantly, but they don't yet have the ability to recognize as they reread their piece that it lacks crucial details.

TARGET

Writing with details and clarity.

Bask in the elegance of the opening lines of Stephen Swinburne's *Turtle Tide* (2010): "A mother turtle swims to shore. She digs a hole in a dune, where she lays one hundred eggs. Following her instinct, she covers the eggs with sand and slowly makes her way back to sea. What happens next, from eggs to hatchlings, is one of the most extraordinary occurrences in nature." Contrast that with how a less talented writer might have begun: "Sea turtles lay eggs in the sand. But only a few of the baby turtles make it back to the sea. Creatures eat them. The baby turtles are cute and black and white." Learning to corral the right words in the right order is a life-long quest, and this activity gets students off to a nice start.

Your Instructional Playbook

Name It: Details are the information and juicy tidbits we add to our writing when revising to make it better. I've noticed in our writing that we have details, so it isn't that details are not in the pieces. Usually, the problem is that there is not enough detail to provide clarity to plot and action in details to support the arguments in our informational writing. In this task, you are going to revise your writing to add details that sharpen your essay or narrative.

What You Might Say Next: "Writing is often bland, like chicken soup that doesn't have enough salt. It doesn't have the detail that makes me want to pay attention. The most important step of writing is revising. Sometimes, we just give up after we write our first drafts, and then we have lots of writing that is *boring and detail-less*. Today we are going to look at how adding details can make our papers clearer and interesting."

Typical Successes

Not Quite There Yet!
Here is an example of a student paper before revision without a lot of detail.

> One day I went into the Kitchen and I said, "I'm Hungry!" Then my dad said "Lets go to Inand out. So we went. Then We order five hamburgers and three fries. After we finshed eating we wen+ home.

Owns It! Check out the same student's paper after he made a revision with details added to the middle.

> begining
> One day I went into the Kitchen and I said, "I'm Hungry!" "sorry I didn't cook anything" said my mom. And my dad was sitting in the Kitchen. And he heard what my mom said. Then my dad said "let's go to Inand out. After he said that we drove to In and out.
> MiddIe
> When we walked in we saw the counter and alot of people talking. Then we order five hamburgers and three fries. Our table was number ten. Then we waited for ten minutes. After the ten minutes we got the five hamburgers and three fries. Then we went on the outside tables. The burger smelled really tasty. And it felt really squishy in my hand. The burger felt squshy as a sponge in my hand. It was really hot. I was hot as a cake in the oven. The cheese felt gooey in my hands. Some of the cheese were dropping off from the sandwich.
> End
> After we finished eating we went home. When we went hom I told my dad I could remember how my brothers face look like before eating.

Model/Do Together: Everyone revises. It is part of writing. Usually students' first drafts are filled with unclear detail and stunted writing. A good way to launch the task of writing with details *for* clarity is to begin by sharing a piece of writing that has a lot of writing in it but doesn't say very much. Share it with the students and ask them to notice the details in the text. Foster a discussion on the details, leading the students to the *ah-ha* moment, when they figure out that more detail would make the writing clearer.

Next, show the same piece of writing revised (make up the writing if you need to, or use my example below). Elicit a discussion about what is different between the first draft and the revised draft. Have students actively mark with a sticky note or highlighter the differences in details. Then, move to creating a teaching chart titled, Pitfalls of Writing Unclear. Sharing the pen with your class, discuss and record what the pitfalls are when the writing is broad and detail poor. Some ideas are the following: hard to understand, cannot visualize it, the point is weak, the plot doesn't make sense, the paper jumps around, and so forth.

Release*:* Now, it is really important that the students are working on their own pieces of writing, as you don't want them copying you verbatim. Have students work on their pieces, adding details by using a caret to insert writing. Having students circle or underline parts of their writing that are vague and need details. Students share their ideas with one another about where to add details in their own writing, and what they will add.

Watch Fors and Work Arounds

Students have a learned helplessness and want you to tell them what details are missing and where they should put it in their pieces. Start a gentle conversation with the student. Ask her what she thinks. If she shrugs her shoulders or stares blankly at you, then ask the student to tell you about her narrative or what the paper is about, if it is a nonfiction piece. Using sticky notes, write down the big ideas she is sharing, one on each sticky note, and line the notes up on her desk. Then, go back over each note and gently ask for details about that big idea. You can use who, what, when, why, and where; sensory details, such as, What did you see, hear, taste, feel (skin), see, or smell? or descriptive details, such as adjectives. Add those notes to the sticky notes. Then go over the notes again, showing how there are recorded ideas on the notes to help develop out the details.

"You become engaged, passionate, and hungry to be different and make a difference. You become an 'infuser' who fills others with energy, inspiration, and hope."

—Simon T. Bailey (2008, p. 42)

WHEN YOU MIGHT OFFER IT

Offer this task at any time you want to get your students writing. Focusing writing is the key to good writing.

TARGET

Write on one topic and go deep so that the piece is controlled and not all over the place.

I grew up on a ranch with 20 acres of orange trees. In the spring, the fragrance of the orange blossoms would hang heavy in the air at dusk. When I walked into the grove as the sun set just over the road running adjacent to the trees, I would be filled with the wonder of a smell that was so heavenly and sweet I felt taken away. Now, when I see orange blossoms, even on a carton of orange juice in the grocery store, I am immediately swept back to my childhood, standing or spinning round and round in a grove of abundant spring blossoms. What triggers my memory is one single thing: orange blossoms.

Your Instructional Playbook

Name It: I want you to think about the one thing you really want to write about in your piece today. I am going to help you plan for it and write it. Writing small means that we rein in our thinking and we keep our thinking about the topic focused. In this task, we are going to write a longer text that is controlled on one topic or one point (moment), if it is a narrative.

What You Might Say Next: "Published authors know how to tell one story at a time. (Here you will show a book and discuss it—I am discussing *Triathlon* by Michele Dufresne.) For instance, in *Triathlon,* the author, Michele Dufresne, writes about one person and his experience in a triathlon (show book, show pictures or text). She doesn't tell us about all people who have ever competed in a triathlon, she tells us about Nick only. She also doesn't tell us everything Nick has ever done during his life getting ready for the triathlon, she only tells us the parts that relate to his training for it and the actual day of the triathlon. And even then, she only shares about when he got to the starting line, not everything that happened before. In this way, the author is keeping the writing small and focused."

Typical Successes

Owns It! Example of a short text that is focused on one topic and doesn't include detail that is about another topic—if a narrative, it is not a bed to breakfast story.

> The first Seed I Planted
> On Saterday morning I saw some seeds at wal-mart I told my mom what are these seeds for she said to plant I said Can I get the seeds she said ok When I got home I got all of the bags cheked in them I got my packet of seeds. I told my mom can I plant them write now my mom said yes. I was very exited I diged and diged with my planting kit And I watered the seeds evry day. On monday I saw their little sprouts I was very happy I took very good care of them. On Tuesday they got bigger. And my mom seen they grew On the next Saterday they grew lots of colorful flowers.

Model/Do Together: Tell a story to students about something that happened to you recently. It could be something funny that happened at the grocery store, or anything really. But when you tell the story, orally, throw in tons of detail that has nothing to do with the story. Basically, bird walk. Once you are done bird walking, talk to the students about how your thinking was just all over the place with sharing your story. Ask them if they think this is the best way to share a story or inform someone about important information or not. Have a discussion about this idea of too much versus just enough.

Encourage students to visualize one specific moment in time or one specific event they want to share in writing. Encourage students to think through this moment in time. What is it? Where is it? What is happening? What do they hear, see, taste, feel and/or smell? Have students really think through their image and then jot down notes in their writing journal (or draw if you work with younger writers) to capture the vividness of their thinking.

Tweak: Have students write about their thinking and the notes (or picture) they prepared. The writing needs to be independent and should not be a story they copy from you; it needs to be their own story.

Release: Writing conferences are a wonderful way to encourage student independence with a task. Conference with the student about what he visualized; allow the student to talk about his notes or picture and then what he wrote. If the narrative doesn't seem to represent thinking small and includes lots of extraneous detail, ask the student where he could "tighten" the narrative to make it reflect his small thinking. Allow the student the time to make a decision about what to remove. If the writing does reflect thinking small, ask the student what worked for him to be able to share his story in a way that he didn't bring in a bunch of extra information. Listen to the student and reinforce his ideas and thinking.

Watch Fors and Work Arounds

Students have a lot of extraneous detail in their piece, but they don't recognize it as not being "small" writing. It can really help to have the student first draw or sketch out the story. Have them sketch out the beginning, a few details for the middle, and the end. If the beginning doesn't have anything to do with their topic (like, "I woke up in the morning and ate"), then have them set aside that drawing for another piece in the future. Help them think through their drawings like this. When done, the student should only have the drawings related to their idea, with the extraneous ideas set aside for another day.

> She asked that I not leave her alone. I said, "Yes." Then I opened the door and closed it so she wold belive I went. Then she said " Cynthial are you there!" I didn't ansewr. When she was done she walked towards the door and then I shouted " BOO!"

Notice in this example how a student used details in the middle of her narrative.

WHEN YOU MIGHT OFFER IT

Offer this task when students are noticing things in their reading and you want them to record their thoughts. This is appropriate for all grade levels at all stages of reading and writing ability (younger readers will rely on the pictures).

TARGET

Students write a bullet point on a sticky note.

I am the queen of short notes. I have jots everywhere—in my car, my office, my kitchen. I jot notes to remember the gist of something important. I first learned about jot writing from Laurie Pessah at a Summer Writing Institute with Teacher's College. Before being in Laurie's class, I thought jots were for taking notes during a lecture. She opened my eyes to the power of getting the gist of an idea down on paper and placing that paper in a place where it will trigger your memory and your thinking.

Your Instructional Playbook

Name It: A jot is a phrase, word, or part of a sentence you write down to remember something. In this task, you are going to write a bullet point on a sticky note (or in a reading journal). The bullet point will be about what you read in an article, book, or text, using succinct text to remind you of what you read.

What You Might Say Next: "When you are reading, it is important to take notes about what you read and what you think about what you read. You can do this by writing a jot. A jot is a short statement about your thinking. It is not a sentence but might be just a word of a few words. The jot is to help you remember what you were thinking while reading."

Typical Successes

This is an example of a jot on a sticky note taken from a student notebook. Note how they didn't give all the information, just a snippet of student thinking.

> Character Thoughts
>
> • He is going to replace a brain for a computer, he thinks it will never be replaced.

> Text to Self Connection
>
> "One time I watch "Friday the thirteen" It was scary. This is scary.

Model/Do Together: Students don't always know to keep notes of the thoughts that run through their heads while they are reading. They can take jots on things they find interesting, pictures, or main ideas in a text. The list of things students can jot about is only dependent on their range of thinking while reading. They can also take jots on words that appeal to them or words they don't know.

It is important to model first how students should take jots. Start with lots of discussion about what a jot is. Create a teaching chart with students watching you. (What they participate in will be more supportive for them as a reference tool when working on the task independently.) On the chart, record a class-written definition of a jot and write several jots, as examples, from a current text you are reading with or to the class.

Tweak: As students begin writing jots on their own while reading, stop and check in with the class as a teachable moment. Facilitate class discussion about how the jot taking is going and share a few of the jots students are making in order to support and celebrate the efforts students make in thinking for themselves and noting their thinking.

Release: Have students write jots on their own while reading and share jots with one another, discussing what they wrote down and why.

Watch Fors and Work Arounds

The jot is only one word. The best way to work around this problem is to help the student think aloud about what they can remember from the one word. You might set up the coaching session by asking the student to open to the page the jot refers to then ask, "Tell me what the word means? What were you thinking about your reading when you wrote it?" Once the student clarifies (they usually give more information or context), encourage her to write that down as the jot.

Prepare students for independence—the following are suggested ways to do this:

- Give students sticky notes to mark their pages.
- Model how to write a jot on a sticky note and put it on the edge of a book, like a bookmark.
- Display books in your room filled with sticky notes with jots. These can be jots you modeled or jots the students wrote.
- Model writing jots in a reading notebook.
- Keep a reading notebook near your reading chair or area in your room where you model lessons. When it is appropriate, stop and jot in your reading notebook to model the action for the students. Show the jot by holding it up or displaying it under a document camera for all students to see.
- Point out that a jot is not a full sentence.

WHEN YOU MIGHT OFFER IT

This task works well for students who work forever but never get any writing done. Offer this task in small groups as an intervention for students who need help with their writing.

TARGET

Students should be able to complete writing that doesn't just repeat the same few sentences over and over again in a single text.

This situation can be a cause of our own romantic ideas about our classroom: Create the perfect context and students will jump into flow and write up a storm. Well, this just doesn't always happen, and there can be several reasons why. Some students might need direction on how to organize their writing; others might feel good with the production of writing so much that they write and say the same thing over and over again. Others might write a lot but not know how to add in new information—in other words, they play it safe. There are several teaching moves you can make to support students when writing, and the key to all of these teaching moves is that they lead to the independent task of writing on your own.

Your Instructional Playbook

Name It: Sometimes we are working hard and writing a lot, but we never get anything finished. In this task, we are going to practice being able to write about an idea, including at least one big idea and details, in a format aligned to the chosen genre, like beginning, middle, end, or sections with headings.

What You Might Say Next: "It can be hard to make sure we are really saying something new when we make our writing longer. Let's take a look at an example of this. (Show a sample of student writing from your class with someone who is having this issue.) Let's brainstorm how to help (student's name) with her writing (then, show the writing and have a positive peer-coaching conversation about how the author could delete repetitive information and add detail)."

Typical Successes

Name _____ Date _____

I dinit know how to bild a snowman and so didtt my sister. then we cold are dad are dad just know how to bild a snowman. I dinit know how to bild a snow man. I dinit bild a snowman.

Not Quite There Yet! Example of student writing that shows student needs to learn how to elaborate.

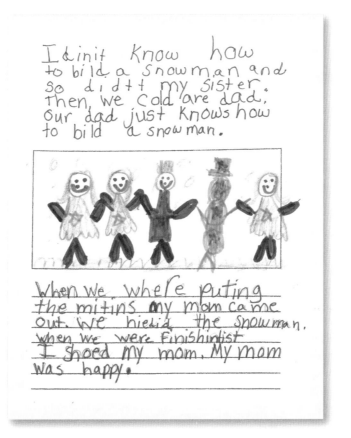

Owns It! Here, the same student has revised so she tells a wonderful focused story.

Model/Do Together: Students are not always aware of how repetitive their writing is. So you can gently point this out by creating a text of your own that is repetitive and doesn't say much as a model. Read it aloud to the students; preferably have it posted on a chart or a document camera so the students can see the writing. Discuss with the student by walking through a series of questions: Is this good writing? Why or why not? What do you think about this line (point out one sentence) that basically says the same thing in the middle (point it out) and at the end (point it out) of the writing? Did we learn much reading this? What is missing?

Hopefully the questioning process you started will help students as they think through what could be added to the writing. Record student thinking on a chart. Then, have them self-reflect. Ask, "Do you ever get stuck saying the same thing in your writing? What makes you get stuck? What do you think would help you get 'unstuck'?"

Tweak: If students cannot think of a way to unstick themselves from lengthy, repetitive writing that doesn't say much, you could have them use a FOCUS Framework. The focus of a FOCUS Framework is for students to think of the following (see next page):

F = Does my writing include *facts* (nonfiction) or *favorites* (narrative)? Favorites are details that a student brainstormed when thinking of writing small (see the writing small task) for narrative writing.

O = Is my writing *organized*? Does it include a beginning, middle, end (B-M-E) for a narrative or topics and heading for nonfiction writing?

C = Does my writing show *care* in the information I wrote about or the details I included in my story?

U = Is my writing *understandable*? Did I use full sentences? Did I provide enough detail?

S = Was I *specific* in sharing my thinking or the information?

Release: Support students as they dive into a revision or take on a new subject or idea to write about, helping them to FOCUS their writing. Students share their old writing and new writing with a partner to see how they improved what they wrote and what they shared in their writing.

Watch Fors and Work Arounds

This task is a work around for students who get stuck in the writing process. So the biggest watch for is identifying students who might need the additional support of this task.

A Drinking Habit
By Nathan Rocha

Along time a go when I was about 2 years old, I made a habit. Let's just say I got a little curious and trust me this I really regret. I started to climb things to see what was on top of it. Then I started to push the limits. For some weird reason I wanted to go on top of the refrigerator. But as I was climbing the chair of books I thought of how I was supposed to get away with this I just grabbed a chair and stacked a bunch of books on it. So I just went on climbing. When I finally got to the top I saw a bottle of nail polish remover. So I grabbed it and threw it on the ground. When I threw of nail polish remover fell under the refrigerator where only I could get it.

After that my mom came back from vacuuming the house and then she caught me. She put me on the ground and picked up all the books and put them back. The next day I sat next to the refrigerator. As I sat down I began to feel a little thirsty. Then I found the bottle of nail polish remover I picked it up and drank it. When I was drinking it I thought it would taste good but boy was I wrong. It tasted as if I just licked a toilet seat and then put peroxide on my mouth. The smell got worse as I drank it. Then my mom ran to take the bottle of nail polish remover. Then she got the phone and dialed 911. Then the ambulance came to pick me up.

I was very scared because I didn't know what was going on. I arrived at ht hospital where I got emergency treatment. I was there for about 2 weeks. When I got home I was back to snooping around.

This example from an older writer has been revised. At first, all he said over and over again was how he climbed up and drank the polish remover.

Name:_____

Date:_____

My Strategies for Independence
Reader and Writer Reflection Checklist

Please circle the answer that seems most true.

As a reader, do I:

Feel confident in finding books I love?	Yes	Sort of	No
Have a few favorite authors?	Yes	Sort of	No
Talk about books with others?	Yes	Sometimes	No
Know how to ask for help when I need it?	Yes	Sometimes	No

Right now, what I want/need next as a reader is _____

My reading goal is _____

As a writer, do I:

Have a favorite kind of writing I like to do?	Yes	Sort of	Not yet
Feel confident coming up with ideas?	Yes	Sort of	Not yet
Share my writers with others for feedback?	Yes	Sometimes	Not yet
Have strategies for problem-solving?	Yes	Sometimes	Not yet
Know how to ask for help when I need it?	Yes	Sometimes	Not yet

Right now, what I want/need next as a writer is _____

My writing goal is _____

WHEN YOU MIGHT OFFER IT

Offer this task when students can write their own thoughts using mostly conventional spelling. Dialogue journals work best with students who are ready for virtual conversations (usually third grade on up).

TARGET

Write thoughts and message to the teacher and respond to the teacher's comments.

I admit I struggled with dialogue journals for a while, as I used to think I had to be perfect and always respond, all of the time. But in reality, you don't. Realize that being imperfect is a gift and allows you to be more real with your students. So lean into using dialogue journals, even if you are afraid of the commitment of writing back to them often. You can write when you can; this task is still a powerful way for students to work through their thinking and for you to formatively assess their comprehension of text.

Your Instructional Playbook

Name It: A dialogue journal is a journal where you write to me and I write back. In this task, you are going to write to me and I am going to write back to you. I won't be able to write back every single time you write to me, but I promise I will read it all, and then I will write back and also leave stamps or my initials.

What You Might Say Next: "Everyday I wish I could sit down with you and have a conversation to learn more about you—things like what you think about a book, what you do everyday, what your favorite things are, and bunches of other things. I cannot do that because there is one of me and many of you—so we are going to write to each other in a journal. You will write to me, and I will write to you."

Typical Successes

Teacher,
why I Let the baby snake go because I Think I shall LeTit go Safe and sound. The next day I was Looking for him and he was the behind That rock going to the water. But when I saw him again he was trying to bite me. I got a stick and scared it away.

Dear Bee,
I enjoyed hearing about when you saw a snake. I am glad the snake didn't bite you. What else can you tell me about the baby snake?

Mrs. Athavan

Not Quite There Yet!
This is a page from a student dialogue journal that shows how teacher feedback can gently encourage focused elaboration.

Model/Do Together: Get the journal organized. If you don't want to purchase one, you can put a construction paper cover on a stack of binder paper and staple, or you can use a tablet or other device to create an online journal. You will write back and forth with the students in the dialogue journals. To get started, write a welcoming sentence in the journal inviting students to share something, perhaps what they do everyday after school.

Model how to write a journal entry. You can create a journal entry on a chart (or device if you are using a tablet), thinking aloud as you write. Show how you start the entry, add in details, and then close the entry with a sign-off (your name and any closing). It might help to have students write to you the first time while you are nearby to check them and help them if they get stuck. You will need to periodically collect the journals and write back to the students. Write from your heart. Don't correct their work, but share your thinking with them and encourage them to keep writing.

Tweak: Students may need to start their dialogue journals by creating a brainstorm list of topics to write about that they can refer to often. This will help them to not get stuck.

Release: Once ready, have students make a few entries and turn the journal in to you when they are ready for a response from you. Ask them to note in the journal what they want you to respond to so that they will be controlling the conversation. Encourage students to decide on the next topic for the dialogue journal.

Watch Fors and Work Arounds

Student entries are repetitive or about non-important topics. Work on brainstorming an idea list again. You might brainstorm in a group, having students share ideas with each other about what they can write about. Keep their lists in their dialogue journal—glue it in, save it in a file on the device or cloud—so that students can refer to it often. Many times our students think that they have to just know, everyday, what to write about. They need to know that writers keep notes to help them get started on days they are stuck.

"Maybe that's all happiness really is, a series of fine and careless moments.

Gingersnaps and the pure color of a clear sky. Mice and hummingbirds and cats that hide in the rug and . . . the first bite of a turkey on French bread with mustard and tomatoes."

—Adair Lara
(1999, p. 193)

THE GOOD, THE BAD, AND THE UGLY

As a way to wrap up the tasks in this section, I turn now to share my own experience in implementing the tasks! I do this so you can learn from my missteps and see that getting great at giving high impact, meaningful tasks takes time. Even when I plan around higher-order thinking skills, there is no way of totally foolproofing my teaching. Or to cut myself some slack, I can never predict or completely control for what students will do. What we plan to teach and what we actually do in the teaching moment might be two different things. Analyzing what we *actually do* can help us plan and implement better in the future.

Let's analyze the good, the bad, and the ugly of daily activities I have taught in an upper grade classroom.

The Good	
What I Planned to Do	**What I Actually Did**
Higher-Order Thinking Skills– **Analyze**	**Higher-Order Thinking Skills–** **Comprehension**
Have students work in groups of four, discuss, choose, and record the strongest theme in the first four chapters of a novel. They would write their statement of the theme on a chart paper, add their evaluation about the strength of the theme, and add two supporting details about the theme.	Students worked in groups of four but only discussed how the theme emerged in the first two chapters. Students used reading notebooks to write a chapter summary and then to write one sentence to describe the emerging theme.

My Thinking About the Lesson in Action
This Was Ok.
While I wanted the students to discuss the emergence of one strong theme (I was using a novel with two themes that twine together throughout the novel), they got confused about which details related to which theme. I realized it would be better for them to just identify a theme and then describe it rather than evaluate the theme with supporting details. I *made a conscious choice to lower the level of the task during the lesson; this just didn't happen by accident.*

The Bad

What I Planned to Do	What I Actually Did
Higher-Order Thinking Skills– Comprehend and Evaluate	**Higher-Order Thinking Skills–** Knowledge
After reading a book and discussing it a few times, students were to write 1-3 descriptions about each main character in the book, describing the character with one adjective or phrase and providing 1-2 supporting details to justify the chosen adjective or phrase. Next, students were to work in pairs and give their partners the descriptions they had written but without the characters' names attached. The partners were to decide which character was which in a matching activity.	Students discussed the characters in groups of four. But they did not have time to write out an adjective or phrase describing the character and decide on supporting evidence because the discussion took a long time. So I quickly went around the room and created flash cards with adjectives describing each character and then proceeded with the matching activity in pairs.

My Thinking About the Lesson in Action

Slow Down!

I blundered by feeling pressured to finish the lesson in the time I had allotted. If I would have paused and reflected on the great conversations the students were having, I could have seen that they were highly engaged and involved in a task that took me by surprise – deep thinking. *I should have just stopped the lesson after they were done discussing and picked it up again the next day.* Then, I could have finished it out as planned and not done the thinking for the students and by doing so, not eliminated the evaluation part of the lesson.

The Ugly

What I Planned to Do	What I Actually Did
Higher-Order Thinking Skills– Comprehend	**Higher-Order Thinking Skills–** Knowledge
Organize students in pairs. Have them look through the books they read and talk about the book they read that day using both social and academic vocabulary. This activity focuses on discussion, as students will be recalling ideas from the book they read.	Students were sitting in pairs, but did not have the books with them. I forgot to have them pass them out. I asked them to start talking about the books they read the previous day during the reading workshop. One child even raised his hand and asked to get his book, and I said no. I did not understand what he was asking as I thought they had the right books with them.

My Thinking About the Lesson in Action

Train Wreck!

I was in a hurry and trying to get this activity slipped into the ten minutes I had before the bell rang for recess. The students did have their book boxes with them, but I had forgotten the previous day I had collected the books I intended to use for the activity and set them aside. So the students didn't have their books to refer back to, and I got so flustered wondering why they were not having focused conversations with books in their hands that I didn't even "hear" the young student ask me to get his book. A lot of students were making stuff up to say just to please me.

WEEKLY TASKS

for Reading,
Writing, and
Thinking

The plot thickens—now we move into fourteen tasks that you would introduce or have students practice only once a week or so. These engagements nourish learners' independent reading and writing yet should never be repeated and required to the point that students get tired of them. Eighty percent of reading and writing time should be students doing their own choice reading and writing.

Section II ● Weekly Tasks for Reading, Writing, and Thinking

	Task	Genre	Skill	Transfer to Independence! Learners can:
36	Analyze for Author's Purpose With a Text That Is a Little Too Hard for Students to Read on Their Own	Fiction, literary nonfiction, informational text	State author's purpose	Make a statement about why an author wrote a text using a complex piece of text.
37	Create a Structured Outline of a Text	Nonfiction, informational text	Identify important facts and details	Record and discern between important facts and details in an outline to understand the text.
38	Collecting Research and Organizing Notes for Writing	Report writing	Investigate a topic and write a report	Choose a topic for a research project, read and take notes on the topic from 3–5 sources.
39	Plot Summary Snapshots	Fiction	Summarize	Summarizes plot and include points on the beginning, middle, and end of the text.
40	Writing Information in a New Format	Informational, literary nonfiction, nonfiction, writing in any genre	Writing fiction, report, response to literature, functional text or poetry	Analyze a topic through several lenses and choose best genre to showcase writing.
41	Stay on Point in Writing	Personal narrative, report writing, functional writing, response to literature	Write with length and clarity	Write longer pieces with control and excluding extraneous detail.
42	Productive Use of the Author's Chair	Any genre	Share own writing and describe reaction to others' writing	Share writing appropriately and acknowledge others' writing contributions.
43	Write a Short Research Report	Informational, nonfiction	Write research report	Explore topic in depth and write report with organizing structure.
44	Write an All About Text	Informational, nonfiction, literary nonfiction	Write research report focused on one topic or subject	Choose topic, read about topic, research, organize, and write about the topic in depth.
45	Your Students Have a Voice: Writing an Opinion Text	Nonfiction, fiction	State opinion	During or after reading, write an opinion and provide a statement backing up opinion.
46	Arguing the Solution to a Problematic Situation	Fiction, nonfiction	Identify a problem and write a solution or additional solutions	Solve a problematic situation related to and researched from the text.
47	Writing the Recipe for Success: How-to Texts	Functional nonfiction	Write how-to text	Provide a guide to action, show steps in the action in detail and include relevant information.
48	Writing Explanations, Be Like an Encyclopedia	Report writing, explanatory writing	Write explanatory text	Write to explain a concept/phenomena using appropriate facts and explanations as necessary.
49	Inquiry for Smart Minds	Nonfiction, informational text	Conduct investigation	Participate in a group investigation and ask questions, find information, and discuss or write about findings collaboratively.
50	Responding to Literature With Some Kick to It	Informational report	Write a book report	Write about a book by stating opinion and include a claim, evidence for the claim, and a recommendation.

WHEN YOU MIGHT OFFER IT

You might offer this task when teaching close reading to your students.

TARGET

Students make a statement about why an author wrote a text using a complex piece of text.

When we ask students to determine the author's purpose, it can devolve into our students guessing what's in our head—as though we have the 100 percent correct answer! So I want you to go into this task with my blessing—it is OK if students think the author's purpose is different from what you think; the point is to let them figure it out for themselves. If a student is working with a complex text and can make a statement about what he or she thinks the author's purpose is and be mostly spot on, this is a win!

Your Instructional Playbook

Name It: In this task, you are going to learn to say the author's purpose for writing with a text that may be a little too hard for you to read on your own. This will be challenging because the author's purpose is the *why*—it describes the reason the text exists—and even the strongest readers can't fully know an author's intentions. Getting a pretty good idea of the purpose makes it easier to get into reading.

What You Might Say Next: "Here's the good news: You can make an educated guess about the author's purpose when you don't yet really understand what you read. How? Because there are some clues in the text that can help you decide why an author wrote what he or she wrote. Scan the page or the section. Ask yourself, "What is it mostly about? What does the author seem to be saying about the topic? Is there one point or thing that the author writes about more than one time?"

Typical Successes

Owns It! A student creatively shared what he thought the author's purpose was in the complex text. He created a political cartoon based on an article published in the *San Diego Union-Tribune* on March 30, 2017. The article is titled "California Can't Afford to Lose Immigrant Workers. These Two Bills Protect Them" by David Garcias.

Model/Do Together: Hand out texts or make the text large enough for all students to read in a shared reading. Demonstrate and think aloud as you scan the text for clues about the meaning. Strategies may include the following:

- Find words that repeat or words that mean the same thing.
- Look for words about the subject, like *is* or *was, certainly, however, on the other hand.*

- Check the first sentence on the page or section and the last sentence on the page or section. What do they say? Do the ideas in these sentences go together? What do they mean?

- Look for ideas that repeat, often by finding recurring words.

Invite students to make suggestions as you read aloud the sections. Facilitate a discussion about what they think the text is about. Next, share a flow of questions that are great for determining the author's purpose, such as the following:

- Who is the intended audience for the text?

- What is the text about?

- What ideas does the author write about? Are any ideas or information repeated?

- Does the author make any statements giving advice to the readers?

Record students' ideas on a chart as they answer these questions. Ask, "What do we see?" Circle, underline, or star important phrases, words, and information as students respond. Ask the students if they put all this together, can they determine the author's purpose for writing the text?

Release: Using a different text and working together with the class, scan and read the text. Then, release—give students ample time with a partner to go through the text and ask themselves the questions above to see if they describe what the text is about. Come back together as the class and reread the text together, encouraging students to annotate their copies of the text. Then, give students ample time to work with a partner to decide what they think the author's purpose is. Have the paired groups share with other groups.

Watch Fors and Work Arounds

Students look at you blankly or shrug their shoulders when you check in on what they think the text is mostly about. Have the student scan the text and write jots on sticky notes about what they think each section of the text is about. Then look at the sticky notes to see if there are any common words, ideas, or thoughts between the jots. Help the student see a connection; if he still can't, repeat the process. Allow the student lots of think time.

Students cannot articulate what they think the author's purpose is. Use a sentence strip to jumpstart the student's sharing. "The author's purpose for writing (title) is _____. I think this because_____. I also think this is true because_____." Have the student write their thoughts on sticky notes or an index card and then point to each line they wrote as they share using the sentence starter to help them.

"Out of the questions of students come most of the creative ideas and discoveries."

—Ellen Langer (2015)

WHEN YOU MIGHT OFFER IT

You might offer this task when working with nonfiction text in an inquiry study or as part of a text set on a specific topic.

TARGET

Students record and discern between important facts and details in an outline to understand the text.

I recently bought a writing desk that I had to assemble—need I say more about the trauma that ensued? The directions were unclear, but more to the point, I'm not a linear thinker. So I had to jot some notes that helped me see the structure of the directions. It got me thinking about my students and how being able to structure an outline by recognizing the structure of texts is really important. This is my secret.

Your Instructional Playbook

Name It: In nonfiction texts, information flows from point to point. In this task, you are going to learn to notice the important facts and details and organize them from beginning to end, which will help you see how the piece flows from point to point.

What You Might Say Next: Project an image of a river and say something like the following; "Imagine seeing a river from above; you can see how it flows, bends, and notice big rocky points or evergreen trees or other features along its banks. In nonfiction, the author's main points are like those major rocks or trees and all the facts and details flow like water into them.

"When reading nonfiction, it can be hard to tell which are the major facts to hang on to and which are not. But here is a trick that helps me. When a fact interests me, I look to see if there are other details that tell *more* about the fact or not. When there isn't additional information, then I decide it is a cool thing to know, but it is not an important fact. Authors give weight to the important points."

Typical Successes

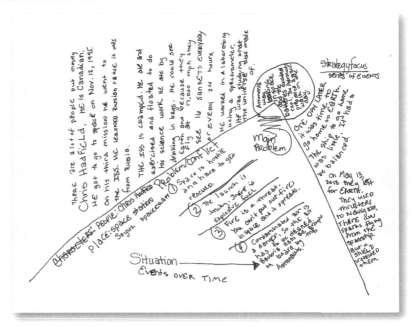

Owns It! Check out the creative use of a Rising Action Story Map to outline a nonfiction text Chris Hadfield and the International Space Station by Andrew Langley.

Model/Do Together: Start outlining the text by skimming and looking for facts and details worthy of bulleting out in order on a chart (or use a document camera to project). If the text is long, don't outline the entire piece; pick a part that has meaty engaging information. Use these steps:

- Identify three important facts from the text or section of text. Write these down in bullet points leaving space between them to add more later.

- Identify one to three details that support each important fact. Write these down in bullet points beneath the important fact they connect to.

- Help students think through the main points by asking questions of the text to ensure they have picked important details for the outline and not just cool stuff to know. Model asking yourself, "Is this a point I think is really cool?" "Does the information repeat in the article, or does it appear in the text only once?" "Do I see details that give more information (explain) about the fact?"

- Ask yourself, "What makes this a detail? How is it connected to the important fact?"

Tweak: To help students who need a "roadmap" create the structured outline, you can create a graphic organizer based on the plot summary task on page 94, just modify it for nonfiction. You can also show students how to draw it out on their own. For younger readers, add pictures to the outline you create on a chart and keep bullet points to one word or a very short phrase.

Release: Using a different text that students can read on their own, encourage them to create their own outlines of the text focusing on a few important points and three details to back up each important fact. Young children can create pictures and label their pictures in a linear timeline to indicate the beginning, middle, and end of the text.

Watch Fors and Work Arounds

Students identify "interesting points" that are not essential to understanding the text as a whole. Point out that nonfiction texts are often organized in sections that make it easier to identify important information.

Students cannot find the main idea of the text they are reading. Help students learn to identify main ideas and details by creating a structured outline. For older students, they can create a structured outline in their notebooks, but younger students can use a graphic organizer. The youngest students can do this on chart paper by sharing the pen with you.

Reflect on your **Teaching**

- Do you use fiction story organizers that could be adapted to nonfiction? Use what students know and modify.

WHEN YOU MIGHT OFFER IT

You might offer this task during a class investigation on a topic or when preparing to write explanatory reports, after students have chosen a topic.

TARGET

Students will choose a topic for a research project, read, and take notes on the topic from three to five sources.

It's so easy for our students to get lost in looking at really cool information in books or on a website and neglect their main research purpose. I am guilty of this too! I often Google a topic and then I just keep looking at different websites and suddenly an hour has gone by! This task is all about avoiding that vortex.

Your Instructional Playbook

Name It: In this task, you are going to learn to record notes when reading materials that help you with your project.

What You Might Say Next: "Today is the day that we get to dig deep into the topics we have chosen to research. I think today is the most exciting day because we can begin to learn things we never knew! Or we can look up facts and details to extend our thinking about something we do know."

You might continue for younger students: "Remember I told you that my daughter got a new dog? He is a Belgian Malinois/Labrador retriever mix. I want to learn more about this type of dog, so I am going to go to our library to see what books they have. I am going to write down what I learn in my research journal. I predict that I will need to look at a few books, because some books might have interesting facts about dogs in general and others might have interesting facts about these kinds of dogs."

You might continue for older students: "Remember we read *We Elect a President, the Story of Our Electoral College* by Tara Ross last week? I really want to know more about how we elect a president in our country, so I can go find additional sources to help me learn about the process. I might do an Internet search, or I could check out the library. I can even go back and reread the book we read last week for facts that I could write down on my note cards."

Typical Successes

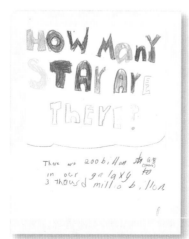

Owns It! **Roselle, a second-grade student wrote ten pages of notes on stars. She organized them in categories. Some of her information is not correct, but this is her first draft.**

Model/Do Together: Think fun size! Help students get confident taking notes from just three sources (you can expand the number later on). Choose an accessible, super-engaging topic (you know what floats your students' boat) and find three sources. First, think aloud how you decide if the sources you chose are in fact on point. Talk about how you look at the table of contents and headings and notice the categories and which source offers subtopics that are different. Choose categories for your modeling (3–4 is a good amount). Next or possibly in a follow-up lesson, demonstrate how you determine when a source is not credible. Ask questions like, "Is this source credible?" "What is the author's expertise?" "Do I recognize any organizations mentioned?" "Is it a sponsored piece?" "Does it include a reference list or a good amount of expert quotes? "Does the resource provide facts, data, graphics, and information related to what I want to learn from my topic?" "Is what I am reading based on fact or opinion?" If the source is credible (if not, choose a different one), model how to take notes from the source.

Tweak: Model recording information on a large chart paper, on 8½ × 11 inch paper, or note cards (depending upon the age and ability of the students). To keep students from getting swamped by too wide a topic, think aloud how you focus research as you read. For example, "Belgian Malinois/Labrador" retriever becomes "Pure bred dogs: Separating Myths from Facts"; "Sharks" becomes "Is there a rise in shark attacks?"

After taking a few notes, think aloud how you organize them. Do you put your notes in order or use color to highlight for order or big ideas versus details?

Release: Have your students talk with a partner about their topics and the kinds of sources they want to check out. Then, over the next few days, have students find two to three sources and take some notes about the topic.

Watch Fors and Work Arounds

Some students have trouble discerning important facts from minor details and take too many notes. Have them read through the text first and ask themselves, "How does this information relate to the big questions I have about my topic or my angle?" "Is this nice to know or important, *need*-to-know for my reader?"

Students have trouble getting started with looking up their sources. First, check that they still are interested in their topics and that their topic isn't too hard to source. Then, check that they know how to look up sources; they may be overwhelmed by the sea of possibilities. If they are still having trouble, focus the choice by saying, "You can start by looking online at the Scholastic Kids website or going to library to see if we have a book on your topic."

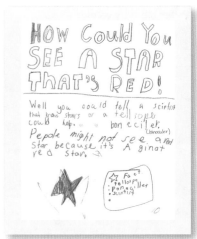

WHEN YOU MIGHT OFFER IT

You might offer this task when reading fiction texts that have a strong beginning, middle, and end.

TARGET

Student summarizes the plot in a fiction text to show how the beginning, middle, and end of the story unfold.

My friend is super-organized, and after she comes back from a vacation, she creates one of those fab photo albums on fancy paper with a gorgeous cover. I swear it's delivered and on her coffee table before her suitcase is unpacked! The other day, I finished a plot-twisting, visually rich summer novel, and I wished I could make a fab memory book of it. I could capture pictures that reminded me of the scenes in my head, like snapshots in a row, bound up in a beautiful book. It prompted me to think about this activity.

Your Instructional Playbook

Name It: When you say or write the gist of a text you read, you are summarizing. In this task, you are going to summarize the plot of a story, by describing the beginning, middle, and end. Not a retelling—not every detail— just these three stops along the way!

What You Might Say Next: "What's a snapshot? (Chart ideas from students.) Yep. Snapshots are pictures that give us a glimpse of a memorable moment. What if you posted a bunch of images from, say, a surprise birthday party? You would probably show the start—the moment of surprise, then snapshots of fun and games—the middle—and then maybe the cake and present opening—the end. Lots of things in life are told in sequence, just like the stories we read. To learn to summarize fiction, we are going to create three snapshots with words and pictures: Beginning, middle, and end. Then, we can give the gist of the storyline by reviewing and adding to our summary statements if needed."

Typical Successes

Owns It! Student "snapshot writing" of *Katie's Trunk* by Anne Turner in a reading notebook. Notice how she added in transition words. She had first brainstormed on sticky notes and wrote ideas out in her notebook.

Model/Do Together: Using any story that you have recently read with students, write on chart paper or a tablet what students recall happened first and have them share the pen, capturing it in three or four sentences (or less). Encourage them to include setting and how the characters get introduced and to add pictures.

Next, move onto the middle. You are going to focus the discussion on the plot but also get at character motives and interactions a bit. What happened in the story *and why*? What was the big problem the character(s) was facing? Record his or her thinking on the chart. After working with students to record a summary of the middle, move to the ending in the same manner. For the ending snapshot, focus students on the problem and how it was resolved at the end of the story.

Tweak: Sticky notes come in handy here also, and you can use larger sticky notes to have students jot out the beginning, middle, and end. Give them three sticky notes and encourage them to write out words and phrases from each part of the story.

Release: Using a new text, have students work on their own to create a storyline describing the plot through the beginning, middle, and end. Students may be ready to expand the middle and have two or more snapshot summaries of the plot development if they read longer texts, like a chapter book.

> *"Character is plot, plot is character."*
>
> —F. Scott Fitzgerald

Watch Fors and Work Arounds

Students seem unsure of how to notice the most important action as they summarize the middle. If that happens, have them first simply retell the events. Once students share all the details, focusing on the plot, ask them, "How could we say that in just a couple of sentences? Let's think about what the main character did and felt and what it might mean and make sure that our few sentences include that."

A student's writing is a retelling and not three summaries for beginning, middle, and end. Meet one on one with a student and help him pare down his words by creating a graphic organizer with three boxes running down the left side of the paper and lines on the right side of the paper. Have him draw pictures or jot notes in the boxes corresponding to beginning, middle, and end. Then, he can write out his corresponding summaries on the lines to the right of the boxes. The lack of writing space will encourage the student to be spare and avoid retelling the entire story.

and quickly hid in an old wedding trunk.

When the patriots came in they caught notice of the trunk and got some of the dresses. Warren (one of the Rebels) touched Katie. Then he told the others someone was coming left the trunk open so Katie could breath.

Finally her family came and had a sigh of relief. She got a little mad at the patriots but, then thought. Even though they were enemies, Warren had a seam of goodness inside him.

WHEN YOU MIGHT OFFER IT

You might offer this task when students are working with a topic and they are ready to show their learning in a nontraditional format.

TARGET

Students analyze a topic through several lenses: from the role of the writer and the audience and by choosing the best way to present their writing (letter, article, poem, multimedia presentation).

Repurposing is the new DIY. I follow at least three blogs where people are flipping old furniture into new, taking thrift store finds and making them gorgeous, or finding some way to decorate their home with items never meant to be decorations (like vintage hubcaps turned into mirrors). Students can DIY their writing too, and in a way, the tweens and teens bullet-journaling is all about that inventive formatting. When they write about something they are interested in in more than one way, they are repurposing their knowledge in a new format.

Your Instructional Playbook

Name It: With this task, you are going to learn to think creatively about how you might present the information you want to share with others.

What You Might Say Next: "There is writing all around us. Writing informs our lives. But we don't always think about the writing we see everyday, and we don't think about who wrote the text. For example, when you go to a restaurant and you read the menu, who wrote it? Why? When you watch TV, someone had to write out in a script everything that the people on TV say. Why did they write what they wrote? How did they write it? We are going to think about communicating an idea about a topic we are studying in a new format, a new way. I want you select an important idea or two about the information you want to share, and as we look at various formats, see if one seems a really good fit for your content.

Typical Successes

Owns It! Here is a snippet of a three-page alternative text written by a student who had been studying ancient Egypt. It is a written as the narrative of a tour.

> Who Said Anything about Ancient?
>
> Ahhh, sorry I just woke up. Are you new here, where are you from? Oh well, as long as you're here I may as well give you the grand tour of my life. There's not much to talk about though. Here we go.
> Let me introduce myself. My name is Amesis. I'm a normal 12 year old Egyptian and I'm living a perfectly normal Egyptian life, fasinating huh?
> Ussually when I wake up I put on my best white linen dress. It's made to fit me nice and loose so I'm not uncomfortable. Next I put my hair up in a sidelock (a braid on the side of my head). Most Egyptians wear make up and wigs but I'm too young.
> I follow my nose to the sweet smell of beer, bread, fresh pomegranits and milk for breakfast.

Model/Do Together: Review different writing formats that writers choose to communicate with and draw out students' thinking about how the format itself serves the purpose. Bring in real examples, such as letters, eulogies, menus, directions, recipes, feature articles, travel brochures, advertisements, news feeds, advice columns, speeches, and diary entries. Then, brainstorm ideas for the format and topic columns of a chart like the one shown below. Next, think of specific writing roles they could assume as the author of a piece written in that format. Then, name the audience.

Different Formats for Helping Students Write in New Ways

Format	Audience	Role	Topic
News release	News feed readers	Reporter	
Travel guide	Other Girl Scout cookies	Girl Scout cookie	Journey through the digestive system
TV script	TV viewers	Rachel Ray	Eating vegetables instead of meat
Letter	Book character (name one)	Book character	Why . . .
Complaint letter	Bus management of buses in 1955	Rosa Parks	Why she should be allowed to sit at the front of the bus.
Advice column			
Diary	Self	Lewis & Clarke	Hardships of traveling west
Instructions			
Letter	U.S. senator	Self	Gun control
Public service announcement	Public	Advertiser	Importance of exercise

Release: Have students meet in triads and plan out their pieces focusing on topic, role of writer, audience, and format. Check in with the groups to see who might need guidance.

Help students get launched in their writing by reviewing the different writing formats that the students chose and the text features of those formats.

Watch Fors and Work Arounds

Students get stuck writing in their chosen format. Review the text features of the format and help the students identify a timeline, planning what part of the text they will write first, second, third, and so forth. Breaking down the task into smaller parts can help make it more manageable for students.

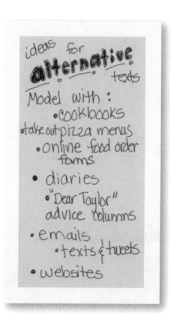

ideas for **alternative** texts
Model with:
• cookbooks
• takeout pizza menus
• online food order forms
• diaries
• "Dear Taylor" advice columns
• emails
• texts & tweets
• websites

WHEN YOU MIGHT OFFER IT

You might offer this task when students are writing longer pieces, but their pieces meander and lose focus.

TARGET

Students stay on point and do not add details that distract from the meaning and intent of their writing.

Okay, I admit it. Sometimes I read letters and essays from the eighteenth and nineteenth century and I find myself thinking, *sheesh*, hurry it up, buddy! What's up with these long, circuitous asides! Often, even our Snapchat-era students presume that if they write more, they are writing better. Not true. When students add extraneous details to their writing, they take away from their writing. The piece can be so embedded with adjectives and asides that the reader cannot keep track of the main idea of the text.

Your Instructional Playbook

Name It: In this task, you are going to learn to take out details that weaken your writing. We call these extraneous details, and they are like clutter in a house or weeds in a garden that distract us from what we are really meant to focus upon.

What You Might Say Next: "When we have been writing recently, we have focused on being reflective and expressive in our writing. This is great, because it makes our writing personal and more interesting, even when we are writing a report or literary nonfiction text. We have a little problem though; we are getting caught up in writing a lot of words that don't really say anything at all. This type of writing weakens our writing."

Typical Successes

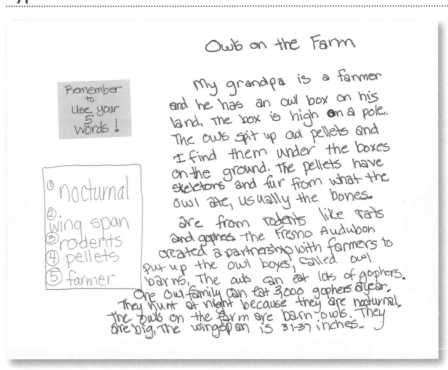

Owns It! In this work sample, you can see how the student used their five words to keep the piece simple. It is based on research the student did on owls.

Model/Do Together: Teach the five-word focus, a mnemonic device to help learners narrow down their thinking for a paper. They have one word for each finger on one hand that is a big idea that needs to be in their writing. These five words might hold the paper together. For example, in the sample student writing above, the student's piece is about owls. The five-word organizer is in the picture beside the student's writing (it reads, *nocturnal, wing span, rodents, pellets, farmer*). You can use the five-word organizer or just sticky notes to have students organize their papers. Line through the details that distract, and highlight the big idea and details connected to those big ideas that relate directly to the five words. Students rewrite the paper leaving out the extraneous details to get to a better final piece of writing. Some tools that help with this are sticky notes—one for each word—highlighters, and thick-point, black pens for lining out extraneous details. Give your students the opportunity to choose what to line out and what to keep; don't do the thinking for them.

Tweak: If you have a student(s) that are struggling to keep their writing to the point, have them write five words that their paper is about and organize their papers by the five words, so the five words would become headings.

Watch Fors and Work Arounds

Even after organizing with five words to focus the piece, students are still adding tons of extraneous details in their pieces. First reread mentor texts (published texts that you come back to over and over again as examples) that provide clear examples of focused writing. Discuss these examples with the students and look at how the author kept the details focused on their big ideas. Then, have the students identify one big idea for their piece and write it on a sticky note and place it in the students' work area, so they can focus on it. Once they write about that, you can add to the piece by writing out other big ideas on sticky notes.

"Research is formalized curiosity. It is poking and prying with a purpose."

—Zora Neale Hurston
(1979)

WHEN YOU MIGHT OFFER IT

You might offer this task after the students have finished writing a piece of text. The text doesn't have to have gone through the writing process; it might just be writing you want students to share part-way through a writing unit.

TARGET

Students share their writing appropriately and acknowledge others' writing contributions.

My husband and I are like the yin and yang of public speaking. I am out in front of people all the time, helping teachers teach. At work, my husband is content to stay in the background and let others take the lead. Truth be told, we all need experiences being both out in front and also in the background. In the classroom, some students find it hard to leave the author's chair, and other students are timid about sharing.

Your Instructional Playbook

Name It: The sharing chair (or podium for older writers) is a special place we have designated in class for the student who is sharing. "In this task, you are going to brainstorm some norms or expectations for our classroom community when sharing our writing."

What You Might Say Next: "Lately in class, I am noticing people talking over someone who is reading their story. Now, I am really happy that we are all excited to share our writing, but we have to remember that when someone is in the sharing chair or at the podium, it is his or her turn to read and our turn to listen. I know you can get very excited about what you wrote, but in our classroom, we honor everyone's voices and everyone's writing. This can happen too when you want to share every day. As a good classroom citizen, we need to remember to take turns. Really good audiences listen when the author is sharing his or her writing, and good audiences know when to offer suggestions and compliments and when it is time to be quiet."

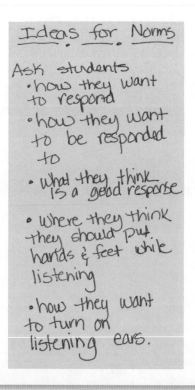

Ideas for creating norms with students.

Model/Do Together: Have a class meeting and set norms for polite audience participation. As a class, you can write, together, what good audience members should do. Then, practice and role-play the agreements that have been made, so that everyone in class is clear with each other about their expectations for respect. You can also pump up attention by suggesting students write author notes. This is particularly a good activity for older readers. The students can write notes to the author sharing and give them to the student as feedback. Notes can also be done in a shared Google Doc, and students can work in real time together while listening. Of course, you will need to facilitate the conversation about what makes an appropriate or inappropriate author note.

Watch Fors and Work Arounds

Young students have not learned to regulate all of their excitement and emotions, and older students have inappropriate outbursts or are derogatory. Help children who are overly eager to share by setting up norms for sharing. Norms might include the following: give only positive feedback, listen carefully when the person is sharing, offer insight, don't just repeat what the reader said, no heads down—everyone should be looking at the reader, no putdowns, and no yelling out.

Some students of any age are too shy or are not mentally prepared for public speaking. Help children too shy to share to visualize themselves going through the process of sharing their piece. Having visual clues on what to do once they are in the writers' sharing chair can help them have more confidence.

"There's not a subject you don't have permission to write about. Students often avoid subjects close to their heart . . . because they assume their teachers will regard those topics as stupid. No area of life is stupid to someone who takes it seriously. If you follow your affections you will write well and will engage your readers."

—William Zinsser
(1976, p. 91)

WHEN YOU MIGHT OFFER IT

You might offer this task once students have spent time exploring a topic in depth.

TARGET

Using notes, students write a short research report independently. For K–1 the "notes" would be their sticky notes. For 2–6, notes would be in a reader's notebook.

I can still remember the parents' faces at the writing celebrations held at my school many years ago. When parents saw how much their young children wrote about their selected animals, their faces lit up. I could tell it was a moment they would remember the rest of their lives. I get the same thrill when middle school students are able to write a short report and give a presentation that knocks it out of the park. Truth be told, my graduate students even struggle with this from time to time, and when they nail it, they and I get the same thrill.

Your Instructional Playbook

Name It: Research papers share information with people on questions that you investigate. In this task, you are going to learn to pull all your notes together and write a draft of a research report.

What You Might Say Next: "Today is a big day. We are going to use our notes, and our organization cards and write a short research report. I want you to get very comfortable in your writing space (on the floor or in a desk). You will need a highlighter, your notebook, a favorite text about the topic, and some writing materials (or device). Using our notes, I want you to write a report on what you have investigated. You are going to have to think about how to organize your writing. What are the main idea(s) you want to share? What details about the main idea(s) do you want your reader to know? I recommend at first that you write in any order, to get all your ideas out. You can revise later to organize your report in a better way."

Typical Successes

Owns it! This younger reader wrote a 15-page report on sharks! Here are two pages to get the idea of what the work can look like.

Model/Do Together: As students read the texts they are using to investigate their topic, have them record questions that come up on cards. Save the questions in a wonder card box (you can use an inexpensive plastic pencil or index card box) or punch a hole in the upper left corner and save them on a ring. Wonder cards will help students write notes about their topic in their notebooks and will help them when they write the first drafts of their research reports. Questions might include the following:

I wonder how . . .?

I wonder why . . ?

I wonder if . . ?

How . . ?

Why do . . ?

Who . . ?

Did . . ?

Once students are satisfied they have enough on their cards, they can start their drafts. Let them know it will be easiest if they create headings (from the big ideas on their cards or in their notebooks) and then draft their report writing under each heading. You can model how to create headings and then write a paragraph or two under each heading by making a teaching chart or using a document camera.

Tweak: If students struggle with what to gather in order to write, have them use wonder cards to collect information (see above). Then, get your students writing by having them use their wonder cards and their notes to start putting their ideas down on the paper.

Release: Writing reports takes time, so on the first day of drafting, you may need to model how to write big ideas and details organized by headings. On subsequent days, don't model, but instead remind students what they can work on and then roam around the room helping students as necessary. Let them do the writing; you should be the coach.

This older reader wrote a report on Egyptians. In this snippet of the report, you can see the student used metaphors.

Watch Fors and Work Arounds

Students are prolific writers and can write volumes in a single sitting. Help them organize their writing to go deeper on a topic rather than broad. Show them how the reader will learn more from a singular idea with details than multiple singular ideas strung in a row. Teach how to use subheaders to organize a paper and dive deep into a topic, writing about a few details.

Students are reluctant to write. Remind them that they don't need to wait for you to start; you will come and check on everyone. They might say they don't know what to write. Remind them that they do because they have lots of information in their notes, and they can begin by restating some of it in their papers.

WHEN YOU MIGHT OFFER IT

An all about book or piece is a simple form of an informational report. It is a good starting place for students who are learning to write reports. It is also a playful genre for students to explore even as more accomplished writers, if they want to focus deeply on one topic and share information about that topic. Offer this task when students want to write about one topic, idea, phenomenon, or thing in depth.

TARGET

Students will choose a topic, read about it, research it, organize, and write about the topic with the goal of sharing everything learned about the one topic.

I own so many books my husband had to build a library in one of the rooms of our house. Two entire shelves are filled with cookbooks. I have what I call "all about" cookbooks where the chef zooms in on a topic—French cooking or all about cooking vegetarian or Paleo or baking bread or the art of soufflés. In any nonfiction genre, from cookbooks to ornithology, there are "all about" texts, and they can be fun to produce with your students.

Your Instructional Playbook

Teaching a writing genre takes many days. This instructional playbook is not designed for you to teach it all in one day but over a few days. You may need to repeat steps as needed to help your students own the writing and be able to write for themselves with you supporting and coaching.

Name It: You need to become familiar with several types of all about books, so I am going to be reading different books to you that are all about one subject. In this task you are going to learn to create your own all about book.

What You Might Say Next: "For the next couple of weeks we are going to work on a form of informational writing called all about books. An all about book is a book that focuses on one topic or one thing. Some alphabet books are all about books, many nonfiction books are developed as all about books. (For example, *The Sea Mammal Alphabet Book* by Jerry Pallota is an all about book on sea mammals.) I cannot wait to see what you are going to write! We are diving in to learning about all about books by reading lots of all about books first. So, let's get reading."

Typical Successes

Owns It! Here is another snippet of the younger readers report. This is his table of contents and a page showing headings.

Model/Do Together: Get started by reading several all about books to the class. Depending on the grade level, you can read an entire book (as in an alphabet book, like *All About Boats: A to Z* by Zora Aiken) or an excerpt from a longer book (like *Devoted: 38 Extraordinary Tales of Love, Loyalty, and Life with Dogs* by Rebecca Ascher-Walsh).

Engage in a variety of instructional opportunities where you model how to organize an all about book. Display charts of various formats you and students have cocreated. Model how to collect information from print sources. Model writing a page of text about an all about book. Perhaps you write all about trucks or lions or for older students, plant and animal cells.

Release: Students need to write texts over several days. The first text they write should not be the only all about book they write, as they will gain ability to write all about books as they write more. Younger writers may benefit from writing books or texts that use a four square model (see below). As students produce writing, give them time to share their writing with each other to learn from each other and encourage them to keep writing.

"The first piece of advice I have to give is that reading is subjective. I may love something, you may hate it. That's true with any art form, visual, music, movies, and the written word. You must be true to yourself."

—Heather Graham (2010)

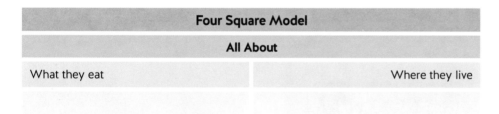

Four Square Model
All About

What they eat	Where they live

Watch Fors and Work Arounds

Writing is scattered and not one topic. While sitting with students, examine several samples of all about books and note how the books are focused. Encourage the student to notice the focus. Ask students for ideas about how they can keep their text focused on one topic or idea. Come to agreement on the student's next step and write down the "next step" goal on a card or sticky note and place it in the student's writing folder to remind her of what she is focused on. For example, "Keep your writing only on what lions do to eat, sleep, or raise their cubs."

Student hasn't organized the all about book, and it is going on and on and on. Sit with the student and work with him using sticky notes. First, ask the student what he wants the book or text to focus on and write it on a sticky note. Then, go through his text, together, line by line, and ask, "Does this connect to your topic and how." If what is written does connect, the writing stays, if it doesn't, then show the student how to delete the writing, either in pencil or on a device. Work through the text in this way, but be supportive and let the student drive the work. Let the student do the thinking about, "Does it match?" The key is that the student can justify why the writing matches their topic or not.

When students are exploring a topic in nonfiction or are reading a fiction text that provides an opportunity for discussion regarding differing opinions about what a character might do/feel/act. As a first grader recently said to me, "It's the stuff we know about what we learned." A fifth grader said, "I formed an opinion based on the facts that I have about the topic."

TARGET

During or after reading, students write an opinion and provide a statement backing up their opinion.

It's probably not a big surprise if I admit to you that I have strong opinions about teaching and learning. Over time, I have learned that opining with force and passion can make others resist buying in; I have learned that when I do state an opinion or write about it, I need to provide evidence for my opinion so that it's well-reasoned rather than just an emotional reaction. We want our students to learn too—to put their facts on the table!

Your Instructional Playbook

Name It: Opinion is our thinking about something. We use knowledge to form an opinion. In this task, you are going to learn to form an opinion using facts from text.

What You Might Say Next: "Today we are going to form opinions about a text we are reading. When we form an opinion, we use information from the text to help us think about what we know and about what we think about what we know. Then, because we are using facts from the text, we can be confident and make a statement about a text, about the character in a story, or about the reasons for something. We can be confident because we are using knowledge or information that we have in our heads."

Typical Successes

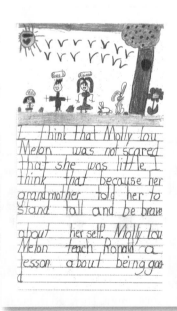

Owns It! In this example from a younger reader, the student used two pieces of textual evidence.

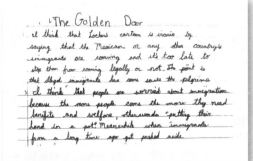

This example is from an older reader who reacted to a political cartoon and feature article.

Model/Do Together: Illustrate the point of making an opinion using facts from a current study or information from a text you are reading. If you are reading a picture book, perhaps only read part of the picture book, and discuss what is happening in the story to the characters. When working with nonfiction text(s), review the known facts. When appropriate, you can also review inferences students might have made about the plot, character's thoughts and feelings, or about the causes or effects in a nonfiction text.

Model how to form an opinion and express the opinion in writing. For example, you might create a teaching chart to record information about what an opinion is and how to form an opinion (see below). Also, you can have students write a bullet point about their opinion while reading on a sticky note and then transfer that sticky note to their writing paper once they are ready to explain their thinking about their reading.

Release: Have students pair up and tell their partners what they think an opinion is and then share their opinion about a text they are reading on their own or the text you read to the whole class. Remind students to record their thinking on sticky notes so that when they later write out their opinion, they can remember all the facts that back up their thinking.

Watch Fors and Work Arounds

Students copy other students' opinions and don't form their own opinion. Help the student feel confident about their opinion. Invite the student to orally tell you their opinion first and then rehearse the best way to write it down. The mental rehearsal will help the student be able to write when you move on to helping the next student.

Students that cannot put the clues or facts from a text together in order to form an opinion. Students who are struggling to make an opinion grounded from evidence in the text can really benefit from the creation of a teaching chart that they can refer back to when working on their own. Create a teaching chart with the students before releasing to independent work. One part of the chart might say, "Clues" and another part say, "Our Thoughts." Model how to connect the clues or facts in the text to the thoughts the students are forming.

WHEN YOU MIGHT OFFER IT

You might offer this task when you are working with a text that has a problem/solution text structure.

TARGET

Students are able to read a text with increased comprehension when first solving a problematic situation related to the text.

There are always two sides to a coin; likewise, there are at least two sides to any problem. When working with a team, sometimes the best solutions to problems never see the light of day. This happens when the person with the great idea doesn't know how to argue her point. I want all students to know how to be flexible problem solvers that know how to get other people believing in their solutions. This takes practice, and you are a master coach, so get practicing with those kids!

Your Instructional Playbook

Name It: A problematic situation is a situation where something is happening in a book and the problem needs to get solved. We are going to make up our own endings for some of the books we read (for example, an intruder named Goldilocks broke into their home—how should Goldilocks be punished for her crime? Or for older readers in *Mick Harte Was Here* by Barbara Park—Mick doesn't die in the beginning but only goes into a coma). In this task, you are going to learn to write and orally share your solution to a problematic situation.

What You Might Say Next: Many books are written in a problem–solution structure. Both fiction and nonfiction books share this structure. We are going to dig deep into a text and figure out the problem in it and then pose our own solutions. We don't have to come up with the same solution that the author did, or if it was a real situation, we don't have to implement the same solution the people in the story did. Let's have some fun.

Typical Successes

Example of a group's solution to a problematic scenario on the rainforest destruction.

Model/Do Together: Present a problematic situation. (You can take any story or cause and effect nonfiction text and provide an introduction on the story plot or event/issue as the problem). Don't provide the resolution or effect; let the students brainstorm that. Provide relevant information about the situation so that students will be able focus on the key ideas in the text. Be as clear as possible. Working in groups, have the students come up with a possible solution to the problematic situation *while* they read the text. Provide 18 x 24 inch paper and markers for students to record their answers. Students may present more than one solution, and if they do, ask them to elaborate on which solution they think is best. Then, tell students they will be able to validate or test their solutions by reading the text and gathering evidence that their solution(s) would work.

Release: Organize students back into trios or quads; have them choose the roles they will take while reading. There should be a fact finder (a fact checker also if working in groups of four), a recorder, and a timer. Double check that the team members know their roles and they know how to work together. Remind students to think about solutions to the problem while reading, and encourage them to read and then see if they can validate their solution. If not, encourage them to modify their solution as they come up with new ideas from the information in the text.

Watch Fors and Work Arounds

Groups get stuck and are unable to come up with a solution. Sit with the group for a few moments and facilitate a discussion. Ask each student in the group to say what they think the problem is and how it could be solved. Write down the students' ideas on a big piece of chart paper, then ask the group which one they think they want to have as their group solution.

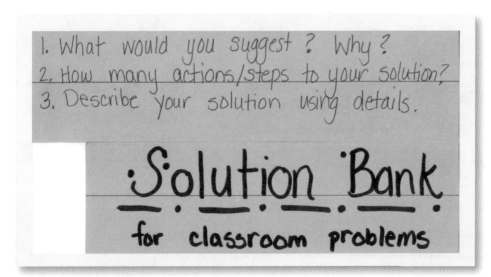

1. What would you suggest? Why?
2. How many actions/steps to your solution?
3. Describe your solution using details.

:Solution :Bank:
for classroom problems

WHEN YOU MIGHT OFFER IT

You might offer this task when reading and writing about how-to texts. This is a good task to introduce students to drafting the how-to.

TARGET

Students will write a how-to text in order to provide classmates with directions on how to do something.

I am a sucker for well-written directions. Whenever we purchase some new item for our home that has to be put together, I dive into the box, fishing for the directions. I feel such a sense of accomplishment when I can follow the directions and voila—get to put my new item to use. I also feel an intense sense of frustration when I cannot make heads or tails out of the directions (see page 92 for that X@%% writing desk manual episode). I usually stomp around my house and threaten to throw the screwdriver—all avoidable behaviors when beautifully laid-out directions accompany products.

Your Instructional Playbook

Name It: A how-to text is a text that gives directions. Common how-to texts are recipes and directions that come with products or toys. In this task, you are going to practice writing a how-to text and see if a classmate thinks your directions make sense.

What You Might Say Next: "Directions help us get all sorts of things done in our lives. Sometimes I give my family and friends directions on how to do something that I know how to do that they are learning or wanting to recreate. (Have a how-to text with you—a recipe or product directions, for instance.) In this how-to text (hold it up), the directions tell us step by step how to . . . (cook a turkey). We are going to think of something we want to teach people to do and write up our directions in a how-to text. How-tos can be really fun. You can write a how-to about putting on socks or washing the dog or making an ice cream sundae or . . . anything you want!"

Typical Successes

  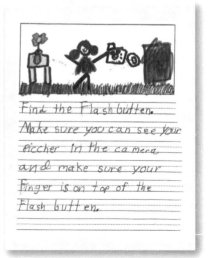

The student first brainstormed this how-to piece in boxes and revised using a different color pen, then wrote it out in paragraph form. This is a snippet of the three-page piece.

Model/Do Together: Play a few minutes of a favorite cooking show video (or any how-to) and then ask students to tell you what they noticed and record ideas, such as materials are organized, the steps shown are in sequence, the chef tells you exactly you what to do, and so on. Next, model for students how to prep writing up directions. Have a chart or blank page on a device ready and draw a box for each step you plan to write. For example, if you are going to model five steps, you will draw five boxes. Let the students know what you are going to write (and draw for younger writers). In the first box, write the first step (add a picture if appropriate). Then facilitate discussion about what they think the next step might be. Go on adding descriptions of directions to the boxes while facilitating discussion with the students about what they think would be clear.

Invite students to brainstorm what they would like to write their directions about. Create an idea bank of direction topics.

Release: Send students off to write their how-to pieces. Encourage them to start by drawing boxes for each step in the directions they are writing (prepare this ahead of time for younger writers and give each student a copy). Once students are finished drafting their directions, encourage them to pair up with another students and share their directions. The partner should listen and let the writer know if they think something is missing from the how-to.

Corn Tortillas
By Mrs. Robbins/Ms. Gonzalez' class

Ingredients
Masa Harina
Water

- First you put 4 cups of Masa harina (corn flour) in the bowl so it looks like snowy mountains.
- Then you put 2 1/2 cups of water that is hot like hot cocoa so it melts the snowy mountains.
- Turn the melted mountains into falling rocks by swirling the masa and the rocks.
- Then add a little more water and squish and push the snowy rocks until it turns into a snowy ball that is soft.
- Keep smashing the snowy ball until it feels like playdough. Smashing for about 3 minutes.
- Take a little piece of the playdough mixture and roll it into a snowball. Then spank the snowball in your hands until it is flat like a pancake.
- Put the playdough pancake in plastic wrap and squish in a squisher until it is a smooth and flat like a plate.
- Pull the plastic up and put the flat plate on the steaming sizzling hot griddle.
- Turn the flat plate over when it's smoky like a candle when you blow it out.
- Then the top of the flat plate should look bumpy like crunchy peanut butter.
- Turn the flat plate over when smoke comes out like a BBQ.
- Take the flat plate off the sizzling griddle when it fills up like a balloon.
- The tortilla will dance in your hands because it is still steaming hot.
- Then you take the beans and you spread it like spreading peanut butter on bread.
- Then you roll it like a flute and then you may eat it.

In this piece, the class wrote the how-to piece after making tortillas.

Watch Fors and Work Arounds

The students have written out their directions, but the directions are mixed up. A pair of scissors can help. Have the student cut up their directions and tape their how-to piece back together in the correct order. Talk with the student to help her brainstorm how she might be able to write the next set of directions in the correct order.

WHEN YOU MIGHT OFFER IT

You might offer this task when students are involved in an inquiry into a subject they are interested in.

TARGET

Students will write an explanatory text that gives facts and an explanation for the facts in the form of an explanatory book.

When I was young, my mother and father were proud owners of an encyclopedia. I would pull it out and sit with my father and thumb through the bird section. That memory is precious to me, and I can't believe that bound encyclopedias are a thing of the past! I remind myself that writing explanations well is just as relevant today—just the platform has changed. I want all students to be able to write clearly. This task is great practice.

Your Instructional Playbook

Name It: When we explain things, we tell people why something is the way it is or why something happened. In this task, you are going to learn to organize a book into explanations to inform others.

What You Might Say Next: "We can learn lots of different things when we look closely at a nonfiction book and read both the words and the pictures. Let's talk about how we can learn facts or make opinion statements by reading the paragraphs, headings, index, and other text features (or for younger readers—just reading the pictures closely)."

Typical Successes

Check out this cute explanatory text page from a younger readers' penguin report.

Model/Do Together: After reviewing a couple of texts filled with facts and explanations, model how to write a fact on a sticky note and place on a T-chart with the headings: Facts/Explanations. On the fact side of the T-chart, put the sticky note that states the fact, and on the other side, put the explanation—for example, birds of prey have sharp beaks (fact). They have sharp beaks in order to tear apart their prey (explanation). Explanations will include words like *because, therefore, in order to, the reason is, being, due to, for, in that,* and *since.* Share several more examples of facts and their explanations and invite students to think of some too.

Have a mock-up of an explanatory book ready to show younger writers (or binder paper with headings written out for older writers). An explanatory book includes five to six pages of writing paper and a cover stapled together. Model writing in whichever format you are using for the age of your students (book or binder paper). Write out the facts and the explanations in full sentences using the sticky notes from the T-chart to help. Do a think-aloud while you write so how you transfer from the sticky note jot to the full sentence is clear for students. Younger writers may also want to draw pictures.

Release: Invite the students to continue to take notes on their own and create an outline for their books, organizing with facts and explanations. Students can explore many formats, but the simplest format is the fact on the top of the page and the explanation on the bottom of the page.

Watch Fors and Work Arounds

Students fill their explanatory books with lots of facts and no explanations—or vice versa. Go back to the sticky notes and the T-chart. Have students line up their facts with an explanation, drawing an arrow between the facts and their matching explanations. Then, double check the book they are writing to see what matches up and what is missing and needs to be filled in. You are guiding the student to look for the gaps.

Facts and explanations are mixed up. Students who are writing about facts and explanations that are incorrect need to go back to the texts where they gathered the facts and check themselves. You may need to go through their text and (gently, not in red pen) mark the pages you think have mixed-up information. Then, the students will know what they need to focus on in their fact checking.

"There is a learning revolution under way because of the confluence of forces. These forces are urgency, knowledge and capacity."

—Michael Fullan (2016)

WHEN YOU MIGHT OFFER IT

You might offer this task when students raise questions about an unknown phenomenon, event, or issue.

TARGET

With facilitation of an adult, students will participate in a group investigation and ask questions, find information, and discuss or write about findings with a partner.

Both of my daughters have degrees in a STEM area. I had a colleague ask me how I did it—how did I get both young women to stick with their scientific, inquiring mind? I attribute that to all the fun and exciting investigations we did together as a family. First, there is the thrill of knowing you can dig up info on something you and only you want to know about. Then, in the end, there is the satisfying sense of accomplishment when you find out something you didn't even know you wanted to know.

Your Instructional Playbook

Name It: An investigation is when you research something you are interested in. In this task, which we are going to do together, you are going to learn to ask questions about a topic and then look up information that helps you answer your questions.

What You Might Say Next: "We are going to launch an investigation into a topic we have been discussing lately (name topic). Investigations are fun and exciting because we delve into a subject that is exciting. After we do a few investigations together, like we are starting today, you will know how to do investigations on your own. Let's get started by reviewing what we know and what we wonder about (name topic)."

Typical Successes

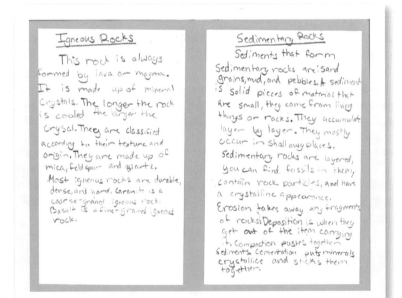

An older reader created an investigative board on rocks. Notice how she organized her information.

Model/Do Together: Ask a launch question to get the investigation started. Your question may be broad, like "What do we already know about dogs' dietary needs?" Record students' answers. Next, focus on a "next step" question. A next step question takes you deeper into the investigation. Perhaps, with the example I have given, it comes up that dogs should not eat chocolate. So a next step question might be, "What happens to a dog's body if it eats chocolate?" This next step question should be narrow enough to go deep. Brainstorm with students what resources you can use to look up answers to the question. Investigate with the class and record findings on a chart or in an electronic document that can be shared with students (if appropriate). Model for students how to set up an investigation report. This type of report has the question at the top, resources listed next, and then findings written out in paragraph form, with pictures as needed.

Release: Organize students into pairs. Invite students to work together to review the question and the findings and decide how to write the report paragraph. Students will work together to produce the report, with one report being authored by two students.

> *"Embrace the attitude of progress, not perfection, and if you find yourself falling down a notch or two, don't fret—just dust yourself off, lift yourself up and keep on climbing."*
>
> —Gabrielle Bernstein
> (2010, p. 119)

Watch Fors and Work Arounds

Some students were not fully engaged during the whole class discussion and recording of findings, so when you release them, they don't know what to do. This happens often as students sometimes are not used to engaging in tasks where they are fully responsible for completing the work on their own once you release. It teaches bad habits for students if you simply sit with them and repeat everything, as then they will learn they really don't have to listen the first time. Instead, organize a "study sheet" where they go back and check the information you have recorded from the whole class conversation and write down notes for themselves.

Students brainstorm a different question than the one investigated with the class (which is all right if they are ready to move forward on their own), but they are having trouble knowing how to find resources of information. Students who are ready to investigate on their own may be ready for a WebQuest, where you compile a list of websites that are appropriate for the students to visit and then list what they should look for on that website. So the students essentially go on a quest looking for information you identified.

WHEN YOU MIGHT OFFER IT

You might offer this task when working with literature or literary nonfiction or when focusing on response to literature as an assessment.

TARGET

Students will write a book review (opinion writing) that includes a claim, evidence for the claim, and a recommendation.

It doesn't matter that I am a grown woman, I still have favorite parts in novels, and when I recommend a book to a friend, I am usually swooning over my favorite part or character and explaining why. Responding to literature should rock our souls, and it needs to be so much more than a book report. I have not once picked up a book to read because someone gave me a jilted book review. I have, however, rushed to Amazon to order the book my best friend just talked up with passion. We want our students approaching literature response with this same purpose of voicing their honest stance.

Your Instructional Playbook

Name It: In this task, you are going to learn to make a recommendation to someone to read a book or not read a book.

What You Might Say Next: "We are going to learn about how to write a response to literature that makes others know *why* we are giving it a thumbs up or a thumbs down. A response is a piece you write where you tell about something you read and what you think of the story. To get ready to write about books, I want to review one of the stories I love. After I read the story, we are going to talk about the story, if we like it or not and why, and whether we would recommend the book to someone else."

Typical Successes

In this piece, a student writes three points from the book and then puts her claim and recommendation at the end of the text.

First Ameya and Koragu went into the woods to discover something. They went through the woods and finds a beautiful web. They both decided that they should study it. When they reached for the web it collapsed. They felt sad and returned home.

Second they went home. Afiya, Ameyai's wife asked what happend. They then decided to go back thei next day, just to see and study it.

Today I read The Spider Weaver by Margaret Musgrove. This is a realistic fiction books, it is true because people could really go into the woods and find a web.

The main characters are Ameyaw and koragu. The are important to the story because they are the one who sees a web in the woods. The story takes place in Ghana. Ghana is where the web was found.

Third, Ameya and Koragu began to Weave the beautiful cloths. The cloths looked like the webs. The beautiful cloths inspired others to weave to.

I recommend this book because it is interesting and because today cloths are made like the beautiful webs. You will find the designs interesting because the webs are intricate.

Model/Do Together: Take a book that you've already read to the class (perhaps a picture book, which works well with all grade levels depending on the complexity of the text), reread all of it or parts of it if it is a long text, and stop and discuss parts you like or dislike about the book. Do a think-aloud and be precise in what you share. Discuss with students what makes you like or dislike the book as a whole, after you finishing reading it, and tell them if you would recommend that another class at school read it. For example, "I really like this book, and I think Mrs. Harrington should read it to her students because on page . . . ".

Review a second picture book; it should be a book you've read to the class at least once, so they can think about their opinion of the story. Discuss if the class liked the story or not and why. Have the students refer back to specific pages in the book to back up their choices. Modeling on a chart, facilitate a discussion with the students, writing out a short book review. Ask what their opinion is about the book and which parts of the book are strong examples to show evidence for their opinion. In the modeled writing, ensure the response includes your opinion and evidence to back up your opinion.

Release: Remind students of what they have learned about writing a book review that includes their opinion and a recommendation. Invite the students to write a good book review with a claim, details to back up their claim, and a recommendation.

Students can refer back to the teaching charts you've created to help them write a claim and a recommendation to read or not read the book. Invite the students to share their recommendations about the books they chose with each other.

Watch Fors and Work Arounds

Students response doesn't have anything to do with the text they read. Sometimes students get swept up by their imagination of a character's life or how an event should end. That is a natural part of reading; so get swept away. However, when writing a response to literature, the student needs to know the difference between what they want to have happened in the text and what actually happened. It is all right for students to respond with how they wished a text would have ended, but they need to say that it is their thinking and ideas. If they really believe what they wrote occurred in the text or is a logical conclusion but not actually written in the text, guide the student to check the facts in the text that lead to what they write.

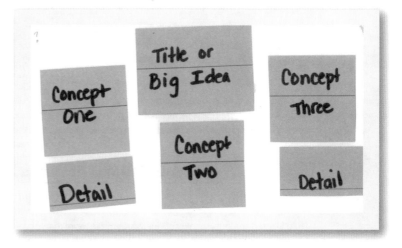

THE GOOD, THE BAD, AND THE UGLY

My own blog-like review of how the tasks actually went down . . .

Here I have provided different examples for The Good, The Bad, and The Ugly reflection. I focus on tasks in this section that were a little more complex than the tasks I reflected on in section one.

The Good

What I Planned to Do	What I Actually Did
Higher-Order Thinking– *Abstraction*	**Higher-Order Thinking–** *Abstraction*
Students were to interpret the theme of a story by writing a summary paragraph of a picture book (a difficult or complex text) and then depict the theme in pictures from a magazine.	Students wrote a short summary paragraph, on their own, about the theme after we discussed the book. Then, they used magazines and a 9 x 12 piece of construction paper to create the theme in photos.

My Thinking About the Lesson in Action

Great!

I had wanted students to think about the theme in more than one way. First, I wanted them to summarize the story theme by stating the theme, justifying it with a quick story plot summary (on their own), and then interpret the theme through pictures. They did it! I used scaffolds to help them think through the story plot, and we discussed possible themes of the book together, but after that, they were on their own. I went around the room coaching and nudging, but I didn't write any of the summary for them. They did it on their own.

The Bad

What I Planned to Do	What I Actually Did
Higher-Order Thinking— Synthesis	**Thinking— Apply**
Students were to synthesize two texts on the same topics. I had a fiction and nonfiction text on the black plague. Students were to consider the theme of the fiction text and the main points of the nonfiction text and write a statement about how the texts were related and why they thought that.	Students regurgitated the main points of the nonfiction text in their notebooks, and they took the main points of the nonfiction text and applied them to the fiction text. The students struggled with the deep thinking of coming up with their own statement of how the texts connected beyond the obvious thing that the subject was the same.

My Thinking About the Lesson in Action

Could Have Been Better

The fact that the students could only look at the surface level of both texts was my fault. I didn't scaffold the activity enough. We read the texts aloud the first day, with me reading, then on the second day, student read and annotated the nonfiction text and the short story. I created a teaching chart of the main ideas of the nonfiction text, but I didn't create a teaching chart of the historically correct facts that were in the story. So in the end, when they had to write their own thinking out, they simply applied the nonfiction main points to the story. They did not synthesize their understanding about the two books to have a deepened understanding of the texts topic.

The Ugly

What I Planned to Do	What I Actually Did
Higher-Order Thinking— Synthesis	**Thinking— Knowledge**
Students were to read two texts with a partner. Then they were to write down all the connections between the texts, discussing their ideas with their partner. Then they were to come up with their own statement about the topic that both books shared.	I read the texts aloud to the students and got caught up talking about the connections between the texts. I ended up doing the analysis of each text while the students listened to me. I stopped there as I realized they didn't need to watch me also synthesize the ideas between the texts, as they wouldn't grasp my thinking.

My Thinking About the Lesson in Action

Yuck!

I got too caught up in the work myself. I guess I was having too much fun thinking through the main points and I forgot the point was for the students to do the work, not me. After I had them copy down my analysis of the texts, I abandoned the lesson, vowing to do a reteach.

SECTION THREE

In this next set of engagements, students take on a more ambitious amount of thinking and doing. Writing a complete fairy tale or fable, learning to distinguish quality information from fake news, practicing think-aloud as a strategy to become a fiercer reader—all sophisticated academic moves. These are "sometimes" tasks because they take more time and you only want to spend the time if your students are ready for them or need a refresher on them. You model and have students do them to a point of independence, so they are skills students can call upon always, adapting them, combining them, and making them their own. To borrow from the nursery rhyme, whether your students become a butcher, a baker, or a candlestick maker, these thinking abilities will serve them well.

SOMETIME TASKS

for Reading, Writing, and Thinking

	Task	Genre	Skill	The Transfer (What students eventually are able to do—independently, and for a lifetime!)
51	Identify Theme in a Complex Text	Fiction	Identify theme.	Synthesize clues to identify the theme, state the theme, and back it up using evidence from the text.
52	Posing Questions for Easier Inquiry	Fiction, literary nonfiction, informational text	Design an inquiry.	Choose topic for inquiry and shape question(s) to guide research.
53	Writing a Fable or Myth	Writing narrative, fiction, realistic fiction	Write a fable or myth.	Create a believable world, introduce characters with sufficient detail, use descriptive details in plot, and have a conclusion that conveys a message.
54	Writing a Fairy Tale	Writing narrative, fiction, fantasy	Write a fairy tale.	Create a believable world, introduce characters with sufficient detail, use descriptive details in plot, and have a conclusion that conveys a resolution or happy ending.
55	Justifying an Answer With a Claim and Evidence	Argumentative writing	State an argument.	Write a claim and then provide evidence that supports the claim.
56	Use Known Info to Help Others Learn New Info	Nonfiction	Collaboratively discuss nonfiction text and write summary of discussion.	Listen to add information to a conversation and then write about the discussion making salient points.
57	Connect Ideas Between Texts	Fiction, informational text	Identify common themes or points of information from multiple texts.	Identify relationships between information or ideas in multiple texts, reflect on the sameness of the relationships in order to name connections.
58	Identifying Real Facts From Made-Up Facts: Fallacious Reasoning	Nonfiction, or *fiction* if you are reading the *National Enquirer!*	Identify fallacious reasoning.	Identify and provide evidence for logical mistakes in reasoning made by persuasive information.
59	Brainstorming Multiple Valid Answers/Responses	Fiction, literary nonfiction, informational text	Brainstorm topics in collaborative conversations.	Brainstorm ideas, group ideas into categories in order to own information, and transform information into opinion or argument texts.
60	Concept Mapping Between Big Ideas	Fiction, literary nonfiction, informational text, nonfiction, functional text	Create mind map.	Design concept map of two big ideas presented in one or more texts.
61	Make Me Ponder: Questions That Get the Thinking Juices Flowing	Fiction, literary nonfiction, informational text	Ask and answer questions of text.	Identify literal, interpretive, and applied questions and answer questions alone or with partners.
62	Writing Compare and Contrast Response to Literature	Response to literature, fiction, literary nonfiction	Write a response to literature.	Write a response to literature where students compare and contrast ideas, texts, or information.
63	Peer-to-Peer Analysis and Response	Fiction, literary nonfiction, informational text, nonfiction	Choose an appropriate comprehension strategy: summarize, question, clarify, or predict.	Summarize, question, clarify, or predict in order to help each other comprehend.
64	Critique a Functional Document or Text	Nonfiction, functional texts, literary nonfiction	Analyze a nonfiction text.	Analyze information in a functional text that indicates the text's purpose, functionality, and sufficiency of information or analyze author's purpose, article context, and relevance.
65	Visible and Visual: Use Known Concepts and Vocabulary to Understand a Text	Informational text, nonfiction	Use prior knowledge.	Use known information to relate concepts to new concepts and information.
66	Summarize a Text That Is a Little Too Hard for Students to Read on Their Own	Literary nonfiction, informational text	Summarize.	Make connections between concepts in the text and prior knowledge and state new information succinctly.
67	Student Think-Alouds	Fiction, literary nonfiction, informational text, nonfiction, functional texts	Monitor comprehension.	Apply coping strategies to handle a difficult text and have a think-aloud conversation to monitor comprehension and visualize new concepts or ideas.
68	Separate Central Idea From a Big Idea	Literary nonfiction	Differentiate between the central idea and big ideas.	Analyze causes, motivations, sequences, and results of events to identify the concepts and relationships between concepts.
69	Writing in Different Genres or Multimedia to Engage and Persuade	Fiction, literary nonfiction, informational text, poetry, music	Rewrite text in a new genre.	Build on the thread of an idea by extending the interpretation into a new genre; go beyond retelling when writing appropriately in new genre.
70	Creative Debate	Fiction, literary nonfiction	Debate a topic from multiple viewpoints.	Make claims and state evidence on a topic from character's point of view (fiction) or from a person's/stakeholder's point of view (nonfiction) utilizing opposing viewpoints.
71	I Am a Reader			Consider oneself as a reader.
72	I Am a Writer			Consider oneself as a writer.
73	Look Up			Take on a new perspective,
74	Goodbye, Perfect Teacher			Move away from the hazard of perfectionism.
75	Teacher and Learner			Because life-long teaching and learning = a literate life.

WHEN YOU MIGHT OFFER IT

You might offer this task when you have been reading texts to students that have a strong central message or when students are talking deeply about texts they are reading and the ideas in the text are coming up in their conversations.

TARGET

Students use clues in the text and synthesize them together to discover the theme in the text; they state the theme and back it up using evidence from the text.

I love theme. My husband, the master coach I mentioned in the intro, loves theme too. It seems that we look for theme everywhere in our lives. The theme of a friend's career journey, the theme of my mom's phone call last weekend (those are often multi-theme), the theme of a movie or current politics; we just love this pattern seeking, and once you are well past your twenties, life gets, well, more thematic! Still, our young students are up for the challenge of recognizing themes too, and it's rewarding when you see them link book themes to real-life themes on their own.

Your Instructional Playbook

Name It: The theme is the idea that holds a story together. The theme is what keeps the plot moving forward, to some sort of resolution. In this task, we are going to practice recognizing the theme.

What You Might Say Next: "Let's mark a place in the book (text) that relates to what you predicted this part (or section of the text) would be about. (Students each have copies of the book or text and sticky notes or highlighter pens.) Now, let's talk about it. What is happening in this part of the book? Take notes and then we can keep reading until we get to another spot where things are happening that also seem charged with importance. We'll do this to the end of the book (or chapter) and then talk about how the happenings seem to work together. That's how we can identify what the theme of the book is."

Typical Successes

Not Quite There Yet! This first try at identifying theme by a younger reader for the book *Gaston* by Kelly DiPucchio, is a good example of how students can begin to think about what they read.

> I perdict that ther are going to have a argument and have a agreement and a switch. also bark at each uther. The text said Gaston slobered and he raced and went ruff and the others walked good and they sipped. The theme is be yourself. The puppies and their familys need to like them as they are.

Model/Do Together: Model first by reading aloud a text that is different than the text that the students will read on their own. As students look/listen for clues in the text that they (not you!) think are important to inferring theme, coach as needed. Students do the highlighting, not you! If you are working with young readers, list Clue #1, Clue #2, Clue #3, on chart paper and then read aloud and invite students to raise their hands when they spot clues to the theme. Write the clues on the chart.

Continue reading and recording clues to the story's end. Then, ask, "Do the clues add up? What would you say the theme is?" Encourage students to do the thinking, go back to the story for support, and gently nudge them to the connections between the clues only if necessary. Remember, theme is often best captured in a few words (not just "love" or "loss" or "injustice").

Release: Guide students as they work to identify theme on their own in a text they are reading in a group. Circulate, and check students' thinking to see if they are able to identify clues that they can knit together. Prompt by asking, "What are you noticing? What information does one clue give them? How does that information or idea connect to the next identified clue?" Encourage students to think about the connections between the clues and what they mean. Once students indicate that they have figured out the theme of the text, have them tell a partner their thinking; make sure they back up their thinking by sharing why they think the theme is what it is, sharing their clues and referring back to the text.

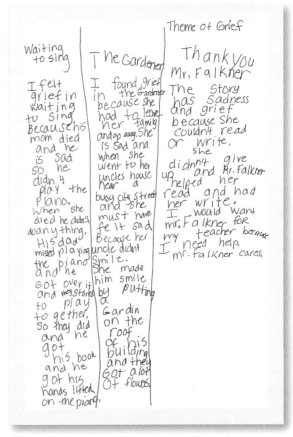

Owns It! Notice how this student identified the theme of grief in three texts, almost comparing them. The texts were *Waiting to Sing* by Howard Kaplan, *The Gardener* by Sarah Stewart, and *Thank You Mr. Falker* by Patricia Polacco.

Watch Fors and Work Arounds

Students are lost in the text and overwhelmed by the length of it, Break complex text into parts or chunks and have students identify what is occurring in each chunk. Then, they can string together the big ideas from the chunks to come up with overall ideas or things happening in the text.

Students check out because the text is hard. Help them think about connections they make to the text while reading. How do the things they identify connect with their personal experiences or knowledge?

WHEN YOU MIGHT OFFER IT

You might offer this task after digging into an inquiry as a whole class, and you are ready for students to design questions and work on their own inquiry project.

TARGET

Student designs an inquiry into a subject of interest.

My husband just got home from Home Depot where he went on a search for how to build a workbench and the materials. He was exasperated from waiting 45 minutes just for someone in the lumber department to recommend the type of wood to use. "You might have just looked up your questions first on your iPad," I said, not meaning to sound like Little Miss Smarty Pants. So don't tell him I'm immortalizing this moment in a book and going on record saying, he could have designed his inquiry first.

Your Instructional Playbook

Name It: An investigation is when we dig into a topic through books, texts, articles, and digital sources. In this task, we are going to decide on what we want to investigate and learn how to shape our question(s) so it helps us do our research.

What You Might Say Next: "When we get ready to investigate a topic that interests us, we first come up with questions that help us focus our research. We need to ask questions that don't result in yes or no answers. We ask questions by thinking about what we want to know, and then we think about, *What if? In which way? or How?*"

Typical Success

> Internet
> The Rock Cycle
>
> 1• group of changes
> •rocks can be broken up
> •form crystals from heat
> 2• heat comes from plate tectonics
> 2• plate tectonics build things
>   from colliding
> 2• things get washed away and
>   get formed again
> •never stops
>
> Guiding Question:
>   What is the rock cycle?
>
> 1. Look up facts
> 2. Organize in groups 1, 2, 3, 4
> 3. Get more details
> 4. check vocab. for glossary
> 5. Write!
>
> Internet
> Igneous Rocks
>
> •form from cooling and solid-
> ification
> 1• mineral crystals
> •longer cooled the bigger they get
> •made of feldspar, quartz, and
>   mica
> •Granite: coarse grained
> •Basalt: fine grained
>
> Text Book
> Metamorphic Rocks
>
> 1• change form
> 1• heat and pressure changes the rocks
> 1• everything about the rock
>   changes
> •most used rocks are marble
>   and slate

Check out how this student has started her notes and where she is planning to go next with her inquiry.

Model/Do Together: Talk with students about setting themselves up for an inquiry. What do they want to investigate? Have them do a few minutes of brainstorming ideas and writing a few questions. Think aloud your process for honing a topic and a few questions. Nine times out of ten, students pursue too big a topic, and if you can help with that, you set them up for success. For example, from "Are humans polluting the oceans?" (*hmmm, too broad*) to "What is bleaching the coral reefs, and why does this threaten ocean life and humans?" (*Yes, more manageable.*) Push students to design questions at an interpretive level; that is, those for which you can't merely look up information and record it, but for which you have to analyze it. For example, in the coral reef inquiry, a student would discover that different scientists recently had a few theories! Was sunscreen the culprit? Warming oceans because of climate change? Also, focus on the quality of questions rather than a hefty amount of them. Maybe the best inquiry a student will design has only one big question that starts like, "What do we know about . . . ?" and "What if . . . ?" or "How would . . . be different if . . . ?"

To support students, share supplies and classic methods of note taking for a report. Sentence strips and index cards are tactile, and the beauty is that students can shuffle them and then staple them together as a reference once they are farther along in knowing sections of their report. If students prefer to use a notebook or a computer, they can go back through and use various colors to highlight and organize information

Release: As students work, they are going to need encouragement—but ask questions and redirect rather than tell them exactly what to do. When they are done and ready to share, ask them to comment on what kept them going; learners love hearing that their peers caught the fever of some aspect of their topic. Point out that real scientists and researchers face the same formidable slog, and it's their curiosity about at least one thing in particular that kept them going. One fourth grader beamed as she talked about investigating whether all newborns—human and mammal—prefer sweet tastes. She had a new baby brother at home, and that was her "spark."

Watch Fors and Work Arounds

Students don't have a lot of practice asking deep questions on their own. Instead of having students focus on "right there" questions that can be answered in a text, have them practice with questions that make them think and search. Think and search questions are interpretive questions where the student has to make inferences and decide on relationships between information sources.

"What makes me want to keep reading a nonfiction text is the encounter with a surprising, well-stocked mind as it takes on the challenge of the next sentence, paragraph, and thematic problem it has set for itself."

—Phillip Lopate
(2013, p. 6)

WHEN YOU MIGHT OFFER IT

You might offer this task after students have read a lot of fables or myths, discussed them as a class, and are ready to write their own fables or myth.

TARGET

Students will write a fable or myth and make sure their writing is focused, has a theme, and has characters developed.

I once taught a third-grade student who really hated riding the bus home everyday. The seventh and eighth graders rode the bus with her. They were not the nicest kids, and I soon learned, they were bullying her. One day, she wrote the loveliest fable about a little girl who stood up to the bus bully. It prompted me to tell the vice principal, who called the school, who put an end to the problem. Not all of our students' issues are solved by writing fables, but it can certainly help them think through difficult things and dream up an answer to the problem. They can explain their worlds through myths and fables.

Your Instructional Playbook

Name It: In this task, we are going to write a fable or a myth—your choice! To get this done, we will organize our writing around a central theme and the structure of the writing type we choose and include what we want the message of our fable or myth to be. All fables have a story that is intended to help or explain—we call these lessons— and myths usually just explain some sort of thing (or phenomena).

What You Might Say to Introduce It: "We have been talking about how a central idea or message is written into the fables and myths we have been reading. *Pride goes before a fall . . . A lie is discovered in time . . . Beware of flatterers.* It's like a theme, but often so clearly stated that it reads like a lesson, right? We are going to jump into writing our own fable/myth, so begin by thinking about the theme or big idea you want to teach. Then think about your characters. Who are they? What are their traits? How will they help you teach your theme or big idea? We are going to start by planning our writing."

Typical Successes

The Pow! Zing! lesson in this fable is about a crazy runaway baseball.

> ### Greatest Hit Superpowers
>
> It was the first ining. Our team was tired and probably had lost all hope. The other team was winning by 12. The hot Sunday air was bringing gallons of sweat down our cheeks. "Strike." I yelled the umpire. "Your out." Now we were in field. "Crack!" went the bat. "I got it." I said. Running to the ball I realized that I had gone to far that ball was after me! "Bong!" The ball wacked me strait in the forhead. For a moment every thing was pitch black.
>
> "What happened?" I said, still feeling woozie. Suddenly I could feel pumped up blood runing through my venis. I felt much stronger. "Wow that hit must of done more to me than I thought." I said
>
> It was 2nd inging. We were out feild I was up to bat. I was sweaty and nervous. I hope I can usualy hit this one. I thought. The pitcher through the ball With out looking I swang. "Crack!" the ball flew out of the feild. I ran to the base. 1st, 2nd, 3rd, home run! It was like super stunth! After 4 home runs, we were winning! We were infeild now. The last inning "Crack! went the bat. I ran to the ball. Suddenly the ball came crashing down. "Bam!" I was hit. I got up. "Ouch" I said My blood slowed down. I got weaker "Oh no not now!" I thought. But I still had hope.

"What!" the team said. "How are we going to win now!" said a player, "Don't give up now," I said. Besides, we're winning by 22 points. They all moaned, but half way were proud. I was up to bat. I got a tight grip on the bat and "wong! Crack!" went the bat. I was off! 1st, 2nd, 3rd. I was almost to home and the catcher was after me. Inches away I slid. Dust scatered every where "Homerun!" yelled the umpire. We had won! We cheered and celebrated. Well I didn't have super powers but I learned that if you lose all hope and a crazy ball starts chasing you, let it hit you and you will have superpowers!

> *"Boundaries that you establish in your life as protection for yourself today will feel like constraints tomorrow."*
>
> —Sadhguru (2016, p. 92)

Therefore, don't set up regretful boundaries in your classroom.

Model/Do Together: Model this writing in a think-aloud, so you can be explicit. For example, "The squirrel was fighting with the other animals, and in the end he got_____and learned_____." Continue writing your fable—have it fill up the chart paper, with enough space for you to draw a picture of the story at the top of the page.

Now comes the fun part. Invite the students to add in their message or lesson. Pass out sentence strips to the students; invite them to think up a lesson they wish they could teach everyone in the world. This can be a really funny lesson (or an explanation for something cool if you are focusing on myths)—for example, never drink Kool Aid before recess. Brainstorm silly and fun ideas with the students and write these ideas out on a chart to create an *idea bank*. Then, invite the students to write out their fun ideas for a lesson on their sentence strip. Once everyone has a lesson written out in one sentence, invite students to share their funny lessons with each other.

Release: Next, it is time to move on to writing the story that goes with the lesson or explanation. Remind the students to think about what happened first in the story and what the big problem was (you can use the story plot map from the Plot Summary Snapshot Task on page 94 to help students brainstorm their stories). Encourage students to revisit their pieces and see if they have a beginning, middle, and end. Then, remind them to add the Pow! Zing! to their stories by adding in the lesson or the fun explanation.

Watch Fors and Work Arounds

Students cannot get started writing. Have students brainstorm their Pow! Zing! lesson first and write it out on a sticky note. Then, tape it to the students' desk as a visual reminder of their writing goal.

Student writing begins to ramble, and the closing point of the myth gets lost. To reteach beginning, middle, and end, use one of the picture books you've read to discuss each section of the story, pointing out the pages that best illustrate.

WHEN YOU MIGHT OFFER IT

You might offer this task after students have read a lot of fairy tales, discussed them as a class, and are ready to write their own fairy tales. This is a companion task to Task 53.

TARGET

Students will write a fairy tale, and make sure their writing is focused and includes a beginning, middle, and an end that solves some magical problem.

I have been called a Pollyanna on more than one occasion—as if that is a bad thing! I see the best in everyone and hope for the happy endings, always! I am known around my house for having a good talk with the writers for *Grey's Anatomy* (the only TV show I really follow) when they don't have Meredith and Derek end up with their happy ending, or when some other character forgets that the point in TV-show life is the happily ever after.

Your Instructional Playbook

Name It: In this task, we are going to write a fairy tale. Fairy tales are so fun because you can make any imaginative idea come true in your story.

What You Might Say to Introduce It: "We have been reading a lot of fairy tales and noticing that in these tales the heroine or hero has a BIG problem and endures hardships and set backs, but the story resolves with the good characters living happily ever after.

Typical Successes

The Wolf Girl

By: Mai Xiong Vang

Once faraway in the woods there lives a husband and his wife. The husband was Max Billmock and his wife was Maria Hannah they both were named after their grandparents. They live alone in the forest because they have no moneys and were too poor to lives in the city. They have no kids, so they pray and pray for a child and at last Maria were about to give birth to her first child. They named their child Vermonica.

It was rainy and lighting on that day when Maria was about to give birth to her child. Her husband took off with the horse to their nearest neighbor about two miles away. He told them that his wife is giving a baby and to come help them. Their neighbor Lucy and Eric Marshall told Max that they will come right away. So Max hurried on his horse as fast as he could back to the woods, but a bolt of lighting hit him and he is soon dead. When Lucy and her husband came to Max's and Maria's house they found out that Maria already give birth to her child because they heard Maria speaking that she already give birth to her child. Then after a while they found out that she was dead. Max was no where to be found. Also their baby was no where to be found. but wolf tracks was marking around.

This fairy tale, written by an English learner, has all the parts that make fairy tales fantastic—wonderful heroine, scary characters, and a big, fat problem. Here is a snippet.

Model/Do Together: It can help by writing a class fairy tale first. You don't have to write out the entire text, just brainstorm the story conventions like characters, plot, and resolution. Facilitate a class discussion, encouraging the class to think of a fantasy and decide who is going to be in it (characters), where is it happening (setting), what is the big problem they are facing (plot), and how the big problem gets solved (resolution).

Next, move into developing your students as independent fantasy writers! Help students make a fairy tale map. Take a large piece of construction paper (12 × 18—you want it big, so students have room for lots of brainstorming) and fold it in quarters. In the first quadrant, students can brainstorm their characters. Younger writers can draw and label, while older writers can name and describe character traits. In the second quadrant, students can draw, label, and describe the setting. In the third quadrant, students can plan the plot. Invite students to write bullet point to describe the big problem and the events leading up to the problem. They can save the resolution of the problem for the next quadrant. Dedicate the last quadrant for the plot resolution. How will the fairy tale get "tied up" at the end? Will everyone live happily ever after? Will the evil queen die or be banished? Now, encourage your students to take their fairy tale maps and write out their stories. Younger writers may need to draw first.

Release: As students write, move about the room. If someone signals they need help, guide with prompts that get them referring back to their fairy tale maps, such as, "Tell me what happens first in the story," or "What was the big problem?" "When did the problem get to be a really, really big problem that needed fixing?"

Watch Fors and Work Arounds

Students don't know what they want their fairy tales "happily every after" to be.
Brainstorm with the class possible fairy tale plots. Make sure to go slow. Students need time to think through the problems and how to solve them.

"For those who immerse themselves in what the fairy tale has to communicate, it becomes a deep, quiet pool which at first seems to reflect only our own image; but behind it we soon discover the inner turmoils of our soul—its depth, and ways to gain peace within ourselves and with the world, which is the reward of our struggles."

—Bruno Bettelheim
(1975)

You might offer this task when students have been investigating a topic or idea and are ready to present ideas about it or any other time that you are ready for students to practice writing argumentative texts.

TARGET

Students answer a question by making a claim and giving evidence.

When it comes to getting our way, we are all suddenly world-class experts or trial lawyers! If I want to splurge on something like visiting an eyelash salon, I say to myself, "Well, everyone is having eyelash extensions to look good in all the selfies," or "Longer eyelashes will keep the stuff flying in the air out of my eyes!" Our students are the same! "Expert" opinions fly when they want something, whether it's no homework or they are desperate to be seen as correct about a topic in front of peers. Saying anything, no matter how unfounded, is a human trait. So let's arm students with the true power of persuasion by teaching them how to back up our claims with evidence.

Your Instructional Playbook

Name It: In this task, you are going to learn to back up your opinions. This is a fancy way of saying you will write a claim and then provide evidence that supports the claim. You might launch yourself into making the claim by asking an inquiry question and then focus on answering it. A claim is a statement you make about a text, and evidence is the part of the text that supports your statement.

What You Might Say Next: "When you are asked a question based on something you know, read, or researched, what you want to do first is to make a statement—and then state what you know that makes your statement true (or real). What you know about or read about becomes the evidence for the statement you made. Make sure you can back up what you know with something that is in a book, text, or on the web."

Typical Successes

These are two examples of claim and evidence. The first comes from a younger reader who wrote "[Dolphins] never harmed people." The second example comes from an older reader who wrote about Alice Paul and how she changed the fact that women were not equal to men.

Knowledge Connections

Draw or write something you already knew about the topic.

Draw or write something new you learned.

Alice Paul

When women were not allowed to vote and were not equal to men, Alice Paul changed that. Alice Paul is a famous person in women's history because of her work.

While going to the University of Pennsylvania to get her Ph.D, Alice Paul began to think about women's suffrage. She studied politics, biology, economics, and social work. Then she met two ladies who worked with her for women's suffrage. Their names are: Lucy Burns, and Christabel Pankrust. Alice also joined the National American Women Suffrage Association, (NAWSA). She led several parades and marches. One of the marches she led was on June 9, 1911, another on March 13, 1913, she also wrote the Equal Rights Amendment, worked to include women in the Civil Rights Act, and earned a law degree.

Alice Paul worked her whole life for women's suffrage. She led marches, protested, gave speeches, and worked really hard. Women finally are allowed to vote. Women would not be able to vote today if it wasn't for Alice Paul!

Model/Do Together: Most often, opinion or argument writing succeeds when students focus on a topic that is appealing to them and relatively easy to research—and for which strong evidence exists. Ask students if anyone wants to volunteer a claim and evidence. Demonstrate how you pick a good topic and name a claim. You model doing an online search or pose a few juicy topics to get kids inspired, such as school should start later in the morning (the claim), and then evidence would be the neuroscience on the sleep needs of the adolescent brain. Older readers and writers can complete a topic search in a similar way. For young students, have them focus on a topic that you have been reading about in class or a point of information they find interesting from *Time for Kids* or *Scholastic News* or some other current events source.

Once students have decided on a claim, they are going to need to back it up with evidence. Questions you can ask include the following:

- What information have you learned about in your topic search?
- What do you think is important about the topic?
- Can you say what you think in one strong sentence?
- What backs up your thinking, and where did your evidence come from?
- How can you say your evidence clearly?

Release: As students write with their claims and evidence, move about the room in case someone needs your coaching. For younger students, sentence frames can be useful:

"I think . . ."

"I think . . . and my evidence is . . . "

However, the strongest claims are not written from the first person viewpoint, and older readers and writers should begin to write their claims by just putting their strong ideas on paper. Sentence frames that support include the following:

" . . . is (good/bad; right/wrong) because . . . . My evidence comes from . . ."

"_____author says . . . . The author says this because . . ."

"_____ is _____. The first reason is . . ."

Writing claims and evidence can be a quick task or a longer task that grows into a full opinion or argument piece. Give students lots of opportunities to share their claims and evidence with one another before they try to grow it into a full writing piece. Writing claims and evidence is a skill, and it takes time—sometimes I find even my graduate students are uncertain about how to write with the voice of authority.

Watch Fors and Work Arounds

Students make claims wildly and without any evidence. Redirect students back to their notes or the text to see if their claim matches or not.

Students use resources that are not credible. Helping students find credible sources to back up their claims is one way for students to learn to make claims that are credible, honest, and real. All students should have two or three evidence points.

"If you were to choose something more significant at this time you might get tripped up over the results. Therefore, keep it simple at the beginning."

—Gabrielle Bernstein
(2010, p. 167)

56 Use Known Info to Help Others Learn New Info

WHEN YOU MIGHT OFFER IT

You might offer it when students are ready to have deeper discussions on a topic or when they have been participating in "dialogue" but discussing rather than dialoguing. As in discussion, students don't closely listen to one another.

TARGET

Student will talk about a text with others using their own written notes to help.

Students will talk over one another to the point they don't learn anything new. Funny thing is, so will adults. We just go on, pitching our voices higher or louder and do not fully listen to each other or respectfully comment on other's contributions. Or we might even say something completely different from what was shared—hmmm . . . reminds me of my last wine club meeting—I mean, book club! Our students can learn to do this better, by dialoguing with one another in class and then writing about that dialogue. The key to dialogue, of course, is honest listening.

Your Instructional Playbook

Name It: We are going to participate in a group discussion about a text using our notes as reference to make valid points about a text or story. In this task, we will listen to add information to a conversation and then we will write about the discussion.

What You Might Say Next: "Let's get eye-to-eye (and knee-to-knee, if appropriate) with a partner. Using your notes in your reading notebook, discuss with your partner what you learned from the text. Remember, you all read something different, so those of you listening, be a good listener (as we have practiced before) and listen to the big ideas your partner is sharing. Do you know how to listen like that? Let's practice (role-play deep listening with another student). I want you to keep your conversation going and take your conversation deeper. So listeners, your job after listening is to ask a thoughtful or clarifying question (role-play listening and then asking a clarifying question) or make a statement that deepens your conversation."

Typical Successes

Owns It!
This snippet of student writing bubbled up after two students were having a discussion about how old Egypt is and so fascinating. The students compared it to how long an Everlasting Gobstopper can last in your mouth!

> Find Draft for W.W. Assignment:
>
> Introduction #5.   (4)
> Have you ever had an Everlasting Gobstopper—the candy? You know how the taste stays in your mouth for a long, long time? Well it and Egypt have a lot in common. Egypt once was and still is called the "Gift of the Nile." That has been Egypt's nickname for about 2,500 years. And it will most likely stick with it for at least another 2,000. If you don't get what I'm saying or don't believe me, than I suggest you read the rest of this feature article.

Model/Do Together: Students participate in group discussions more robustly if you use a protocol, which also assures quiet students contribute. Give each student a notecard and have them write two notes on it that they want to discuss (younger readers can add a picture). Have each student write a number on their notecards, number one through four. Then, write the numbers one through four on four corresponding Popsicle sticks and put the sticks in a can or jar. Have students take turns pulling the Popsicle sticks, and the number that is pulled out of the jar is the number of the student who will talk. Have students launch their conversation by stating what they knew first and what they are adding on. For instance, if students read a text on Rosa Parks, a student might say, "I know Rosa Parks was famous, but I didn't know how brave she must have been to sit down [on the bus] when she knew it wasn't allowed." Guide students in groups as they pull the Popsicle sticks and continue sharing.

Release: Guide students through the conversation with prompts. *For the student sharing their notes, questions they can ask themselves include the following:*

- "Can I support what I have to say? What evidence (or "connection" for younger students) do I have to make my point?"

- "Does what I have to say connect to the topic or the question?"

- "Am I being accurate? Is what I am going to say from my reading or from a personal experience? How can I double check my information is correct?"

For the student listening and asking questions or making statements they can ask themselves the following:

- "Can I ask a thoughtful question about what was shared?"

- "Is what I am going to say connected to the topic?"

- "If I disagree with what was said, can I restate what I heard the other person said and explain how my thinking is different?"

Facilitate a class discussion about what the students knew before they read the text and what they think now, after reading the text. How did the information help them change their thinking? Talk through these questions, encouraging students to reflect.

Watch Fors and Work Arounds

The student who is sharing might not be confident in what he or she wants to share. Have students go back to their notes for support. Use a sentence starter written on a note card to prompt the students.

Students' thinking comes out obtuse or halting, students talk in such a low voice that their partner cannot hear them, or they don't have any notes in their notebook to rely on for help. You can get around these issues through lots of modeling. Model being a thinker, sharer, and questioner. When you are modeling for the class, think aloud about your actions, sharing what you are doing and why with your students. Often, what we think is transparent to students isn't. So we have to practice, practice, practice before we hand off and have them work together on their own.

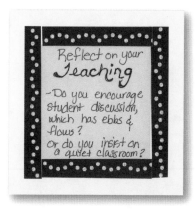

Reflect on your *Teaching*

- Do you encourage student discussion, which has ebbs & flows?
- Or do you insist on a quiet classroom?

You might offer it when students have been reading (or you have been reading to the students) several texts about one topic.

TARGET

Students gather information, think about the relationships between the information, and reflect on what is the same about the relationships in order to name connections.

This story comes from my editor. She told me how she'd edited umpteen books that described text-to-text connections, but it wasn't until her fifteen-year-old daughter recently was reading a *New Yorker* magazine article for school that she literally got misty-eyed about the skill. Her daughter came across a quote asserting that the gig economy and app-based businesses benefit the educated middle class more than the poor and said, "Mom, just like in English history! The rich get richer." It was the first time that she heard her child make a spontaneous text-to-text connection—and one that linked ideas from a textbook the previous year to a current article no less. All of which is to say, it takes a lot of authentic practice and time—years— for learners to connect the dots.

Your Instructional Playbook

Name It: In this task, after reading a variety of texts, you are going to write an explanatory essay/text connecting ideas together among different texts, stating the relationship between information and ideas or identifying a common theme.

What You Might Say to Introduce It: "We have been reading for a while now about (state topic), we have been talking about how there seems to be a theme running between the books. I think you are right; there are some definite connections, so we are going to start working on identifying the connections together so that later on you can identify more connections on your own."

Typical Successes

Model/Do Together: You will be helping students find the patterns or connections between different texts they have read, so you will start by brainstorming information to develop class notes. This can also be done by creating a matrix (see below). Start by having two to three chart papers ready, with an area for the heading marked off, or display a blank matrix. It helps if you create the matrix out of butcher paper, so it is large and you can hang it on the wall. Start the conversation by asking students what they think the big ideas are running throughout the texts. For instance, in the sixth-grade sample on viruses and illnesses, the headings are *Plagues and Epidemics, Viruses and Bacteria, Immunizations and Other Measures,* and *Other Information.* In the first-grade sample, the headings, which are the common points of information, are *Type of Insect, Looks Like, Metamorphosis,* and *Habitat.*

Taking the first text you want to discuss, review it with the students and ask them what they think the big points are. Write down their thinking as they discuss it (on a separate paper than the matrix or chart). Invite all students to share their thoughts and ideas, and ask them if they remember what part of the text spurred their thinking. Then, decide as a class what would be the best information to record on the chart(s) about the first heading the class came up with. Record that information, and then, go on to record information on the next heading/topic. Complete this process with the book, going over each text and discussing each heading. So for example, in the sixth-grade class, I talked with the students specifically about *It's Catching: The Infectious World of*

SIXTH-GRADE EXAMPLE: Viruses and Illnesses

Text Title and Author	Plagues and Epidemics	Viruses and Bacteria	Immunizations and other measures	Other information
Text One *It's Catching: The Infectious World of Germs and Microbes* By Jennifer Gardy	There are 2,000 diseases that make people sick. The WHO has a category called great germs and they keep information on each germ with how its transmitted, the symptoms and the danger of the germ. The plague has wiped out huge numbers of people on several occasions, it is caused by bacterium. The plague has interrupted politics and governments when large numbers of people get sick.	The greatest germs infect 4.6 billion people with diarrhea every year, and 446.8 million will get respiratory infections like bronchitis or pneumonia. There are a total of 7 billion people on earth so these two germs alone infect a large part of the population. There are three words to describe the scale of an infectious disease- epidemic, endemic and pandemic. A pandemic is when a disease spreads to all parts of the world.	In the 1800's, cities were dirty and crowded. People would go to the bathroom in a pot and then throw it in the street. Sanitation was the first action taken and an engineer designed a sewer plant. His name was Bazalgette and this was the start of sanitation. In 1796 the smallpox epidemic led to the discover of vaccination. Penicillin was discovered in 1928, but the age of antibiotics didn't arrive until 1944.	The World Health Organization, WHO, tracks all the diseases in the world.
Text Two *Typhoid Mary* by Susan Campbell Bartoletti	A family became sick with typhoid fever. Mary, the cook, caused the outbreak because she didn't wash her hands well after going to the bathroom. Also, she would never be able to get the germs out of her fingernails without harming herself with hot water.	Germ Theory was accepted by the medical community in 1900–six years early than the typhoid outbreak. The intestinal track, a coiled tube is an ideal place for germs to grow at 98.6 degrees.	An immunization for typhoid was developed in 1911, but not all people were vaccinated. Antibiotics were not yet discovered. Mary, the cook, and many others couldn't accept that microscopic organisms caused disease.	Mary was a healthy carrier of typhoid. She needed medicine.

FIRST-GRADE EXAMPLE: Bugs				
Text Title and Author	Type of Insect	Looks Like	Metamorphosis	Habitat
Text One **Insects and Crawly Creatures** by Angela Royston	Spider	Brown, with 8 long legs and a round body	They hatch as spiderlings.	Lives in a web.
	Bumblebee	Black and yellow round body, wings, 6 short legs	Start as larvae and after they grow they form a pupa and then the bumblebee comes out of the pupa.	Lives in a nest in a ground.
	Butterfly	Small body, big colorful wings	The start as caterpillars turn into a pupa after eating a lot of leaves.	Plants where they can eat lots of leaves.
Text Two **Caterpillar to Butterfly** by Laura Marsh	Butterfly	Caterpillars have lots of colors or are green, they have lot of legs	They start as eggs, and hatch into caterpillars. Then they form into a chrysalis.	Branches, plants, leaves. flowers The butterfly drinks nectar from flowers

Sources: Marsh, L. (2012) *Caterpillar to Butterfly.* Washington, DC: National Geographic Society; and Royston, A., (1992). *Insects and Crawly Creatures.* New York: Scholastic.

Germs and Microbes by Jennifer Gardy and what was in the book regarding plagues, viruses and bacteria, immunizations, and medicine. I then repeated the process with the book *Typhoid Mary* by Susan Campbell Bartoletti. Complete this process with one more text the class read all together, and then give students time to see if they can come up with their own ideas about what to put in the matrix on their own. Have them work with a partner to provide the students with a thinking partner, and then have the students record their thinking on a paper and share their thinking with the class. Once the students all share, decide as a class what to write down on the chart. Continue with the process until all the texts read have been analyzed and discussed.

Once all the texts have been analyzed, talk about the points (or dots, figuratively) in the texts that seem to connect together. Working on the class-brainstormed chart, circle, star, and highlight the ideas or points of information that go together. Share with the students that when we reflect on things in our lives or information we are learning and we see connections between different sources of information, which is known as *connecting the dots. This reference to connecting the dots comes from an activity called Dot-to-Dot pictures where if you follow a number sequence, drawing lines between dots, a picture emerges.* The students "picture" is their understanding of the topic studied together.

Release: Have students write their own short text about the connections that they made between the texts. They can write in pairs if it helps them to collectively analyze and express their thinking.

Watch Fors and Work Arounds

Students make connections that don't really exist between texts. Have students go back and carefully check the charts/matrix. Have them find the point on their chart that provides evidence for what they have written. If the evidence is there, then perhaps, the students writing wasn't clear and they need to revise. If the evidence isn't there, encourage the student to go back and think about what evidence actually exists and what could be written about it.

"I would not want to speculate on what larger social forces in our culture may be militating against the willingness to think on the page. I have no lofty vantage point from which to evaluate these large trends, nor any desire to play the grumpy old professor who laments that his students no longer want to read or think because television has shortened their attention spans . . . On the contrary, it seems to be that my students are very intelligent . . . and touchingly eager to imbibe the reading lists I [give] them."

—Phillip Lopate
(2013, p. 41)

Identifying Real Facts from Made-Up Facts: Fallacious Reasoning

WHEN YOU MIGHT OFFER IT

You might offer it when older readers (standards focus this target on fourth through eighth grade; however, a student maybe ready to think about this sooner) in your classroom are starting to discuss world events and have a firm grasp on facts versus opinion.

TARGET

Identify fallacious reasoning (logical mistakes in reasoning made by persuasive information), false, and misleading information.

Fake news—with the Internet, it's a formidable enemy of the truth that affects everything from science to politics. I used to focus in on teaching fallacious reasoning to help students become good consumers of advertisements, websites, and less than reputable sources. But now, I am focusing on teaching students how to discern real facts from made-up facts because there is so much fake news that looks real. I just see this as my civic duty. If you teach younger readers, don't wait to start teaching this important skill of learning to question what they read.

Your Instructional Playbook

Name It: Fallacious reasoning is thinking that is false or not true. When you are reading a variety of texts, you will be able to identify logical mistakes in reasoning or identify false and misleading information after we work on this task together. In this task, we are going to be naming real facts from fake facts.

What You Might Say Next: "Sometimes, I am reading information that I found online that I just cannot believe is true. Check out this article I found recently (you can use any article from a source that typically reports inflated or false information). While I was reading this text, I was following along, checking my understanding of what I was reading, and all of a sudden I my brain went *zing*. I was thinking, this just cannot be right! So I reread it again (state the inflammatory sentence(s) from the text, for example, one headline I saw in a magazine in a store last week said, 'Lose 100 pounds in one month, try this diet!'), and I realized that the information just cannot be correct. Today, we are going to check out various texts online and see if we think they are true or leading us to only think they are true."

Typical Successes

Owns It!
Check out a student's thinking about the logic in an article titled, "Elephant Theory in Nessie (Loch Ness monster) Search"

> *Falacious Reasoning
> false Reasoning or thinking
> What seems false or illegal
> Dr. Clark said they could have been circus elephants.
> Dr. Clark : quote
> "It's quite possible that people around Loch Ness saw some of these animals."
>
> How Is It Unsupported
> Why Is It False
> How Do We Know It's False
> · This is falacious reasoning because he himself says the latest circus visit was 1933. It's very unlikely that a fully grown elephant survived on its own in a lake
> · They show no actuall evidence that Clark is an actual doctor.
> · It's impossible that the animals survived for over 100 years, and the citizens would have noticed that there were animals going in and out of the water or roming around.

Model/Do Together: Write *"fallacious reasoning"* on chart paper. I know that it's a big term, but your students are not too young to use correct vocabulary. Convey that it is logical mistakes in reasoning made by authors of persuasive information, and it can seem correct! Then, share articles you found ahead of time that show fallacious reasoning or false and misleading information.

Put a piece of text under a document camera. First, read the text aloud. Then do a shared reading, talking about facts and highlighting them as you go. You might use one color for all the facts, whether the students (and you) think the facts are false, misleading, or factual. Ask the students what they think the article is about—what is the reasoning of the text? Write that down on a chart paper or in the margin of the text, if you are using a document camera. Then, invite students to circle and star those facts or statements that you highlighted that seem to be misleading or false. What makes them false? What makes them real? Have students write a couple of sentences about their thinking about the shared reading text.

Release: Now, students are going to jump in and practice on their own. Distribute a different text to the class or have several different texts available and have students choose one. What do they think? Why? Encourage a lot of free flow thinking to support your students as they begin to examine the thinking of a text they are analyzing. Encourage them to think about what evidence makes them think the text/article/ad is factual or not. Invite students to write about what they discovered about the line of reasoning or the facts in the article or advertisements that they analyzed and discussed.

Watch Fors and Work Arounds

Students cannot seem to identify the misleading argument in the articles. Using a list graphic organizer—boxes in a row with plus signs in-between each box—have the students write one detail in each box to see if the facts "add up." You will want them to focus on all the facts, so they can see where the reasoning breaks down and how the false thinking or false facts don't add up to a logical conclusion. Or if the facts presented do seem to be logical but aren't true, brainstorm with the students other known facts or look up other known facts to add to the boxes to "disrupt" the thinking.

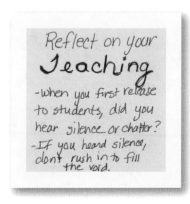

Reflect on your
Teaching
-when you first release
to students, did you
hear silence or chatter?
-If you heard silence,
don't rush in to fill
the void.

WHEN YOU MIGHT OFFER IT

You might offer this task during an inquiry into a subject area, when students are preparing to write opinion or argument papers, during a close read of a text or whenever you want students to get talking about the diversity of ideas and thought in your classroom.

TARGET

Students work with other students to brainstorm ideas about a topic and choose categories to organize the brainstormed ideas.

We just don't do enough to honor student voice. I am fascinated by what students have to offer us, beginning in kindergarten and all the way through high school. I was honored to spend time in an amazing first-grade teacher's classroom this year at Storey Elementary in Fresno, California, and watch her as she masterfully drew her students into a deep discussion about satellites. Her students owned the conversation and were learning with and from one another. During a fifteen-minute conversation, Yasmine spoke for a maximum of two minutes—those first graders owned it! This is the student voice I yearn for in all of our classrooms.

Your Instructional Playbook

Name It: We are going to work on brainstorming. In this task, we are going to work in a large group to brainstorm ideas and then group ideas into categories in order to own information and transform information into opinion or argument texts.

What You Might Say Next: "When we brainstorm, we do our best thinking and then write down all the good thinking. It is really important to capture your thinking, because if you don't write it down, you cannot use it to organize and refine your ideas. It is also important to encourage one another to think up ideas. The more of us who come up with ideas and write them down, the better our class brainstorming will be!"

Typical Successes

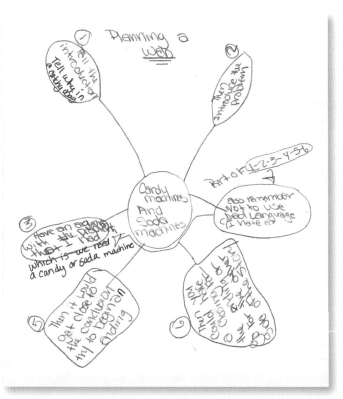

Owns It! In this example of a planning web, you can see how the student organized the writing into six points.

Model/Do Together: Hand out three to four sticky notes or index cards. Bring to students' attention a book or text that you have been reading in class, and let students know that they are going to analyze the text in groups and think about what is important, or they could work to identify theme. Invite students to write down big and small ideas from the text on the cards, *one idea on each card*. Young readers and writers may draw and write one word only on the cards.

Guide students through the brainstorming and categorizing process by acting as a facilitator. Have students come up and post their brainstorming cards on the whiteboard or other surface, where everyone can see one another's cards. Once all cards are posted, ask students if they see any cards that group together, and then invite students to come up and move the cards around, putting cards together that seem to belong together. Having students work in groups of three to four, invite the groups to brainstorm topic headings for the cards in the groups. For example, a group of cards that says "stood up for friends" and "was not scared," might be labeled as *courage*.

Release: Working in the groups of three to four, have students write a short text stating what they think the labels should be and why. Students can refer back to the brainstorming cards, or they can go back and reference the text.

Have the small groups share their ideas about the labels with the class, citing their written texts, and then choose a label and write the label next to the group of cards it represents.

Watch Fors and Work Arounds

Students don't write any thoughts on their brainstorming cards. Create a thought bank first, by working with students to think up terms, ideas, and thoughts about the topic in the text. This brainstorming bank process may be heavily facilitated by you, but it provides independence afterward, in that students can pick what they want from the list to write on their cards.

"We allow the person to say everything that's on her mind; we encourage her to pour everything out and we don't interrupt her or try to correct her in that moment . . . Patience is one of the marks of true love."

—Thich Nhat Hanh (2011)

WHEN YOU MIGHT OFFER IT

You might offer it if you have been working with students on one topic for a while and the concepts are becoming more complicated for them. It is helpful to create concept maps to help connect ideas together and simplify students' thinking.

TARGET

Students will create a concept map of two big ideas.

My husband is a math whiz. He sees the world mathematically, and math comes to him very easily. I'm not like that. At all. So when I am struggling to keep up with his explanation of how curves are designed in roads to keep the cars from flying off and I understand his point well enough, I sketch on a napkin or notepad to see and cement my shaky understandings. Sometimes the best way to really grasp big ideas and new information is to draw it out. This task is about helping students see connections between big ideas in texts. Diagramming works just as well with a reading task as it does with math.

Your Instructional Playbook

Name It: A concept map is a visual that shows our thinking. In this task, after we finish reading our own books (or after I finish reading to you), we will create a concept map of two big ideas presented in one or more texts.

What You Might Say Next: "When we have to bring information together, we synthesize it in ways that help us understand. Sometimes a visual helps us synthesize information and ideas and helps us make our thinking visible. Let's work on making our thinking visible by creating a concept map."

Typical Successes

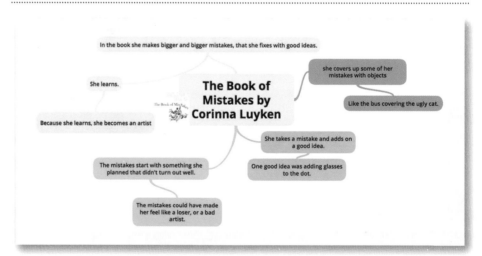

Here is a concept map created using goconqr.com

Model/Do Together: You can create concept maps on paper, or you can create them on a device. The concept map in the Typical Successes was created on goconqr.com; several web-based applications have tools for creating concept maps that are easy to use. One application that is easy to use on a tablet is Explain Everything. You can write words on a concept map, draw pictures, or tape up book pages, articles, or other items. You can do these things also electronically, adding a variety of pinned resources. For this lesson, I will refer to paper but know that "paper" could also mean "screen," if you are using a device.

To get started, draw two ovals or rectangles near the center of a large paper. One oval/rectangle would be filled in with one word or phrase representing a big idea from the book/text/topic you have been reading and exploring. Draw a similar shape near it horizontally (see the example below) and add another word or phrase representing a second big idea from the book/text/topic you have been reading and exploring. As you add the words to the page, you might consider asking your students, "Why do you think I am writing these words here in these ovals/squares?" Explore the conversation with the students, and see what other ideas come up. As they come up, create branches off of the main oval/rectangle and add it if it is another key idea or piece of information. If it is a detail, just write it down with a line connecting it to the big idea. Continue in the discussion until the conversation somewhat fizzles out. You might have to stoke the conversation with tidbits of your own thinking. Discuss the concept map that the class made together to see what insights the students have about their thinking. Help them connect between the ideas by tracing the connections with their fingers (or you can model this).

After creating a concept map with the students, help them to create one on their own. You can do this by facilitating a conversation, while each student is drawing a mind map on his or her own papers/devices. You can compare ideas from a broad topic, or you can compare information from a fiction book with chapters, using an oval/rectangle to represent each chapter. One book that I think works particularly well for creating concept maps is *Animals Nobody Loves* by Seymour Simon. It is a book about animals that people generally don't like. The text structure is a list, with each page providing information about a different animal. It would be important to read this type of book first to students or have students read part of it on their own. Students would be tempted to create an oval/rectangle for each animal, but invite them to think about the bigger ideas in the text that connect the animals together. Perhaps the connecting idea might be the animal traits, habitats, or some other connecting idea.

Release: As students work through the text the second or third time, prompt them to think about what the big ideas are that connect the topic/information together, and encourage them to create the main oval/rectangle for those two big ideas. Then, encourage them to think about what the details are, and have them express those ideas branching from the big ideas in words, pictures, or any other media that is appropriate. Have students stop and think about what *they think* is the information important to record in the text or about the topic. The goal is for the student to engage in the thought process, not create a perfect map, so coach them as they think through by asking encouraging and reflective questions. In pairs, small groups, or whole class, have students share their concept maps and discuss how the thinking on their page connects together and also connects back to the topic or the text.

Watch Fors and Work Arounds

Students put topics that are not connected in anyway into the concept map. Upon first glance, you may believe a concept is unrelated; however, ask students first if they can explain their thinking. If the student can explain the connection and it makes sense, then don't encourage the student to make changes. If the student cannot explain clearly or the topics truly are unrelated, then help the student think through the connections between the topic/information again. Help the student think of terms that describe the big ideas, and then write those on sticky notes (if the student hasn't already identified the two big ideas), then organize the other sticky notes around the big idea as they branch out on the student's desk. Encourage the student to add to the notes as they think of new bits of information. Also encourage them to check the text to see what they might be missing or not understanding.

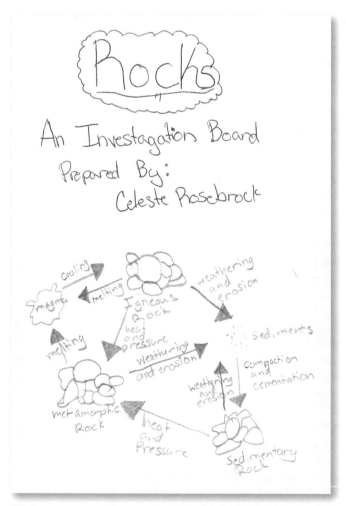

This is a concept map that a student created during her inquiry on rocks.

Make Me Ponder: Questions That Get the Thinking Juices Flowing

WHEN YOU MIGHT OFFER IT

When you realize you have been asking too many of the questions and you want to transfer ownership of question asking and answering to the students.

TARGET

Students ask and answer questions during and after reading a text.

Boy, once in a while I just get really lazy as a thinker. Sometimes, with complicated issues like healthcare or geopolitics, I just want the world to figure things out for me, so I don't have to do it. Students go through this too. Sometimes, students get so used to us figuring things out for them that they don't exercise their deeper thinking "muscles." In this task, you start by modeling thinking processes. Just watch out. Don't spend too much time on right-there questions, as these questions don't take as much thinking as interpretive or applied questions.

Your Instructional Playbook

Name It: It is important to ask questions while we read and after we have read something to make sure we understand what we are reading. In this task, you are going to work at identifying literal, interpretive, and applied questions and answer questions alone or with partners.

What You Might Say Next: "I feel as though I have been doing all the asking of questions lately, so I am going to turn over the asking of questions to all of you. There are different types of questions we can ask each other (explain the three types). I am going to challenge you today to ask a partner three different types of question. The first question is a Tell About It question, the second question is a Make Me Ponder Question, and the third question is What Would YOU Do? question."

Typical Successes

Long May She Wave: The True Story of Caroline Pickersgill and Her Star-Spangled Creation **by Kristen Fulton**	Question One	Question Two
Tell About It	How did Caroline Pickersgill stitch 350,000 tiny weaves to create George Washington's first flag?	What were all the sounds Caroline heard during the battle in Baltimore?
	Answer— She stitched over and under, over and under, for weeks and weeks, even during the battles.	Answer— She heard lots of sounds. First, quiet, then drums and tooting bugles, thumping horses' hooves, and BOOM!
Make Me Ponder	What would have happened if Caroline had not stitched the flag?	What if Caroline's first flag was burned during the battle in Baltimore?

	Question One	Question Two
	Maybe the British would not have attacked the fort in Baltimore. It seems like the flag made the British angry. She was the only one who could have stitched the flag because it was so big they needed a nimble girl.	She would not have seen it waving at the end of the battle. It would probably have been sad. We might not be the United States.
What Would YOU Do	If you were Caroline's mother?	
	I would have helped her more and also the grandmother as they laid it out. I think they were old and tired and that is why Caroline had to stitch it. She could get on the floor and sew on top of the flag as the mom and grandma couldn't do that.	

Here are examples of student-written Tell About It questions, Make Me Ponder Questions, and a What Would YOU Do? questions.

Model/Do Together: Begin by discussing with students the types of questions that readers ask while reading, and reinforce your students that you know they can think deeply about the types of questions they ask of themselves and each other while reading. Tell About It questions are literal questions, and readers can literally put their finger on the text that tells them about something in the text. Maybe the text tells them what it is about or what is happening. Make Me Ponder Questions are questions that get the reader wondering about the author's purpose, predict the ending of the story, or wonder about the possibility of the text's plot. A What Would YOU Do? question is a question that gets the students talking about what they would have written if they were the authors. Would they choose the same special vocabulary words? Would they change the ending or make a character more or less likeable? All these questions are designed to reinforce comprehension while unleashing imagination.

Together with the class or a small group of students, practice having the students ask and answer the three types of questions. There are a few ways you can do this. Students can team up and have Team A ask question and then Team B answers the questions, or students can ask you questions (you might have to bite your lip to not ask questions yourself), and you answer the questions.

(Continued) Make Me Ponder: Questions That Get the Thinking Juices Flowing

The difference between blame and accountability is very similar to the difference between guilt and shame . . . Like guilt, accountability is often motivated by wanting to live in alignment with our values.

—Brene Brown
(2015)

Once students have some practice with asking the questions, model language about how to answer the questions. For example, "It makes me think . . . , is that possibly true or false?" "If I were the author, I would have used a wondrous word here, because this word is really boring (and they could choose a word off your Wondrous Word board) (Akhavan, 2007). They could also close their eyes and visualize a new ending and explain what would happen. If they were asking a What Would YOU Do? question and the text is nonfiction, the students could dream up new angles from which to share the information.

These three types of questions take a lot of thinking, and you might spend some time working through these questions with students. Younger readers can work through these questions as well; just practice with an appropriate text. For instance, in regards to *Maybe Something Beautiful* by F. Isabel Campoy and Theresa Howell, students could ask each other, "What would you do if you were Mira and you only had light-colored (pastel) paints? For older readers, encourage them to ask questions that will encourage them to mine information in other books or on the Internet. Perhaps they will need to conduct a Google search to find information that helps them answer the deeper questions they are asking and being asked. Questions like this might begin with phrases such as *What if, How would this be different if*, and *Can we apply this to, How does this affect*, or *What would you* (or a character's name here) *do if*. With on my own questions, the possibilities are endless.

Release: Asking and answering questions can be done in groups or with students working alone. It will all depend on the types of questions students are asking and answering and their interest in the questions and engagement they might have about the questions. You will need to coach students to success by matching your coaching moves to the type of questions they are asking and answering. You might encourage the use of sticky notes or highlighters to denote places in the text that help them. You might have to cheerlead students on as they grapple with deep thinking about what happened in a text early on compared to later in the text. Students may need help organizing their question, so they are clear about what they are searching for. In all instances, guiding them to write out their questions and answers clearly will help them as they learn from their own thinking.

Watch Fors and Work Arounds

Students get stuck in asking and answering Make Me Ponder questions. When students sit there and their eyes glaze over a bit when you ask them to think deeply, differentiated scaffolding usually helps. For instance, a student having trouble asking questions might need question starter cards (index cards with question frames written out on them) or need two colors of paper to write on. The student can use one color paper for the question and a different color paper for the answer. Another support is helping the student write a "plan." Sometimes students are perfectly capable of figuring out the answer to a question that another student asks of them, but they don't know what to do first and then what to do next. Write out a short plan on a sticky note and place the note in a visible place on the student's desk. Other students might need to work with a partner or in a trio, as they might need some help in connecting the information together.

Name:_____

Date:_____

Checking My Understanding
Reflection Checklist

Before reading, did I:

❑ set a purpose for reading?

❑ know why I am reading the story or text?

During reading, did I:

❑ stop and check that I understood what the story or text is saying?

❑ reread sentences that didn't make sense?

❑ use my fix-up strategies to figure out words I didn't know?

❑ use my fix-up strategies when the story or text didn't make sense?

❑ make predictions about what would happen next?

❑ check to see if my prediction was right?

After reading, did I:

❑ identify facts from the text like who, what, why, when, where and how?

❑ find clues in the text to help me answer who, what, why when, where and how?

❑ name what is happening in the story or what the text is about?

❑ check the text to justify my answers?

❑ point to part of the text that backs up my thinking?

WHEN YOU MIGHT OFFER IT

You might offer this task when your students have been reading a variety of literature or literary nonfiction and have been forming opinions and ideas about what they are reading.

TARGET

Student writes a response to literature where they compare and contrast ideas, texts, or information.

Our world bombards us with so much information it is easy to get overwhelmed on a daily basis. We have a few choices with how to handle all this information. One is to bury our heads in the sand like ostriches and ignore most of what hits our feed. Or we can selectively choose what we pay attention to. In our digital world, a lot is available for students to read—differing opinions on the same subject and differing stories but similar, multiple perspectives on events. We have to learn to hone our attention on what has meaning for us. Then, we need to work on responding to all this information in constructive ways. This task is just about that: constructive response!

Your Instructional Playbook

Name It: A response to literature is something you write to show your thinking and your emotions about what you have read. In this task, when we are done, you are going to able to take two different ideas, points of information, or text and write a response that is interpretive, analytic, or evaluative.

What You Might Say Next: "There are different ways that you can respond to something that you have read. We are going to begin working on a response where you compare or contrast ideas or information that you are noticing in texts that you read that have similar stories. This can help us really think about and consider what we are reading and what we think about what we are reading. Really good readers don't just read something and then move on to the next thing that they read. Often, good readers think through what they have read and make connections between what they have read—how it is the same or different than the perspectives of different authors or even the same author in different texts."

Typical Successes

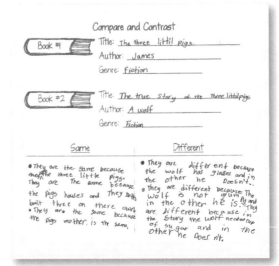

Not Quite There Yet!
In this response to literature, a younger reader compared and contrasted two versions of a fairy tale.

Model/Do Together: There are many ways a student can compare and contrast ideas in a response to literature. There are many types of responses to literature that can be written. A few ideas include the following: Students can write a literary response paper, a book review, a comparison of a literary text with multimedia source of the same information, or a story. When connecting students to responses to literature, you might want to comb through websites or survey magazines to find examples. Students needs to hear, read, and see several examples of responses to literature before they dive in and begin creating on their own. A response is different than an informational report, and you will need to point out what makes a response a response. Typically in a response, the author is formulating an opinion. In this task, students will formulate an opinion by comparing and/or contrasting.

Once students gather information on their topic or story, they will want to check that they have ideas and information recorded that they can compare and/or contrast. Then, help them in setting up their compare and contrast response. Model how to compare/contrast a specific point of interest. This can include, but is not limited to, the following:

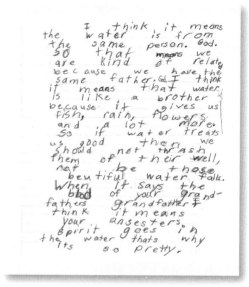

Not Quite There Yet! An older reader wrote about parts of the text from "Chief Seattle's Speech" but didnt' compare it to another text.

- Characters and character traits or motives

- Stereotypical characters versus fully developed characters

- Plot development

- Literary merit of two texts/stories

- Themes

- Impact of author's choice of genre, format, wording, and content

- Point of view of the author, the intended audience

- Historical time and place

- Fantasy time and place (think *Avatar* versus Knights of the Round Table)

- Imagery differences between different stories on the same topic (like Cinderella stories)

- The context in which the piece was written

Release: Working with and modeling for students is very different than when your students need to launch and complete their thinking, note taking, and writing on their own (remember, our goal of the tasks is student independence). The goal of this task is for students to get their thinking on the paper, not to take the piece all the way through the writing process to perfection. You might need to cheerlead students forward, telling them, "You can do this," as when the thinking gets hard, students need encouragement and validation. Coach them as they

"This is one of those moments, in one of those stories, that makes me want to dance around the fire, if I had one, to the rhythm of the drums, . . . because it gets in so deep, as usually only music and poetry can."

—Anne Lamott
(2017b, p. 117)

write; you can ask questions that help them further their thinking and writing process. Questions might be the following:

- What two ideas are you comparing and/or contrasting?
- How does the author show these ideas in words, or how does the illustrator show them in pictures?
- In what way are they the same/different?
- Do you see common connections between the themes in the texts? What are those? Why?

Have students share their drafts with one another. If another student offers ideas for revision, have the author make a note of the idea(s).

Watch Fors and Work Arounds

Students get stuck and cannot make any connections between texts read. Students may need to draw or sketch-out their thinking to show what is the same or different. They can also make a two-column list with the name of one item on the top heading one column and the name of another item for analysis heading the second column. Then, the student can write notes and jots in each column to help them gather information that they can reflect on.

WHEN YOU MIGHT OFFER IT

After students have practice summarizing, asking questions of text, clarifying, and predicting while reading. This task works best when students are reading more difficult material in a group, but they can all be reading different texts.

TARGET

Students engage in comprehension strategies while working with a partner or in a group.

Just a few weeks ago, my daughter accepted a job as a math tutor. She is studying engineering in college, and she felt that tutoring high school students in math would be great. After her first couple of tutoring sessions, she came home and said in dismay, "I really need to brush up on some subjects, like geometry." I leaned in and gave her teacher's insider knowledge: that we all "brush up" to be able to teach something. When we teach something, we really have to know it. Having students work peer-to-peer teaching one another is powerful. They can guide one another's learning in ways that we, as the adults, cannot.

Your Instructional Playbook

Name It: Summaries help us think about what we read and double check that we understood our reading. In this task, we are going to work together with a partner or in a group to summarize, question, clarify, or predict in order to help each other comprehend what you are reading.

What You Might Say Next: "I am really getting tired of doing all the teaching, so from now on we are going to work on you teaching each other. I really think you can do this! And I notice often that you learn better from one another than you do from me. We are going to be reading and working on comprehension strategies, but you are going to be doing the teaching so that I can sit with a group and be a reader too!"

Typical Successes

These two pages show how one group put together their visualization discussion and their predictions in charts.

Model/Do Together: If you start by making a chart for the Peer-to-Peer Analysis that outlines the steps they might take, it can help the groups stay on track. Start by taking a large piece of chart paper (Remember, if you use a PowerPoint slide and project it, the information disappears when you move on to another slide, so if you make an electronic "chart," put it in a shared document and have students access it on their individual devices.) and writing "Peer-to-Peer Analysis" on the top. Then list the following terms with short definitions: *summarizing*—identifying and stating the most important points in the text; *questioning*—asking questions about the text while reading to help you understand the text; *clarifying*—checking in with yourself on what is confusing or doesn't make sense in the text; *predicting*—using information already presented in the text to "guess" about what is going to happen next or where the text is going.

Even though you are working with your students in skills they have been developing over time, since the goal of this task is to hand over the responsibility for the teaching and learning to the students in groups, you may need to check in with students and make sure they remember or feel OK about summarizing, questioning, clarifying, and making predictions. At first, you will need to walk students through the steps and remind them (using the chart or electronic document) what strategy they are using with each other as they help one another learn. Give your students control of what strategy they want to try out first as they read text together. Assign a text or encourage groups or partners to choose a text that they both want to read. As they read together, remind students to stop and practice one of the strategies. Encourage students to all make a comment about the text in relation to the strategy they are working on. If the student is the second or third student to speak, she might start her sentence by saying, "I agree (or disagree) . . . ," "In addition, . . . ," "I am also thinking or noticing . . . ," or "To add on . . . ." Students might need to practice some ways they can join the conversation and add on to what has been said by other group members. The students might record their thinking in a reading notebook or on sticky notes to keep track of what they are summarizing, questioning, clarifying, and predicting.

Release: As students work together, you might need to interrupt the groups for a "stop-and-check moment." As you move from group to group helping each group move along, from time to time (as appropriate), call the students' attention and say, "stop and check." At that moment, group members work together to work through one of the strategies. You can engage students in a short popcorn share (where students "pop" with statements about their thinking randomly), before students go back to reading with their groups and partners.

At the end of the reading session for the day, have a few student groups share what they worked on that day, what they read, and what strategies they were working through. Fuel the excitement of the reading by getting as many student voices in the room sharing as possible.

Watch Fors and Work Arounds

A group of students doesn't have an "organizer" or a student that helps start up the conversation about which strategy to try out at a given time. You may need to assign a leader to the group of students. Sometimes students are shy to step forward or they don't feel confident in leading the group. It can also help to have a little "coaching" session with the student that is going to lead the group to practice with them how to get the group to focus on one strategy and to work together taking turns to say something about their thinking.

Here is a group-developed page on rockets and the planets from a group of kindergarten students.

WHEN YOU MIGHT OFFER IT

You might offer it once students have spent some time working with functional (texts that exist to help us get things done) or complex texts.

TARGET

For *functional text:* Students analyze the information in a functional text that indicates the text's purpose, helps make the document user friendly (context), and considers whether provided information is sufficient or incomplete (relevance).

For *complex text:* Students analyze author's purpose, big idea, or theme (context) and consider the context or audience for the text (relevance).

Complex text may immediately bring to mind Shakespeare or an engineering textbook on a syllabus at MIT but by gosh, it can also be a *functional text*—like those assembly instructions for that darn writing desk! Functional texts can also be less complex, like perhaps a guacamole recipe. What makes a text complex might be more challenging vocabulary, concepts, and organizing structures. In this task, you invite students to critique more simple text that is functional and also complex text that might be in a variety of genre.

Your Instructional Playbook

Name It: "You are going to read texts called functional texts (or complex text). In this task after you read on your own (or with support), you are going to analyze the text based on three criteria: purpose, context, and relevance. Then you are going to share their analysis orally and write about it."

What You Might Say Next: "I have been noticing that sometimes, while we are reading and after reading, we are taking for granted that the author was correct in how he or she wrote the text, and we don't think about the fact that maybe the author could have done a few things differently in writing the text. It is OK to critique what we read, and we are going to get some practice in critiquing the writing of authors. After all, they are writing for us, as readers, so let's spend some time thinking about if they did a good job or not."

Typical Successes

A Student Critique of a Functional Text			
Text Title	**Functionality**	**Clarity**	**Helpful Information**
How to make and ride skateboards By Glenn and Eve Bunting	It was OK. This was a super old book from the library. But it did show you how to balance. It talked about ways to support yourself till you could balance and roll forward. There were several pages that showed the technique.	I think the directions on making them didn't have enough illustrations and was kinda confusing. Check out Page 13. It needed more pictures, or better ones.	The rolling forward and balancing was helpful. The how to make a skateboard was not too helpful cause I don't have the equipment to do it. So, I think all these pages were a waste.

Model/Do Together: First, choose whether students will be working with a complex text or a functional text. Connect students to this task by exploring the text and other texts like the text first. Students will need something to compare to, and if they have seen only one text prior and the one you are now asking them to analyze, they won't have a good reference. They need to see a lot of different texts. To connect to this task, you can explore different texts for more than one day in order to truly ground your students in the type of text they will analyze. While students are exploring texts, invite them to be curious, to ask questions, and to know it is perfectly fine (and encouraged!) for the reader to second-guess the author and to not accept what they are reading as being good, just because it is published.

In order to ground the exploration of the text before beginning an analysis, it helps to ground the discussion of the text into an inquiry. When you frame the reading of the text with a question, you give the students a lens for reading the text, which can help spur their thinking. When focusing on purpose, context, and relevance, these general questions can help: for purpose, "What is the author's purpose in writing this text? and "How is the writer trying to connect to the readers by writing this text?" for context, "What is the author trying to convey to the reader and why?" and "How does the author help the reader understand the timing of the subject or story?" for relevance, "How does this text help us understand the world? In what ways?"

Once students dig into the text through inquiry, record their thinking on charts or documents that students can refer back to in order to help them when they create their personal response. Ask another question that helps spur student thinking about each part of the text that they are considering: "Based on your thinking, how could the author improve the text (if needed)?"

Release: After you have worked through the questions, open up for a class discussion. Ask students what they think and why. Have them go back and show what parts of the text help them with their thinking. Have students jot down their thinking on an exit ticket (for older readers) or on a response page for younger readers (a page with a blank for a picture and a space for writing). If needed, you can provide a frame to scaffold their writing. The frames could be based on the inquiry questions—for instance, "The organization of this text was . . . because . . . ." Or "This text was hard to understand because . . . ." Or also, "This text has [deep meaning], for example on page . . . ."

Invite students to orally share their analysis in groups or with a partner. Then, share out a few students' responses with the entire class.

Watch Fors and Work Arounds

Students might be able to critique the text for purpose but not for context or relevance. In this instance, visualization can help. Students might need to put themselves in the shoes of the intended audience of the text. For example, if reading a functional text on how to do something, help students visualize whom the text might be for. Then students can think about whether the author was helping those people (the intended audience) or not.

Drawing pictures helps also. When analyzing for context, perhaps the students could draw a picture and label it, in order to hone in on the place and time the book is occurring in and the place and time the book is intended to relate to.

> *"Most writers say that Rule 1 of writing has to be 'write' or 'put butt in chair.' I disagree. Before you can start writing, you have to let go of the illusion of perfection."*
>
> —Mur Lafferty (2017)

Visible and Visual: Use Known Concepts and Vocabulary to Understand a Text

WHEN YOU MIGHT OFFER IT

You might offer it before diving into a new text with lots of new ideas and words.

TARGET

Students use prior knowledge to understand a nonfiction text.

The other night when I was teaching a doctoral class, I mentioned to my students that they should do a skim read of the abundant reading materials for class before they dove in. They all politely nodded. I said, "You don't know what skim reading is, do you?" About three quarters of the class said, "No." So I embarked on a think-aloud of how to conduct a skim read. Surveying the text is a skill that all students, of all ages, need. It can help you hone in your attention on where you need to take a deep dive into the reading. When I taught kindergarten and first grade, I focused on surveying the text as picture walks.

Your Instructional Playbook

Name It: Before, during, and after reading, we should be thinking about what we know about a topic/information that a text is about and use our knowledge to understand the text better. In this task, we are going to practice thinking and recording our thinking before we read, while we are reading a text and when we are done. Then we will reflect on what we wrote to see how our thinking changed as we read the text.

What You Might Say Next: We all have tons of information in our brains that we don't even realize that we have. Today, we are going to tap into that knowledge and amp up our awareness, so we can think about what we know while we are reading. It will help us better understand what we are reading, but it will also help us learn information as we read. It's super cool to think that what we already know helps us with what we don't know yet.

Typical Successes

Students can work together or on their own to take notes about their discussion. This is an example from a student's notebook. You can see the page numbers on the left that the group surveyed and their comments on the right.

in the wild Leopards	
Imp	why
12 They hunt alone during the night.	Because the ainmle can't see them.
4 Leopards all have spotted coat	so anmiles cant see them at all.
15 They Practice by playing at hunting.	They practice Because the don't a know how to do it well.

Model/Do Together: Before you read a text that is new for students and is challenging in concepts, survey the text. Skim, notice, get the lay of the land, nudging students to discuss bold words, section titles, table of contents, other features. Remember to be only the facilitator and get students to do the talking. Go to the glossary, select a term, and ask kids: "So what do you think the word means?" When students come up with ideas, jot them down on a chart. Make the discussion visible and visual, which makes it so that no one student secretly thinks he's the only one totally intimidated by the content! Stop, and ask, "So what do we already know about (the topic)?" Identify what students might know, and make this part of the discussion visual and visible also by jotting a few notes down on a chart labeled "Our Text Survey."

As students dive into reading the text, either as a choral read with you, a paired reading, or an independent read, remind them to keep making their thinking visible and visual. Ask them to record ideas about what are they reading that reminds them of something they already know. Or record their thinking about words and word meaning. What is important here is that students actively make connections between what is in the text and their own knowledge. You can model this by stopping students' reading at predetermined places in the text and then first model writing a jot about what you are thinking. Then, encourage them to write a jot in their notebooks.

Release: Once students have a couple of jots written down, have them share their jots in a pair share or in a small group. Encourage them to discuss with their team members what is similar and different in what they are thinking about the text. Remind students to keep going, read, stop, jot.

After students finish reading the text or the class finishes the choral read and makes the last jot, break the class into four or five groups. Have each student share in the group what jots they wrote and what part of the text corresponded to their jot. Have them discuss their thinking together; they can identify similarities and differences or also areas that really made a lot of sense and areas that were difficult to understand.

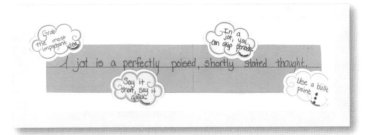

Watch Fors and Work Arounds

Students are not jotting information that seems relevant or important. Sometimes students get lost in the idea of just jotting, so they jot down anything just to fill up the page. Reassure them that you are not looking just for their page to have jots on it but that the jots make sense. Have students review their jots and see if the connections they are making to the text and writing down are actually connected or just a long shot. If the information isn't actually connected, encourage them to remove that jot (or several jots) and then write down things when they read about something that really connects, in some way.

66 Summarize a Text That Is a Little Too Hard for Students to Read on Their Own

WHEN YOU MIGHT OFFER IT

You might offer it when you are reading a book to or with the class; however, the book is a little too hard for students to read without support.

TARGET

Students will summarize in order to comprehend the text by making connections between concepts in the text and prior knowledge.

Gosh, I am glad I don't have to teach my children to ride a bike again. I have memories of holding the handle on one side of the bike and jogging (huffing, puffing) alongside as they wobbled down the road. And when I taught them to mix cake batter, same thing—it was so hard for me to see them struggle with that lumpy mess! That's why I break out into a sweat across my brow when coaching students to read a challenging text—it's so tempting to do too much and turn them into codependent readers. So I have them summarize what we read together. By focusing on what they heard, read, and remember and putting those thoughts into their own words, students take ownership.

Your Instructional Playbook

Name It: A summary of a text is a paragraph or two, written in your own words, telling what a text is about. In this task, you are going to write a summary in your own words about a text that I read to you or that you read with my support.

What You Might Say Next: "I've noticed that after reading, when I ask you to summarize, I get the 'silence.' That's when I say, 'Oh no! You are not going to be quiet and wait for me to summarize this—we are doing it together. Get thinking!' Seriously, though, I'm not just being bossy—when you write your thoughts in your own words, it really helps you grasp the story (text) in a way that you won't if you only listen to what I think or what other students think."

Typical Successes

Not Quite There Yet!
In this group written summary, the students are developing the ideas from the text they read; however, they have written it more like a retelling. They are getting close!

> Legend has it that Rome actually began because of twin brothers, Romulus and Remus, but first they were abandoned close to the Tiber River, rescued by a wolf, and then they were raised by a shepherd. Then when they were all grown up they decided to build a city which will have been soon be known as Rome, but Romulus killed his own brother after he laughed at his wall that he was building and became the first king of Rome. Italy had better farmland than Greece so people came to Italy because of its farmland and one of those groups that came to Italy were the Latinos which built the city of Rome on 7 high hills so it would be easier to protect themselves from enemies and soon they became the Romans. Around 8800B.C. Greeks and Etruscans came to Rome and the Greeks taught the Romans the Greek alphabet, how to grow grapes and olives, and Greek architecture. Soon the Etruscans took over Rome and made it a better place with their metalwork, clothes, and army. Rome became very rich because of the Etruscans. The Romans fought many wars against enemies and soon the Romans ruled most of Italy. Later on, the Romans made the Roman Confederation and made great strategies for wars which helped them win land. Something that helped the Romans a lot was their three part government that kept everything in balance, since patricians were rich and had more freedom then the plebeians, the plebeians got mad, but got equal right. Cincinnatus helped Rome become better by helping the Roman army win battles. Soon the Romans invented the twelve tablets where they wrote their laws.

Model/Do Together: Read aloud (and students have copies) enough of the text that the students can make some connections between concepts in the text. The key is for students to state in their own words what is going on in the text and what it might mean. You want to set up a nurturing, accepting, open discussion so that students can feel free to talk and make mistakes about what they think the concepts are.

Using a chart paper, a document camera, or electronic device, create a page that has the header: Big Ideas in the Text (name the text). Then, using a pair-share approach, have students talk to one another about what they think has happened in the text so far and write down those notes on note cards or slips of paper approximately 3 × 8 ½ inches. These slips of paper are brainstorming tickets. After students pair up, talk and record their thinking; have the students move into groups of four. Each student in the group of four would share what they had thought the big ideas were with their partners. Have the students discuss in the group and see if they agree or disagree with one another. Once they work in groups of four, open the discussion up to the whole class. Invite groups to share their thinking; check the text as necessary to confirm or disprove the statements students are making about the text. Once the class settles on one to two big ideas in the text, ask the students how they relate together. Then, working in the same group of four, students group write one to two sentences about how the big ideas in the text connect together. This is the start of their summary statements.

Read another section of the text and repeat the process, so that students have had the chance to talk about big ideas and how they relate at least twice. Then, move into summarizing what has been read so far. You can model writing the summary or share the pen (or keyboard if typing). End with a group-written summary that includes the big ideas and how they connect together and also how students are connecting to the big ideas. Remember, this is a group-written summary on only part of the longer text you are reading to or with the students.

Release: After modeling the summary process with the students and upon reading another section of the book, ask students to go through the summarizing process on their own, meeting with a partner, then in a group of four. Have the group of four write their own summary statements.

Have the groups share their summaries. As they share, invite students to say what they think about the other groups' summaries. Invite them to add on to what the other students are sharing.

Watch Fors and Work Arounds

Students don't think on their own; they wait to see what you will say the big ideas (concepts) are in the text. Focus on facilitating your students' thinking rather than pushing for one right answer. You can ask questions to get the discussion going:

- What do you think about it?
- What does it remind you of?
- Is there anything else in the text that it makes you think about?
- What did you discuss with your partner? Did your partner have an idea?

Resist giving the students the answer. Productive struggle helps students learn and grow cognitively. It is OK for them to have to work through their thinking for a little while.

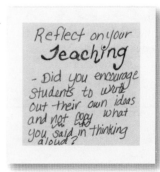

Reflect on your
Teaching
- Did you encourage students to work out their own ideas and not copy what you said in thinking aloud?

WHEN YOU MIGHT OFFER IT

You might offer it any time that you want students to independently engage with a text to help them understand what they are reading more deeply. In a think-aloud they can figure out unknown vocabulary, make predictions, visualize, use fix-up strategies, or apply another comprehension strategy that you often use with your class.

TARGET

Students think about and record comprehension or fix-up strategies on their own. In essence, you are helping them learn coping strategies to handle a difficult text on their own and have a think-aloud conversation with themselves.

I am a YouTube addict. I have learned so much fun stuff to do around the house (like baking cakes) by watching YouTube. In the process, I definitely know I am not going to learn too much if the video is just someone doing something and music playing to accompany the demonstration. Nope. I am going to learn more from a video that has commentary throughout while the person demonstrates exactly what to do. Essentially, these videos are think-alouds; it's like I get to be inside the head of the person teaching, and I get to see how, what, and why they are doing what they are doing. Knowing the why can be the difference between a hit and a flop when recreating what I learn on a video.

Your Instructional Playbook

Name It: It is important for us to focus on how we are fixing up our own reading when we have a problem. In this task, using a think-aloud guide, you are going to use a few comprehension strategies on your own while doing what I do all the time. You are going to do a think aloud and talk out loud as you think about your reading.

What You Might Say Next: "Really good readers have to cope with texts from time to time that seem challenging. It may not show, and you might not realize it, but good readers don't love reading everything they come across or don't find all genres, texts, or stories to be easy for them to read. But I do know what good readers do to get through something that is more difficult, and we are going to do that together today. Good readers stop and think to themselves about what they are reading, what problems they are having, and how they can fix up to understand or be able to read the words."

Typical Successes

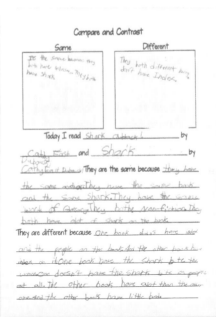

You can create visual self-assessments like in this example focused on the reading strategy of compare and contrast.

Model/Do Together: Invite students to start thinking about their own thinking by letting them know that really good readers have to stop and think about what they are reading all the time, just to make sure they understand. It is just that it is so automatic for them to think about their own thinking, and they do it silently, so other readers cannot see them doing this. Let the students know that they are going to learn to think about their thinking and notice how alive their minds are as readers with ideas, thoughts, and connections as they read. Jump into a read-aloud of a text you have not previously read to or with students. You want the text to be fresh, so as you go through the think-aloud, you can be as authentic as possible. When doing a think-aloud, make your own thinking really visible by discussing everything that is whizzing through your mind connected to the story. You might say, "Wow, this just happened in the text and I wonder if . . . ," or "Now I am thinking . . . ," or any other way to get your thinking visible for your students.

Dig into coping strategies so that students can be strong, independent readers. It is OK to admit to students that all readers have a few go-to coping strategies when reading; good readers are not perfect readers, they need to stop and think from time to time about what they are reading:

- One coping strategy might be what to do when finding difficult, unknown vocabulary or ambiguous wording. Not knowing what the words means hurts the understanding of the text. Develop questions with the students that they could ask themselves to try to figure out the words. Questions might include, Was there anything in the paragraph that gives me a clue about the words? What about in the previous paragraph or the following paragraph? If there is a picture, does the picture help me figure it out? If I am really stuck, and the words seem super important to know, what can I do?

- Another coping strategy is to understand anything, read it to yourself and think . . . "From what the author has said so far, I bet the author is going to have the character . . . ." Or for nonfiction, "From what the author has said so far, I bet the author is going to give us examples of how the students helped the horses."

- You can also have students discuss the mental pictures they "see" in their minds as they read.

- Students can talk aloud to themselves about what they know that has happened in the story already and how that helps them know what is happening next—or in nonfiction, connect to any prior knowledge they might have about the topic.

- You can have students think aloud about any comprehension strategy you have been using with them.

- When it comes to fix-up strategies (I am referring to word-related problems and comprehension problems), have student think aloud about what fix-up strategy they want to apply. Fix-up strategies can include rereading, chunking words, reading aloud, reading slower, asking a friend to read a word or phrase, looking at the pictures or text features, or checking out the sentence structure.

"Synthesis is the combined connections of reader, text, and big world ideas. Readers synthesize when they read, and after reading when they reflect."

—Goldberg and Houser (2017, p. 153)

Release: It can help a lot to have students complete a self-assessment on the think-aloud they did while reading. A think-aloud assessment is a great tool, as you can assess what strategies students seem to be using most often and/or who is just breezing through text and understanding or having comprehension breakdown. Create a quick self-assessment by typing out the areas you want students to focus on. The example on the first page of this task is a self-assessment using the reading strategy of compare and contrast. Model the use of the think-aloud self-assessment. Remind students to think aloud, which might be quietly thinking on their own or subvocalizing as they read their texts.

Watch Fors and Work Arounds

Students sit and pretend to be doing a think-aloud. Once you realize that a student is "faking it," check in and see what the problem is. He might not understand that he has the power of his own reading, or perhaps, reading on his own is overwhelming or "boring." If this is the case, encourage the student to take control of his own reading and try just one of the think-aloud strategies. Maybe trying one thing would be less daunting. It could also be that the text is too hard for the student to read on his own, so ask the student to self-select a strategy he wants to try, then set him up with a text he can read; better yet, encourage the student to pick out his own text to read.

Name:_____

Date:_____

Making Connections
Questions to Ask Yourself

Before reading, prepare for it:

What is this story or text about and what do I know about that topic, idea, or information already?

(If you are reading a story, check the pictures, or read the back of the book to see what it's about.)

(If you are reading non-fiction, check the table of contents, the bold text in the book, and the illustrations or pictures.)

During reading, think about it:

Have I ever heard or read about this topic, situation, information or idea before?

Do I know anything about this topic, situation, information or idea?

How is the situation (if I am reading fiction), topic, or information (if I am reading nonfiction) similar or different to what I have experienced or know?

After reading, reflect on it

How can I connect what I know to what I think the text is about?

How does what I know, what I've experienced, what I've heard or learned already connect to what this text is about?

WHEN YOU MIGHT OFFER IT

You might offer it for students third grade and above who are reading informational text; for younger students, focus on only identifying the big idea.

TARGET

Students can differentiate between the central idea and big ideas in informational text.

I admit that I used to think that the central idea was the same as the big idea in a text. But it's not. The central idea is the broad, overarching idea that holds information together in a nonfiction text. For example, in a sports text, the central idea is playing sports teaches life skills, and the big ideas are competition, camaraderie, and handling defeat. I honestly had to dig in and practice a bit on my own to learn to identify the central idea and then see the big ideas that connect to it. Once I got used to doing this, it made sense—the central idea is that big umbrella over the topic, and the big ideas are the major points of information.

Your Instructional Playbook

Name It: The central idea is similar to theme in fiction texts, so it is different than the big ideas in a text, as the central idea is the broad idea that the big ideas connect to. In this task, after reading a text or passage, you are going to practice identifying the central idea in a text and discuss how it is different than big ideas in the text.

What You Might Say Next: "We have been reading a lot of informational text lately, and you may notice, it doesn't have a theme the way that fiction does. However, informational text usually does have an idea or point that holds all the information in the text together. It works kind of like a theme, but it is called a central idea. Sometimes it can be tricky to figure out the central idea, so we are going to work together to decide the central idea of a text we read as a class."

Typical Successes

After much discussion, a group of students decided the central idea in Gilbert Ford's *The Marvelous Thing That Came From a Spring.*

Model/Do Together: Launch into teaching central idea by initiating a discussion of big ideas about something known to students. For example, at your school, what are some of the big ideas about things happening around campus? Are there sports games going on? Are there clubs? Do students like to play certain games at recess? Does the band have a concert? Ask questions to get the students thinking about campus and all the good or great things happening. Then, suggest students make a statement about all these things together. A statement could be a proposition that could be argued to be true based on all the big ideas about events and great things happening at school. Perhaps the statement is, "Orange School is a fun place to learn and play." This proposition, which can be backed up with the facts that the class listed, is a central idea. It organizes all the big ideas that were brainstormed.

Next launch into a discussion about a text that students have read on their own, with you or in a choral reading, by initiating a discussion of big ideas in the text. Generate a list of examples of big ideas in a text just as you listed big ideas that happen around your school. Generate as long as a list of big ideas. (You can add details to the big ideas if you want, but if a student mentions a detail, it would be better to record details on a separate chart.) Organize the class into groups of three to four and have the groups work together to come up with one to two propositional ideas that organize all the big ideas together. Have groups share out their propositional ideas and their thinking that backs up the proposition. Their thinking should be supported by the big ideas on the charts. Perhaps they use clues in the text to support their proposition. Groups can write their propositions on sentence strips or paper cut into 18 × 3 inch rectangles. Have groups share their ideas and discuss how the idea they proposed as groups might be the point that holds all the other information together. Discuss with the class and have the class chose one central idea from the statements generated by the groups.

Release: Using a new text or a different section from the previously read text, repeat the process, but instead of brainstorming with the whole class, have the groups work together to generate the list of big ideas, and then, have students work as partners to write one central idea, sharing their central idea with their group. Discuss as a class the differences between the central idea and the big ideas and how the central idea holds all the ideas and information together.

Watch Fors and Work Arounds

Students list lots and lots of big ideas but are not able to come up with one or two thoughts about possible central ideas. This can happen when students are unfamiliar with thinking about themes in fiction or they are unable to transfer their skills in identifying themes in fiction to identifying a central idea in informational text. It helps to create a word cloud or Wordle. You can create a Wordle online using a free word cloud application, or you can create a word cloud by hand (the old fashioned way). A word cloud is created by taking a chunk of text and highlighting or circling the words that appear the most times and then writing those words out on a new page, with the words appearing most often printed larger than the words appearing more frequently. Web-based applications will do this automatically for you. Use the big ideas that the students generate as the text that is used to create the word cloud.

Once the word cloud is created, students can usually see three to four words that are larger or appear more frequently in the text. These words can be used to craft the central idea.

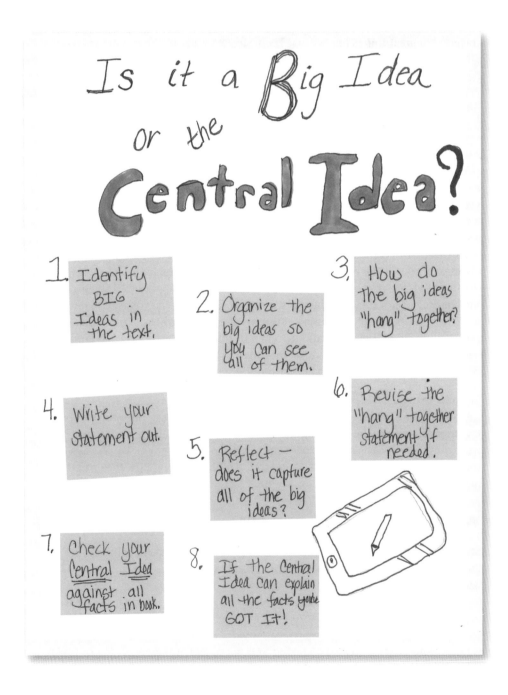

Is it a Big Idea or the Central Idea?

1. Identify BIG Ideas in the text.

2. Organize the big ideas so you can see all of them.

3. How do the big ideas "hang" together?

4. Write your statement out.

5. Reflect — does it capture all of the big ideas?

6. Revise the "hang" together statement if needed.

7. Check your Central Idea against all facts in book.

8. If the Central Idea can explain all the facts you've GOT It!

Name:_____

Date:_____

Identifying the Central Idea
Checklist for Action

Did I?

- ❑ Identify the big ideas in the text

- ❑ Write the big ideas down in my notebook

- ❑ Organize the big ideas in my notebook, so I can check them

- ❑ Think about how the big ideas connect together

- ❑ Write out my statement about how the big ideas connect together

- ❑ Reflect on my statement. Does my statement about the big ideas capture all of my thinking?

- ❑ Revise my statement about the big ideas if I need to

My statement is the central idea. Now, check the central idea with facts from the text, to double check that I am correct.

Writing in Different Genres or Multimedia to Engage and Persuade

WHEN YOU MIGHT OFFER IT

You might offer it when students have written about a topic or subject in one genre or mode and are ready to try writing about it in a different way.

TARGET

Students take a piece they have already written and turn it into a different genre or mode—such as a multimedia text.

When we mix up our practice, we learn more. This fact is not intuitive; rather, we often think that if we practice the same thing, in the same way, we will master it. Peter Brown and his colleagues discuss just the opposite being true in *Make It Stick* (Brown, Roediger, & McDaniel, 2016). They contend that mixed-up practice is the best type of practice, and that it leads to long-term learning. So whether you want students to work with the same content in a new way or work with familiar comprehension strategies but respond to their reading in new ways, mix up how they present the material.

Your Instructional Playbook

Name It: Sometimes authors write about what they know in more than one genre. Genre is a category of how a text is composed, and texts in the same genre share characteristics. In this task, you are going to choose a piece we have already written from our writing folders, and we are going to use that text as inspiration for us to write about it in another genre.

What You Might Say Next: When we mix up our practice, not only do things get more interesting and intriguing, we learn more. By mixing up what we do, we have to really stretch our brains and think in new ways. Check out these ways I have thought to mix up what I already wrote about to create something brand new. (It helps if you have at least a short paragraph written out about a topic you are interested in, say for instance, why bats fly at night. Then, you can show students how you turned the information you wrote about into a PowerPoint slide, a Tweet, or a newspaper article. You can also turn it into a poem, a rap, or an "all about" book).

Typical Successes

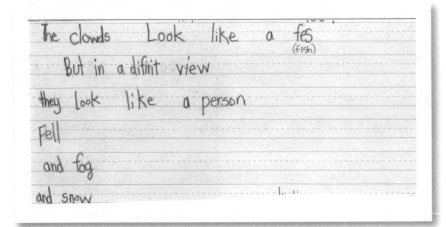

Owns It! Justine rewrote her nonfiction book on clouds into a poem.

Rosa Parks

Hi I'm Rosa Parks and this is my story. One day I went to work. When I was done I walked a long way to be at the bus stop, I was tired of walking that when the bus came I seat on the first chaer I saw, and that Chaer was a seat it was used for white people, Then a white man came in the bus, and said to me, "get out." "I want to seat here." I said "no!" "I paid my same money as you did."

Arely changed her nonfiction report on Rosa Parks into a first-person narrative.

Model/Do Together: Have texts or books on various topics ready to model with. Model for students how to write about your reading as a short summary (see page 118 for an example) after reading one of the texts, so you have one piece written about one topic. Then, introduce to them the idea of mixing up how you write about the information by choosing to write about it in a different genre. The goal is for students to watch you express the information in at least two ways. Perhaps after writing a summary, you write a short poem about the material to model. (It doesn't have to be a great poem, just give it a try.)

As students branch out and ready to write about their reading in more than one mode or genre, they are going to need a plan. Cowrite a class plan for changing writing from one genre to another (see the example above of a class-written plan) or from one mode to another. After writing up the plan, help students begin to implement it. Perhaps first they are going to gather materials or books on one subject or topic. Maybe they want to prepare writing materials or a devise a plan to present it in a different way. Then, guide students to start developing the material in a new way. The goal is to have them write about the same subject in two different ways, and writing may mean representing the material through a multimedia source. Different ways students can write or represent information include the following:

- Short reports, feature articles, informational reports
- Poems, picture writing, songs, raps

"Writers are obviously at their most natural when they write in the first person. Writing is an intimate transaction between two people, conducted on paper, and it will go well to the extent that it retains its humanity."

—William Zinsser
(1976, p. 20)

- PowerPoints, teaching "demos" made in a whiteboard app and recorded, short videos made in an app like Adobe Voice
- Creating graphic novels or storybooks with illustrations or storyboards
- Summaries, retellings, picture boards
- Pictographs, Prezi, Haikudeck
- ABC books, all-about books

Release: Invite students to pick a genre or type of expression they want to create, and help them launch. Students can work in partners if it helps them to think about how to organize their writing or piece and think through what they want to put in the piece.

After students finish creating at least two pieces about the same subject area, organize a sharing day and have students share their two pieces, discussing how they created the first piece and what they did with the information to change it to create the second piece.

Watch Fors and Work Arounds

Students get stuck and cannot think of how to represent the information in a different genre. It is really important to read lots of texts in different genres and note how similar topics are explored in each genre. Talk about those texts, and use them as mentor texts to think about how the author organized the piece. Then, using a favorite text in a genre chosen by the students, walk the students through thinking how the text was composed. You could guide with questions like, "What do you notice the author did first? What could you learn from that to try in your own piece? What did the author do next? How could you try that technique in your own writing?"

Creative Debate

WHEN YOU MIGHT OFFER IT

You might offer it after reading a book that had a strong character that students relate to or after reading a text that was about a controversial subject or issue.

TARGET

Students will debate a topic from character's point of view (fiction) or from a person's/stakeholder's point of view (nonfiction).

My wonderful husband can debate like no other.

I think he learned to take sides when he was growing up with his sister and four brothers. He has lots of stories about how he would take a side to make his sister mad. This takes practice; it doesn't come so easy to learn to stand in someone else's shoes and see the world from her point of view, and there is nothing like sibling rivalry to sharpen it!

Your Instructional Playbook

Name It: In this task, you are going to learn to debate a topic by thinking about an issue from different people's viewpoints.

What You Might Say Next: "How difficult do you think it is to share information or ideas from a different perspective? Today, we are going to debate one another, acting as if we were a character/person in (name the text you have recently read). Each of you will have a role, some of you will debate each other, and some of you will be audience members judging the debate. You will work in teams to debate another team, or you will listen and use criteria to judge the debate."

Typical Successes

Model/Do Together: Prepare to discuss a relevant theme or issue from either a fiction or nonfiction book you have recently read. For fiction, this could include the climax and the plot resolution; for nonfiction, this might be examining cause and effect of a situation, thing, or phenomenon or two opposing sides of an event.

Lead students through thinking about the perspective of the character or persons in the text. Ask questions to help all the students process what the character or person might have thought or felt. For instance, you might ask: "What happened in the text? Why? How did it affect character/person A, character/person B?" For nonfiction, you can also ask how what happened in the text affected an issue, a thing, or phenomenon.

Assign character A or B to two of the groups that will be debating. Give the students time to meet in their group to discuss what their statements and responses could be based on what occurred in the book. Have students prepare their thinking for the debate using the debate-planning sheet (see below) which prompts them to consider (1) the context and what happened in the text; (2) what the character/person thought or felt about what happened in the text; (3) what the character/person might want to say about what happened in the text; (4) what the character/person might want to change or keep the same regarding the outcome of the text. Remind students to go back to the text to check.

Tweak: Students are going to need to take the perspective of another person. Because they will be working in a team, with the team being the "person", you need to give students some practice time. (It is like a team persona, not where one student on the team does all the debating and the others just listen; collectively, the *team* will be the character.) Try this out first in partner groups before having the whole team work together for the debate.

Debate Planning Sheet

Text title:
Theme in the text:

Character 1 Name	What would this character be thinking or feeling regarding the situation?
	What might the character/person want to say about what happened in the text?
	What might the character/person want to change or keep the same? Why?
Character 2 Name	What would this character be thinking or feeling regarding the situation?
	What might the character/person want to say about what happened in the text?
	What might the character/person want to change or keep the same? Why?

This is a graphic organizer you can use with your students to plan a debate.

"Every so often we drop down into another plane, to that trusting spirit that knows that, underneath all things, we are held, that we are [people] . . . But then we have to snap out of it . . . get back to work."

—Anne Lamott
(2017b, p. 109)

Pose a character to the students and have them close their eyes for a moment to imagine that they *are* that person—for example, if they were the principal of the school or the bus driver in the morning. What might that person think or feel? Have them share their thinking with the other students. Once they share in small groups, have them go back to their team to get ready to take on *being* the person that they are assigned to be in the debate. Ponder the situation, the voice, the body posture, the mood. Invite them to practice with one another. Have all the students (even the audience members who will be judging the debate) act out being another person with a partner so that all the students get an idea of how it might feel to think like and be like a character or person in a text.

Release: *How to manage the debate:* Divide class into groups. It works well to divide the class into thirds, with one third being Debate Team 1, the second third being Debate Team 2, and the final third being active observers/judges. Students debate from their character's point of view for ten minutes. Debrief the debate and give time for the audience to share how they judged the debate (see judging criteria below) and why.

Watch Fors and Work Arounds

Some students take over and don't allow others to get involved in the debate. Go over norms for the debate: (1) Each team makes up the character or person, (2) not just one person can do the talking for the team, any team member can answer, (3) if a team member is confused or unsure, the team should confer and support the student in answering rather than one person just jumping in and answering.

Students don't have ideas about what the character/person might think or feel.
Using the debate-planning sheet and a copy of the text, go back and look for textual evidence about what a character might have thought or felt at critical points in the text. Invite students to record their thinking on the debate-planning sheet so they have notes to refer back to.

Students and Teachers—Full Throttle Independence

For the final five engagements of the book, we are shifting gears. I have chosen two tasks for students that are not so much a means to an end, as the other ones are, but ways of being. Let's call them habits or mindsets. One is for readers, the other for writers. Following these are two tasks that are the teacher equivalents—yes, just for you. And the very last one? It's an engagement for you and your students.

I started this book with a mix of bold defense of tasks and a bit of sheepishness, as though anticipating some Amazon reviews would snipe that "tasks" are what's wrong with school. Now, I hope you see that the seventy engagements work the minds of your students, building the academic and "skillsy" abilities of their brains—so they've got the hardwiring to then take creative and cognitive leaps any way they want. The tasks help them *become* readers and writers. Period. So without further ado, these final five ideas are more like inspirational posters you want to hang on the walls of their literate lives. I've chosen photos to match each one.

What is my favorite book, and why?

Which friend do I share books with most?

Can I promise myself that at least once a year, I'm going to choose to read something that is super new territory for me?

How can I use my reading to take action—to improve something in the world?

istockphoto.com/wavebreakmedia

When has writing made me feel smarter or calmer or more connected to another?

What is my favorite kind of writing, and why?

Can I promise myself that at least once a year, I write something and send it to another person who would appreciate it?

What do I know about the writing of my family?

istockphoto.com/stock-eye

A few months ago, a friend noticed I was running on empty and advised me to literally look up.

Look up each day. Look up to gain a new perspective. Here are some questions for you:

What has meaning for you when you take a moment to "look up"?

What time in the school year is your best time to reset?

In what ways do you reset? Do you read?

I invite you to relax, now, in whatever space or moment you are in and read to renew your soul. What will you read?

In what ways will you connect to what you read?

istockphoto.com/zodebala

On Monday, I picked up my daughter from her college summer school math (high level math that only math geeks would understand) and drove her across town. While we were driving, she (who is normally not very talkative) said, "Wow, there is really a difference between good instructors and not-so-good instructors." Immediately, I felt my stomach tighten and those pesky, negative thoughts that plague me jumped up and took a lap around my head.

"Like, what to do you mean, sweetie?" I said, in a voice that was a little too high pitched. I could feel my throat getting warm as the feeling of self-doubt bubbled up. My daughter just pitched a new "standard" that I was going to subconsciously hold myself to.

"You know, teachers who really explain things and don't just jump in and start, where you are left going, 'Whoa,' what's going on," she answered.

"Oh," I said, my voice getting higher. "So, tell me what that looks like."

"Well, they take the TIME to explain why we are doing the math that we are doing. They don't just jump into the material and assume we know why or don't care if we know why or not."

"Got it," I answered, my voice hitting the top octave of squeakiness now as my throat closed. I drove in silence for a few moments while the fearful thought of, Am I a good teacher or not? ran around my head again. So I had to come home and write it out.

Try writing it out whenever you get struck by "perfect teacher" syndrome or whatever other issue eats at your soul.

What can you say for yourself on the page?

Can writing become a "healthy vice" you turn to in order to puzzle things out? To rejuvenate yourself? To reinforce your good teaching?

istockphoto.com/Marjon_Apostolovic

We can call ourselves learning facilitators. We don't just learn; I don't just teach. I help you learn, you help me learn, and you help each other learn.

Let's write about this together. I don't teach; I assist you in your learning and changing your own life. How can we write that out?

You don't just learn; you help me learn too. How can we write about that?

istockphoto.com/monkeybusinessimages

THE GOOD, THE BAD, AND THE UGLY

These tasks were harder, so they are harder to teach, and more complicated to manage. Knowing that, I was kinder to myself in the reflection of what went well, and what went poorly. Check it out.

The Good	
What I Planned to Do	**What I Actually Did**
Higher Order Thinking Skills– *Evaluate*	**Higher Order Thinking Skills–** *Evaluate*
Have students work in pairs, take two argumentative texts or books on the same subject we read in class recently and compare the strength of the authors' arguments, students then create their own argument in writing together.	Students worked in pairs and used a graphic organizer to evaluate the two types of writing. They got a bit stuck when needing to write their own arguments (even though we had practiced a few days prior), and I gave them a scaffold to help them write their arguments. The 'Do you Understand My Point' graphic organizer appears in the appendix.

My Thinking About the Lesson in Action
Right On!
I was very pleased that when my students started to struggle a bit, I didn't just throw out my plan for them to create their own arguments. Instead, I decided to provide a scaffold that was appropriate to the task (not to water it down to me writing the argument for them as a model) and ensure they were working through their own original thinking, but using the graphic organizer as a support.
I carefully planned this lesson to ensure I could keep the task at a higher level and ensure students would be involved with thinking and writing about their own original thinking. To keep myself on track, I kept my notes right with me so I didn't accidentally lower the level of the task.

The Bad

What I Planned to Do	What I Actually Did
Higher Order Thinking Skills– Evaluate	**Thinking Skills– Application**
Students were to plan out a way to collect water from a leaky water faucet in our classroom and use the captured water to water plants in the planters in front of school. Students did have parameters to solving the problem in that they could not miss any class time to deliver the water. They could not carry heavy loads of water. The water schedule needed to be a routine that the groundsman didn't have to worry about.	The class was really excited to get to solve a real-world problem. We had had several discussions about how much water was being lost weekly from the leaky faucet. It was the students' idea to use the water for a greater purpose while we waited for the faucet to get fixed. Students worked in groups of 4–5 to come up with their plans. Their plans were simplistic and didn't account for all the issues that needed to be worked out. For example how to store the water, how to transport the water, and how to get volunteers to water the plants on their own time, and not classroom time. The students did, however, create diagrams and a storyboard to demonstrate how to collect the water and how to water the plants with the collected water.

My Thinking About the Lesson in Action

I Was Close!

I was excited to have the students try to solve a real world problem. What I did not anticipate was their lack of prior knowledge of how long it takes to carry water around to the planters, and also of their lack of knowledge of the weight of the water. They took the literal steps that were needed and put these in their diagrams, but they didn't evaluate the buckets we had available, and whether the classroom wagon was actually operable for carrying the buckets of water. The students just assumed their plans would work and didn't troubleshoot. We did display the plans for a few weeks in the hallway and had students help with water delivery. It is just that I had to figure out all the logistics and it would have been a richer experience for the students if they had thought through the details of implementation.

The Ugly

What I Planned to Do	What I Actually Did
Higher Order Thinking Skills– Evaluate	**Thinking Skills– Knowledge**
Have students work in pairs, take two argumentative texts or books on the same subject we read in class recently and compare the strength of the authors' arguments, students then create their own argument in writing together.	Students read a text silently while I read the text aloud; this happened the day before. I led a discussion in the reason the author wrote the arguments. Students identified the main idea of each text and wrote down two supporting details. However, they didn't participate much in the conversation and they mostly copied my notes from the board.

My Thinking About the Lesson in Action

First Time Was Terrible.

This is the same lesson that I reflected on in The Good example. However, this was what happened the first time I taught it – I didn't follow through with my planning and I got off track. Also, we ran out of time as I didn't allow the students to work together and I was cajoling a lot of the class to keep paying attention to me while I read, and while I thought through the main ideas.

References and Further Reading

Akhavan, N. (2004). *How to align literacy instruction, assessment and standards and achieve results you never dreamed possible.* Portsmouth, NH: Heinemann.

Akhavan, N. (2006). *Help! My kids don't all speak English: How to set up language workshop in your linguistically diverse classroom.* Portsmouth, NH: Heinemann.

Akhavan, N. (2007). *Accelerated vocabulary instruction: Strategies for closing the achievement gap for all students.* New York, NY: Scholastic.

Akhavan, N. (2008a). *Teaching reading in a title I school.* Portsmouth, NH: Heinemann.

Akhavan, N. (2008b). *The content rich reading and writing workshop: A time saving approach for making the most of your literacy block.* New York, NY: Scholastic.

Akhavan, N. (2009). *Teaching writing in a title I school.* Portsmouth, NH: Heinemann.

Akhavan, N. (2014). *The nonfiction now lesson bank: Strategies and routines for higher-level comprehension in the content areas, grades 4–8.* Thousand Oaks, CA: Corwin.

Akhavan, N. (2016). *Instruction of effective reading comprehension strategies with nonfiction text.* Manuscript submitted for publication.

Associated Press. (2017, February 22). *7 Earth-size planets have been discovered orbiting a nearby star.* Retrieved from http://www.wptv.com/news/science-tech/7-earth-size-planets-have-been-discovered-orbiting-a-nearby-star

Bailey, S. T. (2008). *Release your brilliance: The 4 steps to transforming your life and revealing your genius to the world.* New York, NY: Collins.

Barone, T. A. (2012). *Complex assessments, teacher inferences and instructional decision making* (Doctoral dissertation). Retrieved from ProQuest LLC. (3555561)

Beers, K. & Probst, R. E. (2017). *Disrupting thinking: Why how we read matters.* NY: Scholastic.

Berger, R., Woodfin, L., Plaut, S. N., & Dobbertin, C. B. (2014). *Transformational literacy: Making the common core shift with work that matters.* San Francisco, CA: Jossey-Bass.

Bernstein, G. (2010). *Add more ing to your life: A hip guide to happiness.* New York: Harmony.

Bettelheim, B. (1975). *The uses of enchantment. The meaning and importance of fairy tales.* New York, NY. Knopf.

Block. C. (2004). The abcs of performing highly effective think-alouds. *The Reading Teacher 58*(2), 154–167.

Bohaty, J. J. (2015). *The effects of expository text structure instruction on the reading outcomes of 4th and 5th graders experiencing reading difficulties.* (Doctoral dissertation). Retrieved from ProQuest (3689619).

Bray, M. (1998). *Using collaborative writing/planning as an instructional technique to teach elementary school students to create World Wide Web documents* (Doctoral dissertation). Retrieved from ProQuest.

Brock, C. H., Trost-Shahata, E., Weber, C. M., Goatley, V. J., & Raphael, T. (2014). *Engaging students in disciplinary literacy, K–6: Reading, writing and teaching tools for the classroom.* New York, NY: Teachers College Press.

Brown, B. (2015). *Rising Strong.* New York: Spiegel & Grau.

Brown, P. C, Roediger, H. L., III, McDaniel, M. A. (2016). *Make it stick: The science of successful learning.* New York: Harvard University Press/Belknap.

City, E. A., Elmore, R. F., Fiarman, S. E., & Teitel, L. (2009). *Instructional rounds in education: A network approach to improving teaching and learning* (6th ed.). Cambridge, MA: Harvard Educational Press.

Clarke, P. J., Truelove, E., Hulme, C., & Snowling, M. J. (2013). *Developing reading comprehension.* Hoboken, NJ: Wiley.

Clark, S., Jones, C., & Reutzel, D. (2013). Using the text structure of information books to teach writing in the primary grades. *Early Childhood Education Journal, 41*(4), 265–271.

Conroy, P. (2016, March 9). Pat Conroy: Interpreting the world through story. *The Writer,* para. 3. Retrieved from https://www.writermag.com/2016/03/09/pat-conroy/

Davis, M. H., & Guthrie, J. T. (2015). Measuring reading comprehension of content-area texts using an assessment of knowledge organization. *The Journal of Educational Research, 108,* 148–164.

DiCamillo, K. (2006). *The miraculous journey of Edward Tulane.* Cambridge, MA: Candlewick.

DiCamillo, K. (2015). *The tiger rising.* Cambridge, MA: Candlewick.

Dillard, A. (1989). *The writing life.* New York, NY. HarperCollins.

DiPucchio, K. (2014). *Gaston.* New York, NY: Anthenum Books for Young Readers.

Donovan, C. A., & Smolkin, L. B. (2011). Supporting information writing in the elementary grades. *The Reading Teacher, 64*(6), 406–416.

Duncan, L. G., McGeown, S. P., Griffiths, Y. M., Stothard, S. E., & Dobai, A. (2015). Adolescent reading skills and engagement with digital and traditional literacies as predictors of reading comprehension. *British Journal of Psychology, 107,* 209–238.

Dweck, C. (2007). *Mindset: The new psychology of success.* New York, NY: Ballantine Books.

Ediger, M. (2000). Writing poetry in ongoing units of study. *ERIC Documents.* U.S. Department of Education.

Fisher, D., & Frey, N. (2015a). Improve reading with complex texts. *Kappan, 96*(5), 56–61.

Fisher, D., & Frey, N. (2015b). Selecting texts and tasks for content area reading and learning. *The Reading Teacher, 68*(7), 524–529.

Fisher, D., Frey, N., & Hattie, J. (2016). *Visible learning for literacy.* Thousand Oaks, CA: Corwin.

Forman, M., Stocich, E. L., & Bacala, C. (2017). *The internal coherence framework: Creating the conditions for continuous improvement in schools.* Cambridge, MA: Harvard Education Press.

Fullan, M. & Quinn, J. (2016). *Coherence: The right drivers in action for schools, districts and systems.* Thousand Oaks: Corwin.

Fulton, K. (2017). *Long may she wave: The true story of Caroline Pickersgill and her star-spangled banner.* New York, NY: Margaret K. McElderry Books.

Gentry, L. (2006). *Comparison of the effects of training in expository text structure* through annotation textmarking and training in vocabulary development on reading comprehension of student going into fourth grade (Doctoral dissertation). Retrieved from ProQuest Dissertations and Theses.

Goldberg, G. (2016). *Mindsets and moves: Strategies that help readers take charge, grades 1–8*. Thousand Oaks, CA: Corwin.

Goldberg, G., & Houser, R. (2017). *What do I teach readers tomorrow? Nonfiction: Your moment-to-moment decision-making guide* Thousand Oaks, CA: Corwin.

Graham, H. (2010). Writing and publishing advice. In S. Nicholson (Ed.), *Write good or die*. Haunted Computer Books.

Graham. S., Hebert, M., & Harris, K. R. (2015). Formative assessment and writing: A meta-analysis. *The Elementary School Journal 115*(4), 523–547.

Guthrie, J. T., Schafer, W. D., & Huang, C. (2001). Benefits of opportunity to read and balanced literacy instruction on the NAEP. *The Journal of Educational Research, 94*(3), 145–162.

Hanh, T. N. (2011). *Peace is every breath: A practice for our busy lives*. New York, NY: HarperCollins.

Harris, K. R., Graham, S., Friedlander, B., & Laud, L. (2013). Bringing writing strategies into your classroom: Why and how. *The Reading Teacher, 66*(7), 538–542.

Harvey, S., & Goudvis, A. (2007). *Strategies that work: Teaching comprehension for understanding and engagement, second edition*. Portland, ME: Stenhouse.

Henkes, K. (1997). *Sun & spoon*. New York, NY: Greenwillow Books.

Henry, L. A., Castek, J., O'Byrne, W. I., & Zawilinkski, L. (2012). Using peer collaboration to support online reading, writing and communication: An empowerment model for struggling readers. *Reading & Writing Quarterly, 28*(3), 279–306.

Houck, L. C. (2017). An exploration of close reading strategies and 3rd grade comprehension. Rowan *Theses and Dissertations* (2350), **http://rdw.rowan .edu/etd/2350**

Hurston, Z. N. (1979). *I love myself when I'm laughing–and then again. A Zora Neal Hurston reader*. New York, NY: The Feminist Press at CUNY.

Jaeger, E. L. (2012). *Understanding and supporting vulnerable readers: An ecological systems perspective* (Doctoral dissertation). Retrieved from ProQuest.

Jung, C. (1998). *Psychological reflections. An anthology of Jung's writings, 1905–1961*. Great Britain: Routledge.

Keating, J. (2016). *Pink is for blobfish: Discovering the world's perfectly pink animals*. New York, NY: Alfred A. Knof.

Lafferty, M. (2017). *I should be writing: A writer's workshop*. Santa Fe, NM: Rock Point Press.

Lai, T. (2011). *Inside out & back again*. New York, NY: HarperCollins.

Lamothe, M. (2017). *This is how we do it: One day in the lives of seven kids from around the world*. San Francisco, CA: Chronicle Books.

Lamott, A. (2017a). 12 truths I learned from life and writing [Video file]. Retrieved From https://www.ted.com/talks/anne_lamott_12_ truths_i_learned_from_life_and_ writing

Lamott, A. (2017b). *Hallelujah anyway: Rediscovering mercy*. New York, NY: Riverhead.

Langer, E. (2015). Science of mindlessness and mindfulness *On being with Krista Tippet* [Video podcast]. Retrieved from https://onbeing.org/programs/ellen-langer-science-of-mindlessness-and-mindfulness-nov2017/

Langley, A. (2015). *Chris Hadfield and the international space station*. Chicago, IL: Heinemann Raintree.

Lara, Adair. (1999). *The best of Adair Lara: Award-winning columns form the San Francisco Chronicle*. San Francisco, CA: Scottswell Associates.

Lee-Tai, A. (2006). *A place where sunflowers grow*. San Francisco, CA: Children's Book Press.

Logue, C. (2015). Writing with mentor texts. *Scholastic Instructor*, 58–59.

Lopate, P. (2013). *To show and to tell: The craft of literary nonfiction*. New York, NY: Simon and Schuster.

Lutz, S. L., Guthrie, J. T., & Davis. M. H. (2006). Scaffolding for engagement in elementary school reading instruction. *The Journal of Educational Research, 100*(1), 3–20.

Luyken, C. (2017). *The book of mistakes*. New York: Dial Books for Young Readers.

Marshall, J. (2000). Research on response to literature. In M. Kamil, P. D. Pearson, E. Moje, & P. Afflerbach (Eds.), *Handbook of reading research* (Vol. 4, Chapter 23). Mahwah, NJ: Lawrence Erlbaum Associates.

Mcgough, J. M., & Nyberg, L. (2015). *The power of questioning: Guiding student questioning*. Arlington, VA: National Science Teachers Association Press.

Mokhtari, K., Hutchison, A. C., & Edwards, P. A. (2010). Organizing instruction for struggling readers in tutorial settings. *The Reading Teacher, 64*(4), 287–290.

Moss, B. (2003). *Exploring the literature of fact: Children's nonfiction trade books in the elementary classroom*. New York: Guilford.

Nicklaus, J. (1972). The secrets. *Golf Digest*.

Padamsee, S. (2016). *Dancing on walls*. Chennai, India: Tulika Publishers.

Parson, S. C., Mokhtari, K., Yellin, D., & Orwig. R. (2011, May). Literature study groups: Literacy learning "with legs." *Middle School Journal, 42*(5), 22–30.

Parsons, S. A., & Ward, A. E. (2011). The case for authentic tasks in content literacy. *The Reading Teacher, 64*(6), 462–465.

Pennington, J. L, Obenchain, K. M., & Brock, C. H. (2014). Reading informational text: A civic transactional perspective. *The Reading Teacher 67*(7), 532–542.

Pressley, M., Mohan, L., Raphael, L. M., & Fingeret, L. (2007). How does Bennett woods elementary school produce such high reading and writing achievement? *Journal of Educational Psychology, 99*(2), 221–240.

Pytash, K. E., & Morgan, D. N. (2013). A unit of study approach for teaching common core standards for writing. *Middle School Journal, 44*(3), 44–51.

Raphael, T. E., & Pearson, P. D. (1985). Assessing students' awareness of sources of information for answering questions. *American Educational Research Journal, 22*(2), 217–235.

Rasinski, T. V. (2017). Readers who struggle: Why many struggle and a modest proposal for improving their reading. *The Reading Teacher 70*(5), 519–524.

Sadhguru. (2016). *Inner engineering: A yogi's guide to joy*. New York: Spiegel & Grau.

Sandler, M. W. (2009). *Secret subway: The fascinating tale of an amazing feat of engineering*. Washington, DC: National Geographic.

Schirmer, A. (2010). *Mark my words: Tone of voice changes affective word representations in memory*. PLoS ONE 5(2): e9080. https://doi.org/10.1371/ journal.pone.0009080

Sharp, N. L. (2004). *Effie's image*. Freemont Press, NE: Prairieland Press.

Shashiredkha, S. M. (2014). Story reading: Tasks as tools to facilitate values among second language learners. *Indian Journal of Positive Psychology, 5*(4), 531–533.

Snow, C. (2002). *Reading for understanding: Toward an R & D program in reading comprehension*. Santa Monica, CA: RAND.

Stein, Sol. (1995). *Stein on writing: A master editor of some of the most successful writers of our century shares his craft techniques and strategies.* New York, NY: Saint Martin's Griffin.

Stevens, R. J., Lu, X., Baker, D. P., Eckert, S. A., & Gamson, D. A. (2015). Assessing the cognitive demands of a century of reading curricula: An analysis of reading text and comprehension tasks from 1910 to 2000. *American Educational Research Journal 52*(3), 582–617.

Swinburne, S. (2010). *Turtle Tide.* Honesdale, PA: Boyds Mills Press.

Taylor, B. M., Pearson, P. D., Peterson, D. S., & Rodriguez, M. C. (2003). High-poverty classrooms: The influence of teacher practices that encourage cognitive engagement in literacy learning. *The Elementary School Journal, 104*(1), 3–28.

Tompkins, G. E., & Blanchfield, C. (2005). *50 ways to develop strategic writers.* Upper Saddle River, NJ: Pearson.

Topping, K. J. (2001). *Thinking, reading, writing: A practical guide to paired learning with peers, parents and volunteers.* London, NY: Continuum.

Valencia, S. W., Wixon, K. K., & Pearson, P. D. (2014). Putting text complexity in context: Refocusing on comprehension of complex text. *The Elementary School Journal, 115*(2), 270–289.

Wade, S. E., & Moje, E. B. (2000). The role of text in classroom learning. In M. Kamil, P. D. Pearson, E. Moje, & P. Afflerbach (Eds.), *Handbook of reading research* (Vol. 4, Chapter 33). Mahwah, NJ: Lawrence Erlbaum Associates.

Wilhelm, J, & Smith, M. (2016). *Diving deep into nonfiction: Transferable tools to use with any text.* Thousand Oaks, CA. Corwin.

Williams, C., & Pilonieta, P. (2012). Using interactive writing instruction with kindergarten and first-grade English language learners. *Early Childhood Journal, 40*(3), 145–150.

Wixon, K. K. (1983). Questions about a text: What you about is what children learn. *The Reading Teacher, 37*(3), 287–293.

Wood Ray, K. (1999). *Wondrous words: Writers and writing in the elementary classroom.* Urbana, Illinois: NCTE.

Yoo, M. S. (2010). *Students' perceived and actual use of strategies for reading and writing* (Doctoral dissertation). Retrieved from ProQuest. (3527027)

Zaragoza, N., & Vaughn, S. (1995). Children teach us to teach writing. *The Reading Teacher, 49*(1), 42–47.

Zinsser, W. (1976). *On writing well. The classic guide to writing nonfiction.* New York, NY: HarperCollins.

Index

Notes

Notes

Notes

Notes

A SAGE Publishing Company

Helping educators make the greatest impact

CORWIN HAS ONE MISSION: to enhance education through intentional professional learning.

We build long-term relationships with our authors, educators, clients, and associations who partner with us to develop and continuously improve the best evidence-based practices that establish and support lifelong learning.